JADE LADDER

Editorial team: W.N. Herbert and Yang Lian, with Brian Holton and Qin Xiaoyu.

Translation team: Brian Holton, with W.N. Herbert, Lee Man-Kay and Yang Lian.

JADE LADDER

CONTEMPORARY CHINESE POETRY

EDITED BY
W.N. HERBERT & YANG LIAN
WITH BRIAN HOLTON & QIN XIAOYU

BLOODAXE BOOKS

ISBN: 978 1 85224 895 6

First published 2012 by
Bloodaxe Books Ltd,
Highgreen,
Tarset,
Northumberland NE48 1RP.

www.bloodaxebooks.com
For further information about Bloodaxe titles
please visit our website or write to
the above address for a catalogue.

Supported by
**ARTS COUNCIL
ENGLAND**

Cover design: Neil Astley & Pamela Robertson-Pearce.

Printed in Great Britain by Bell & Bain Limited, Glasgow, Scotland.

CONTENTS

PART TWO

1. NARRATIVE POEMS

2. NEO-CLASSICAL POEMS

3. SEQUENCES

The selections in this anthology are presented chronologically by poet's birth year in each section. A number of poets are represented in several sections of the book.

Translators (except where otherwise indicated):

BH   Brian Holton
LMK   Lee Man-Kay
WNH   W.N. Herbert

PREFACE

Modern Chinese poetry is, at least partly, the result of often-tragic pressures exerted on Chinese writers throughout the last century. Firstly, the impact of western Modernism in the form of the New Culture or May Fourth Movement of 1919 moved literary writing decisively away from the rules if not the influence of classical forms. The date resonates throughout Chinese literature almost like that of Bloomsday, symbolising the shift from an embodiment of (then) stifling "eternal" verities to a politicised representation of social realities influenced by Modernism.[1] Secondly, the eventual triumph of Mao in 1949 confirmed and intensified the same tensions between propagandistic "realism" and individual expression that were then afflicting Stalinist Russia.

From the perspective of poets writing in the late 1970s after the terrible privations and intellectual suppression of the Cultural Revolution, the classical heritage (which is as much as most western audiences know of Chinese literature), and the 20th-century influences of western and other literatures (which Chinese writers knew only as far as it was published, translated or accessible, i.e. in part) both seemed equally "other". This moment of equal alienation, from the past, from the rest of the world, and, perhaps most crucially – as is agonisingly played out again and again in these pages – from the self, was the beginning of Misty poetry (Menglong shi), and therefore of this anthology. The 'mistiness' or obscurity of this writing – the term was applied by official critics – served to protect and nurture the imagination of writers through a period of continued persecution.

Since then, Mainland Chinese society (there is no room here for the parallel developments of Taiwan) has been changing radically and with astonishingly sustained rapidity over thirty years of political and cultural tumult.[2] As the Cultural Revolution gave way to the post-Mao era, and the crackdown of Tiananmen Square was succeeded by the

---

1. See Eliot Weinberger's introduction to *The New Directions Anthology of Classical Chinese Poetry* (New Directions, 2003), p. xxi, for one ironic aspect of this influence, where modern Chinese poetry was influenced by Ezra Pound's reading of classical Chinese poetry.

2. For an authoritative overview of Taiwanese writing, consult Michelle Yeh's two anthologies, *Anthology of Modern Chinese Poetry* (Yale University Press, 1994), and *Frontier Taiwan: An Anthology of Modern Chinese Poetry* (Columbia University Press, 2001).

return of Hong Kong, the present period has been one of extraordinary and deeply problematic growth.

Chinese poets, driven by alienation, trauma and exile, as well as the potentially positive opportunity to engage with a global audience, and indeed to re-engage in a fundamentally different manner with their long past, have embarked on one of the world's most thorough and exciting experiments in contemporary poetry. Misty, post-Misty or Third Generation, Fourth Generation; increasingly diverse, indeed bewildering, sub-groupings, including Lower Body, Fei Fei ('Not Not') and Trash; publication in *samizdat*, or in exile, or on the internet – in a nation of billions, it sometimes seems that there are a million ways to write and disseminate poetry.

The ladder our title alludes to – a mythic device, which we might imagine being placed on a mountaintop and leaning against a cloud – symbolises the transit of the Chinese poem between imagination and the world.[3] For most of the last hundred years that movement has been anything but free. However, this anthology is not a selection of political poetry, but the record of an aesthetic revolution, as Chinese writing simultaneously renegotiates its relationship with Modernist and Postmodernist poetry, and re-conceptualises its classical heritage. The cultural crises of political suppression and exile are read principally in terms of the linguistic crises and the crises of form and style they contribute to.

It aims to show for the first time in English the diversity of mainland Chinese poetry today and the foundations of that poetry, which are set in both the stasis of the classical tradition and the uneven ground of the early Modernist and Communist periods, as well as in the partial rejection of that tradition, the gradual reinterpretation of that influence, and, in its key figures, a wholehearted resistance to that regime.

In order to do this, it must both begin with and move beyond the lyric poem to showcase work across a range of genres including narrative poetry, neo-classical writing, the sequence, experimental poetry and the long poem. Diversity of mode, diversity of principle and indeed of formal technique, are all markers of the contemporary in Chinese writing, as poets have responded to the full range of literary possibilities opening up to them in the last thirty years. These diverse modes form, if you like, the rungs of our ladder.

---

3. But see also *The Jade Mountain*, a notable translation into English of *Three Hundred Tang Poems*, the 18th-century collection regarded as the standard Tang poetry textbook, translated by Witter Bynner and Jiang Kanghu, in ten editions from 1929 through to 1972.

Given the breadth of the field and its relative unfamiliarity to many western readers, we have decided to include a supportive framework of essays from both Chinese and western perspectives. Therefore this more general introduction confines itself to presenting the structure of the book, and discussing the principles behind its assembly and the approach to translation we have taken. My co-editor Yang Lian has contributed an "insider's report", based in personal experience, providing his own highly distinctive take on China and Chinese poetry in this period.

We have begun each section with a short introductory essay by our Chinese associate editor, Qin Xiaoyu, presenting each genre from a Chinese viewpoint. These not only provide valuable context, but allow readers to gauge the sometimes significant contrast in approaches between Chinese and western poetry. Finally, our principal translator and associate editor, Brian Holton, concludes the book with an essay based on his extensive experience of translating both classical and contemporary poetry, focusing on some of the issues which arose during translation, and setting those against the more general context of translating poetry from Chinese into English.

We hope the reader will find sufficient support from these complementary critical perspectives in building up their own picture of contemporary Chinese poetry. Our aim in this is, obliquely, derived from the practice of interlinear commentary in classical Chinese criticism, wherein a reader is always accompanied through the reading process by the comments of a famous previous reader. But this is first and foremost an anthology of poetry, and we would always encourage our reader to begin with the poetry, returning to the essays and introductions as and when they see fit.

Poetry has been central to Chinese culture since its beginning, in a way that has few parallels in the west. Partly because of Confucianism's emphasis on the social usefulness of poetry, it is through the poem that Chinese culture has always engaged with itself, asking difficult questions about identity, about the present's relationship to the past, about the good man's response to bad government, and about the eternal questions of who we are and why we are on this earth. But for the outsider, both Chinese language and culture form considerable barriers to understanding the poetry.

Many western readers have some working knowledge of other European languages – or are at least comfortable enough with Roman script to feel that, for instance, publishing a poem and its translation as parallel texts is of some use. But Chinese is an especially difficult language to access, especially in its literary and classical forms, and culturally –

even for the non-native student with a reading knowledge of the characters and a degree of fluency in the spoken language – contemporary Chinese poetry makes great demands upon the reader. For the general reader, for the student or even the teacher, there are few authoritative resources available. That is the gap this anthology aims to fill.[4]

It could be said, indeed, that this anthology came about because a gap of this nature appeared in the midst of a specific dialogue between Chinese and western writers, or rather between the editors of this book. Certainly, it was conceived as the natural result of that process of literary dialogue, relying on the principle that such exchanges between poets can be synaptic, a means of resolving cultural lacunae, that they are engines for generating creative energy, whether in original poetry, literary translation, or a creatively responsible mode of criticism.

Part of the exercise here for western readers and writers must consist of an engagement with our own perceptions of and preconceptions about Chinese language, culture and poetry, the latter in particular being formed at least in the English-speaking world by two early 20th-century readings of the classical heritage, one British and understood as scholarly, the other American and apparently experimental. These are the approaches of Arthur Waley on the one hand and Ezra Pound on the other.

Pound's Chinese translations famously first appeared in *Cathay* in 1916, and Waley's *A Hundred and Seventy Chinese Poems* followed in 1918. They have been seen as in debate over the best way to produce Chinese translations, with Pound's vigorous reshapings of Li Po (Li Bai) being opposed to Waley's championing of Po Chü-I (Bai Juyi), focusing on his simpler, more plangent poems, the Imagist being set against the Bloomsburyite. Eliot Weinberger, for instance, delivers the damning judgement that Waley's 'translations were often sunk by his fondness for Gerard Manley Hopkins and a theory that the number of stresses in the English line must match the number of characters

---

4. That the nature of that gap is not always as evident to Chinese writers as it could be is exemplified by a sentence in Zhang Er's introduction to *Another Kind of Nation*: 'For readers who are interested in a closer examination of the contemporary poetry scene in Mainland China from 1966...the introduction *in Chinese* to this book written by Chen Dongdong...would be a good place to start.' [my italics] *Another Kind of Nation: An Anthology of Contemporary Chinese Poetry*, edited by Zhang Er and Chen Dongdong (Talisman House Publishers, 2007), pp.4-5.

5. *The New Directions Anthology of Classical Chinese Poetry*, edited Eliot Weinberger (New York: New Directions, 2003), p.xxii.

in the Chinese'.[5] In comparison, a key aspect of Pound's approach is generally supposed to be his emphasis on the ideogram, following Ernest Fenollosa's theories regarding the pictorial aspects of Chinese characters.

Except, as Ming Xie points out in *Ezra Pound and the Appropriation of Chinese Poetry*, 'Pound's Cathay versions do not seem to contain any lines or images that are made on the basis of pictorial etymology. It was only much later, particularly during the forties and fifties…that Pound started making new poetic images by analysing the components of some of the Chinese characters.'[6]

Another, perhaps more persuasive distinction between the two writers' initial approaches is hinted at in a remark by A.C. Graham on Pound's relationship with his sources in Herbert A. Giles' *A History of Chinese Literature*: 'Pound emerges triumphantly by discarding Giles'.[7] Here the aesthetic merit of Pound's text is asserted not in relation to its imagistic properties, but as an act of rebellion against scholarly accuracy.

This is the same line taken by Pound when discussing Waley's translations in a letter from 2 July 1917 to Margaret Anderson, editor of *The Little Review*, where he ensured Waley's translations (and, in 1919, Fenollosa's essay) were published: 'Some of the poems are magnificent. Nearly all the translations marred by his bungling English and defective rhythm…I shall try…to get him to remove some of the botched places. (He is stubborn as a donkey, or a scholar.)'[8]

Here the field of classical Chinese poetry is set up as a Modernist battleground between the dead hand of bungling British scholarship and the lively free-spiritedness of American artistry. There is between these two camps a noticeable absence of any mediating Chinese voice. This gap in the discourse, applied to the situation of modern Chinese poetry, was what I felt most keenly before I first visited China to talk to and to translate its poets. What, I wanted to know, do Chinese writers think about their representation in translation in the west?

I have been invited to China several times over the last seven years, usually for the same set of reasons: to read my poetry and hear the poetry of my contemporaries. To talk to Chinese poets about the possible links between our parallel cultural modes – how and why we write. To learn about their relationship, not just with western writing

6. Ming Xie, *Ezra Pound and the Appropriation of Chinese Poetry* (Routledge, 1999), p. 21
7. Quoted in Ming Xie, p. 13.
8. http://en.wikipedia.org/wiki/Arthur_Waley accessed March 2012.

and its influence, but with the powerful continuing influence of their classical heritage. Finally, to translate one or two poems, from Chinese to English and from English to Chinese, by sitting down with together and talking through our poems line by line.

Perhaps because this act of poet-to-poet translation gathers into itself so many of the issues concerning our modes of cultural exchange, it was while we were having these exciting and creatively stimulating dialogues that the idea for this anthology came to me.

We were in a hotel in Yi, or 'Many Black', County, in Anhui Province, as part of the first Yellow Mountain Poetry Festival. Myself, Yang Lian, the eminent Chinese critic Tang Xiaodu, and my fellow British poet Pascale Petit, were sipping red wine and ruminating on the process so far. This was towards the end of my fourth trip to China, in October 2007.

Previously, in 2005, Pascale and I had gone with Polly Clark and Antony Dunn to Wansongpu, a writers' centre in Shandong Province, to translate Yang Lian and Tang Xiaodu, as well as Xi Chuan and Zhai Yongming, two poets who feature prominently in this anthology. Then, in 2006, I had gone to a conference in Beijing along with the eminent critic and translator Eliot Weinberger, and the US poets Forrest Gander and C.D. Wright, at which I had met Mang Ke, Duo Duo, and other founding figures of the Misty movement, as well as Third Generation writers such as Ouyang Jianghe, and younger writers like Hu Xudong and Zhang Er. Also in 2007, at Hu Xudong's invitation and with the assistance of the British Council, I had read at the Guangzhou Poetry Festival. Each time I had met more and more writers interested in the issue of how contemporary Chinese poetry interacted with the west, and how it could be presented to western audiences whether in English or in the other major European languages.

At some point in a sparse function room in the quiet hotel, quite late in the evening after a long day of discussion – after outings to Ming Dynasty villages famous from recent Chinese movies; after a banquet featuring the fresh bamboo shoots for which the province was famous; after climbing the famous Daoist site of Yellow Mountain and viewing the North Sea of dawn mists – I raised the possibility of an anthology. It seemed to me that the English-speaking reader, although they could seek out the work of the major figures known in the West – Yang Lian himself and Bei Dao, for instance; although they could find traces of the extraordinary flowering of Chinese poetry over the last thirty years in anthologies by Michelle Yeh or John Cayley; although they could catch a glimpse of the extraordinary ferment of more recent writing in Zhang Er's *Another Kind of Nation*, lacked a comprehensive overview anthology of what had been achieved in the face of much oppression and official constraint.

As important as this for me was a perception, arising directly from the type of exchange I'd experienced in the translation process, that the point of finish of most Chinese poetry I was reading in translation was premature. That is, I was encountering a poetics in our dialogues which I could not perceive in already-existing translations. I was engaging with a sensibility, and not just the sense. It appeared this was because of a gap in the usual translation process.

It seemed self-evident that Chinese writers translating themselves into English were often not able to achieve the same idiomatic – or indeed non-idiomatic – finish their work had in Chinese. But, equally, the method of many Chinese and western translators, even when it drew on considerable expertise, did not seem ordinarily to put them in a position to consult the author, or even a close associate of the author.

There therefore opened up a gap between the best efforts of Chinese writers and of their translators, in which the danger was an ordinary reader could not know, or could not be expected to understand, the issues of form and content that were at stake. But, I argued to my friends, it was in closing that gap, in positing translation itself as an act of dialogue, not merely transmission, that true communication begins, not just between poet and translator, but between poet, translator and reader. Because the poet's approach is almost always through the processes and techniques of poetry itself, poet-to-poet translation would foreground and could encompass and engage with such issues as an integral part of the act of translation.

I had realised that this was a formal as well as a methodological issue the previous year in conversation with Yang Lian and Eliot Weinberger after a reading. We were discussing *fu*, an ancient form that moves between prose and poetry, which was often used to evoke a landscape or cityscape at a particular time, sometimes in a subjective or fantastic manner.[9] Eliot was enthusiastically discussing its possibilities as a form in English, so Yang Lian was beginning to describe its formal rules, when Eliot remarked, 'Oh, we'd have to set those aside.'

I could see entirely what he meant – the technicalities of *fu* would sound rather strange in English, while the potential of the mode was far more exciting. His response echoes the position taken by Kenneth Rexroth in Weinberger's *New Directions Anthology* in relation to the forms of classical Chinese poetry:

9. See Burton Watson, *Chinese Rhyme-Prose: Poems in the Fu Form from the Han and Six Dynasties Periods* (Columbia University Press, 1971).

22

Learned and industrious people have tried to reproduce in English the original rhythms, but have managed to produce only absurdities. So Chinese poetry has come to influence the West as a special form of Chinese verse...a special kind of free verse and its appearance happened to converge with the movement toward objectivism, Imagism, and even the Cubist poetry of Gertrude Stein and Pierre Reverdy– 'no ideas but in things,' as Williams says rather naively.[10]

This takes Pound's resistance to scholastic translation and aligns it to a particularly American version of the Modernist agenda: Chinese poetry becomes, to the extent that it agrees with this agenda (to the extent that it is separated from its form?) a suitable influence. Rexroth continues:

Today, for a very large sector of American poets, the poetry of the Far East is more influential than 19th and 20th century French poetry, which has dominated the international idiom for so long, and certainly incomparably more influential than American or English poetry of the 19th century.[11]

I'm sure both Rexroth and Weinberger were largely correct as regards the translation of classical forms, and even in relation to the assimilation of such forms into western poetry, but of course we face a very different issue when we engage with the very diverse appearances of form in contemporary Chinese poetry, where form has re-established itself as an aesthetic choice with specific cultural baggage. This exchange therefore made me realise that we now need to reconsider such approaches, and therefore our translation strategies, when considering poetry written subsequent to the Cultural Revolution.

In short, this reminded me of the tension we can sense between Pound and Waley's approaches – except that we have access to, by a simple act of dialogue, the contexts of both culture and form which they could only approach and understand indirectly. Surely the impact of subsequent Chinese history must become, if not as profound, then as technically significant for the translator as it has been for the poet.

Essentially, it is what Chinese writing is doing now rather than what western writers are attempting to do with Chinese writing that is important. Our translation paradigm has shifted, and is no longer adequately governed by the oppositions set forth by Pound, and so we must re-establish the principles by which we define it. I recognised my own impulse was to attempt cultural translation, to engage with

10. Kenneth Rexroth, in Weinberger, p. 209.
11. Weinberger, p. 210.

the formal issues as far as possible, however problematic that may be, rather than to risk cultural appropriation.

Such issues may seem less relevant in the American context within which much Chinese poetry has been translated into English, in part because it is habitual for many American poets to believe Postmodernism means they occupy a post-formal universe. However, the one thing Chinese poetry appears to teach us is that it is very difficult to be entirely post- anything, let alone Modernism. It appears instead to be the case that many of poetry's most key issues, including the nature of its embodiment in specific forms, continue to present themselves in new but nonetheless living guises, rather than merely haunting us with dead shapes.

Form itself is only one, albeit symbolic, element in what I have alluded to as the essential crisis of Chinese poetry: its equidistance from both classical heritage and western influence, its alienation, through political opposition or exile, from contemporary China itself. There appears to be a reluctance to relinquish any aspect of poetic resource, but rather to rewrite or reinvent it. This is not so much a Postmodernist breakdown of hierarchies, rather a sense of equality of potential, a democracy of utility, given that everything must be revisited – anything, rather than nothing, may be of value. In the testing of cultural equivalences which is part of the translator's endeavour, the constant balancing of relative social values, it seemed to me the UK's complex approach to its poetic heritage, in which nothing is entirely ruled in or out, offered a good match.

This formulation of translation process answered another vague disquiet – a sense that the reader must not, as far as possible, be excluded from the negotiation between translator and poet. This disquiet arose from the gap I often experienced when reading contemporary Chinese poetry in translation. What if the act of translation was habitually or predominantly taking place in a grey area rather than at a meeting point, an area where neither party was fully committing to communication in terms the reader had any opportunity to appraise?

Zhang Er posits this as the Chinese-to-English translator's central issue, referring to Wai-Lim Yip's admonitions about English's embedded sensibilities, those linguistic and ideological preconceptions through which we must approach Chinese poetry in translation:

> ...difficulties arise in translation from Chinese to English...not so much from 'tyrannical framing functions of the English language' as Yip put it, but from the fact that each language exists in its distinct domain of metaphysics, at least in part, in different epistemologies. In other words, each language offers a different conception of knowledge, therefore the world.[12]

Partly supported by a surviving notion of the old Poundian version, partly by, post-Language Poetry, the convention of defamiliarising the surface tensions and textures of poetry, the grammatical characteristics of Chinese often felt as though they were being left largely undigested in the translation, as though they were in themselves a marker of experimental writing, a shortcut to postmodernity. A literal translation from Chinese can read a little as though it might purposively be challenging idiomatic convention, whatever its original intent. Every now and then I got the impression translators were content to work from that, while Chinese writers were to some extent assuming that their original intent (a deeply problematic issue rather than an obvious result) would come across whatever form the target language took. Inherent in such a situation are the dangers of both laziness and arrogance, and I felt we had to seek out a method which would work against the possibility of propping two hubrises, one against the other.

Yang Lian talks in his introduction about the idea of Kunlun, the sacred mountain which functions as a jade ladder connecting Earth to Heaven – I realised from the outset that there was a distinct idealism inherent in my intentions for this anthology, which this ladder some-what ironically embodied. To hope that the act of dialogue between poets can lead to a perfect or 'heavenly' understanding of the original poem is of course to prop my own hubris against nothing, or rather against the transparency of Benjamin's 'real' translation: 'A real trans-lation is transparent; it does not cover the original, does not block its light, but allows the pure language, as though reinforced by its own medium, to shine upon the original all the more fully.'[13]

I nonetheless felt strongly that an emphasis on dialogue, on poets and translators simply talking to one another about the text they were hoping to translate and the motives that led to it, meant that a fuller act of transmission could be possible. The possibility arises that that principles and motives underlying the original act of composition may be more fully embedded in those of the translating poet, and that he or she might therefore seek or create more engaged equivalences in their own language and tradition. For that reason this anthology returns wherever possible to translation as an act of dialogue between an author and a translating poet, and between the translating poet and the professional translator.

12. Zhang Er, p. 439; see also Wai-Lim Yip, *Chinese Poetry: an Anthology of Major Modes and Genres* (Duke University Press, 1997).

13. Walter Benjamin, 'The Task of the Translator', translated by Harry Zohn, in *Illuminations* (Fontana Press, 1992), p.79.

It's less elegant than Yang Lian's definition, of course, but my image of the jade ladder is less the link between the human and the divine, and a little more like the stepladder we use to reach a shelf: two poets may ascend, certainly, one to attempt to deposit and the other to try and collect – either separately or at the same time, either on a single occasion or repeatedly – only to meet, if at all, nose to nose a few feet above the ground, by which I mean above the background interference of our own cultural agendas. The ground itself never quite equates to ground level – we stand on that most unnatural of mountains, a heap of our agglomerated habits, ascended by the coiling paths of separate traditions. Translator and translatee have to make sure, as a first step to that ascent, that they are at least on the same mountain. A stepladder on a mountaintop: the image and the aspiration it represents are more than slightly absurd, but the meeting, after all, by whatever means, is the important thing.

What I have been arguing for here is, in essence, a realignment of emphasis toward regarding translation as a more fundamental act of communication in itself, a mode inherent in all dialogue which posits dialogue itself as the process by which the focal point of literary translation transmutes gradually from source to target language. As a result of being translated, of course, the original text, without changing a word, is changed by its new context: its relationship with its own translation. And, inevitably, the poetics of the translator is also changed by the new work created.

The emphasis of this particular process is upon poetic language as a structure composed of musical, metrical, rhetorical and imagistic or symbolic elements, each of which may have a subtly different role or cultural weight in each language, but, I would argue, these relative weights can only be adequately assessed in the act of translating, of taking the poem across into its new form. (By the way, the idea inherent in this last phrase, that the translation is a kind of metaphor for the original, seems a not unimportant aspect of this way of working and thinking.)

There is here a paradoxical focus on accessing cultural depth principally through verbal surface, on moving back and forth from word to word and line to line and stanza to stanza, both within and across languages, while simultaneously moving from poem to poem and poet to poet and period to period both within and across cultures. This valuing of surface, then, moves the translation process toward a simultaneity of perception while accepting such an absolute cannot be more than fleetingly achieved. Instead it sets in motion a kind of oscillatory mode of thought, a constant movement from the specific to the general and back again, from poet to poet, never fully at rest at either point. The ladder, to return to our central metaphor, tends to shake as we attempt to climb it.

This is, again, a kind of interlinearity like the commentaries of the classical tradition, something which embodies the necessary inter-textuality of the translation process, the constant attempt at mirroring and the actuality of substitution which must take into account both poets' apprehension of their own cultures and traditions at the level simultaneously of line and poem and book. Or, as was often the case here, the apprehension of both editors and the principle translator, and the poet, whenever or if he or she could be consulted.

Because, while the kernel of the book remains those pieces done poet-to-poet as described above, the scope of this anthology means its methods have had to be more various. Around two-fifths of the poems were selected either from existing translations or, as in the case of Lucas Klein's marvellous work with Xi Chuan, from translation emerging through similar close dialogue as *Jade Ladder* was being edited. This selection was a two-fold process: Yang Lian and Qin Xiaoyu indicated those poems they knew were available in translation and thought suitable, then I selected those poems I felt worked most strongly in English.

All other new translations were done according to the following system. Yang Lian and Qin Xiaoyu's initial list was sent to Brian Holton, who has been translating Yang Lian's poetry for almost twenty years. This was while he was still living and working in Hong Kong. An initial draft of the book was produced by Brian, either alone or with Lee Man-Kay, his assistant. This was sent poem by poem to Yang Lian for feedback. Then (having relocated to Newcastle in the meantime) Brian brought a more polished second draft to me. The final part of the process involved Brian and I working closely together firstly to establish where my input was most needed, and then, to re-draft yet again.

Some poems needed only to be discussed, or lightly polished, and left. Others had specific issues of form or reference, problems of tone or address to be cracked. Still others needed to be worked through character by character, studied at arm's length till they would yield nicety, nuance, angle of approach. Sometimes idiom was the crucial final layer, the 'last percentile' in Don Paterson's ringing, touchstone phrase; sometimes we had to ensure the poem was, exactly, unidiomatic.[14] At each stage poems were discarded – either found wanting when

14. Don Paterson, *Orpheus* (London: Faber & Faber, 2006), p. 82.

subjected to such intense scrutiny, or simply lacking sufficient impact in English – and emails flew back and forward between ourselves and Yang Lian and, where possible, the poet.

Then Qin Xiaoyu's essays had to be addressed. Initial drafts in Chinese were translated into, more or less, literals by Yang Lian and his associates in Beijing. These versions were then passed on to me to be edited, which, as it involved substantial cutting and rephrasing, as well as fathoming a wide-ranging set of allusions to the extensive past of Chinese literature and history, meant that a secondary layer of translation dialogues had to be held between myself and Brian and Yang Lian. This process was also followed with regard to Yang Lian's own introduction.

The intention, which you are now in a position to judge, was to orientate and acclimatise the reader to the view from the Jade Ladder. We hope you agree with the perspective reached here, that contemporary Chinese poetry, formed in a culture of undeniably global significance, is not only unique in its scope and its depth, but constitutes indispensable reading for anyone with an interest in the future not just of China, but of poetry itself.

W.N. HERBERT

INTRODUCTION

1

Contemporary, Chinese, Poetry – three words that point to three symmetries: between traditional and modern, between Chinese and other languages, and between poets and poetry. I say 'symmetry' and not 'opposition', because each side of a symmetry must treat the other as the premise of its own existence, and its awareness becomes richer based on the other. These three symmetries also hold three themes important to contemporary Chinese poetry: the creative transformation of the classical Chinese tradition by the contemporary; the linguistic inter-dynamic between Chinese and foreign influence; and the linked questions of 'Why do we write?' (based on our interrogation of the reality we are confronted with), and 'How do we write?' (judged by our aesthetic standards). For the past thirty years, Chinese poetry could be regarded as circling around these three themes.

Trying to depict the poetry of an entire language is difficult. What isn't "contemporary"? How many different kinds of "Chinese" are there in the world? So what I want to discuss is one specific cultural landscape: its geography rooted in the complex political realities and experiences of mainland China in the 20th century, especially after 1949; its weather showing the multiple layers of cultural rupture and how they shape people's thoughts; its borders having nothing to do with the actual map, but established by every pen which keeps writing, whichever corner of the world it is in. In the end, this is what we call poetry, the poetry written in a Chinese that has continually experienced the challenge of 'speaking the impossible' after each disaster: this poetry is different from either classical Chinese or imported influences. It's uniquely itself: *contemporary Chinese poetry*.

I remember very clearly a cold, raining evening in the early spring of 1979, when Gu Cheng and I walked into a lane in Beijing, looking for a particular address. Here it was, a dilapidated doorway in a grey wall, and a dark, messy courtyard that led us into a house where a Gestetner printer stood. This perfectly ordinary place shone with a bright and mysterious light in our eyes, because it was where the editorial department of *Jintian* (or 'Today' magazine) was based, the magazine which gathered together almost all the poets who were discovering a modern Chinese poetry for the first time.

By then, although I'd experienced three years of 'Re-education' – as it was called during the Cultural Revolution, when the young were forced to work in the countryside – I had been writing poetry for some time, but the pre-history of my own writing, my apprenticeship, was far from complete. The question haunted me: what is "our" poetry? what poem is really worth writing? There was the painful memory of the Cultural Revolution, but this did not necessarily lead to any profound understanding, it could not create meaningful writing. What gave contemporary Chinese poetry life? This question never left me, even when, one year later, *Jintian* was banned by the government, and, fourteen years later, Gu Cheng committed suicide during his exile in New Zealand.

My writing, our writing, remains part of a process of seeking. What we're looking for is not merely an answer, it is rather the ability to question ourselves deeply. The contemporary Chinese poet cannot help but be a professional questioner, maintaining a constant position of questioning the self and facing up to a constantly changing world. This tendency could be said to go back like a spiritual link to the first poet named in the history of Chinese poetry, Qu Yuan, who lived about 2300 years ago. His great poem *Tian Wen* ('Heavenly Questions'), is built up of two hundred questions proceeding layer by layer, addressing the origins of universal, mythological, historical and political reality but without providing any answers. He already knew the energy of the question is far stronger than that of the answer.

One question which sounds like a joke, but which put us in a hugely awkward situation, was: 'Is there a Chinese language?' In other words, do the characters in which our work is written provide us with unique values? Or, alternatively, do they cancel out such values? What I am trying to point to here is the position contemporary Chinese occupies as a language between two "others". The first is Western culture, which has latched onto China since the Opium Wars of the 19th century. The second is – strange but true – the classical Chinese poetry tradition itself, which must also be seen as an 'other', even though it has lasted for more than three thousand years. Who would dare to describe him or herself as classical Chinese today? When we assume there is a straight line linking classical China directly to the contemporary era, we just fall into an invisible but nonetheless enormous gap. Even most Chinese people are not aware that more than half of the words we speak today are simply not "Chinese", but loan words from Europe which are derived from Japanese.

Without concepts like Democracy, Science, Human Rights, Law, Politics, Socialism, Capitalism, Materialism, Idealism (these last two were extremely important for Marxism but are totally wrong in Chinese translation) how could we talk about "China" today? But these words have no link to classical Chinese meanings except for their visual appearance in Chinese characters. Based on this "Chinese" language, so-called contemporary Chinese poetry is just a rainbow bridge hanging between two mountain cliffs. Put positively, it's creative and transcendent; put negatively, it's broken and shallow. Even 'Anxiety of Influence' is something we thirst for but can't have. To write in a language which is actually younger than American English, but still hope to stand aesthetic judgement by the exquisite standards of classical Chinese poetry is to speak the impossible to a horrifying degree!

However, to be horrified is not necessarily a bad thing. Only those who have to start with the impossible can hope to achieve the miraculous. Something interesting happened. In the wasteland of Chinese culture after the Cultural Revolution, the last thirty years of Chinese poetry has created an era that is one of the most quick-witted and exciting in the whole history of Chinese poetry. It is not too much to say 'one of the most' here because, if we compare it with Li Bai and Du Fu, the great poets of the Tang Dynasty, the beautiful forms they wrote in were the great results of a long evolution, based on generations of poetic explorations over thousands of years. Furthermore, they shared the same rules and critical judgement of poetry with their predecessor and contemporaries. But what we had to face was much more challenging: to create a form for each individual poetic, and to try to build up our own judgement based on a multiplicity of influences, all within a single generation.

The following steps have been completed: we began at the 'Democracy Wall' in Beijing at the end of the 70s, and developed 'Menglong Shi' ('Misty Poetry') through debate at the beginning of the 80s. We established philosophical and poetical depth in the so-called 'Xun Gen' (Roots Literature) – actually a meditation on Chinese history and cultural tradition which took up the whole of the 80s. We developed a Poetry of Exile after 1989's Tiananmen Massacre, and, more recently, a poetry which faces up to today's weird, raucous China where power and money unite. During this time, when the first group of poets are still writing, several "new generations" have already been born.

We can see three clear stages to the journey: the previous, propagandistic, officially-sanctioned 'Non-Poetry' has been abandoned; the individuality of poets and poetry has been re-built; and healthy and positive debate between different kinds of poetry has spread out to a point where it has become our common understanding. However difficult the situation, a living tradition called 'contemporary Chinese poetry' has nonetheless been created. It is rooted in each individual's creative energy, and gathers materials together from no matter where

31

or when. Perhaps T.S. Eliot's title is particularly apt for Chinese poets: we are all 'inventors', and our poems are inventing a new tradition. We had to invent because there was nothing we could simply copy. Perhaps the great Classical poets can smile again, because individual energy has once again become where we stand. Only with this root can thousands of years of Chinese poetry properly be called a tradition, otherwise, it's just a long-winded past.

In 121 AD, Xu Shen, the author of *Shuowen Jiezi*, the very first Chinese dictionary, defined the meaning of 'poetry' as 'expression of will'. This pointed immediately to the expressionist nature of Chinese poetry. It also explained why there were no epics based on linear narrative in Chinese tradition. Instead, the Chinese achievement was to create a concept of poetic space as a timeless constant and view history in relation to this. This same desire has continued, transforming the Gestetner used by *Jintian* into countless computers accessed by the young poets of the 21st century. Now, at every minute, poems fly in flocks from all corners of the Chinese language, crossing millions of miles of the internet in seconds.

This makes me think about the role played in Chinese mythology by a mountain in the far west of China, Kunlun. It was well known for its beautiful jade, and was often called 'a Heavenly Jade Ladder' that the holy could use to climb between Earth and Heaven. When I read this description by the great Tang Dynasty poet Li He, 'Jade breaks to pieces and the phoenix cries / Lotus drop their tears while the perfumed orchids smile', I thought that this 'Jade Ladder' might also be a metaphor for contemporary Chinese poetry. Unlike the biblical story of the Tower of Babel, building work on this tower has never stopped. The Jade Ladder stands on every poet's desk. We write to climb upon it, and the journey of life between Earth and Heaven is endless.

2

Language and reality always test each other. In Beijing in early 1988, some young poets including myself set up the Survivor Poets' Club. The name was chosen to hint at two kinds of death. One was physical: the nightmare of Cultural Revolution was not far behind, and countless ghosts still haunted us. The other was a spiritual death: as some friends gradually came out from the underground and got better known, being published and even visiting foreign countries, we felt that their works had become slippery and shallow. 'Survivors,' we thought, must fight both deaths. At that point, we never thought that a bloody reality was secretly stalking our choice of language. After the Tiananmen Massacre in Beijing in June 1989, who could dare to say that 'I am not a survivor'?

The Tiananmen massacre shocked the whole world – everywhere, people wept for the dead. But another question came to me: if we were shocked to tears to see the killing for the first time, then what had happened to our memories of previous deaths? Weren't we also those millions on millions who had died in political disasters like the anti-Rightist 'Hundred Flowers' campaign in the 1950s, the Great Hunger in 1959-1961, and the Cultural Revolution? If so, what were our tears for? Were we lamenting the dead or betraying them, washing them away? Which is more terrifying: the huge number of the dead or the emptiness of death itself? My tears were for what and who we were forgetting. Thus my poem '1989' ended up with a line all my friends thought must be a misprint: 'this is no doubt a perfectly ordinary year'. Ordinary, yes, and universal, because the destruction was never over.

The Tiananmen Massacre is therefore an important coordinate for contemporary Chinese poetry. It completed a circle of thinking that started with a question asked about the Cultural Revolution when it ended in 1976: 'Whose fault is this?' This was deepened by our painful introspection throughout the 1980s, contemplating how our history and tradition was rooted inside us, until people's eyes turned again to the political system that continue to produce this malignant and vicious situation. This line linking cultural research to realistic resistance was very clear. It could be seen as one process followed through three tumultuous periods of time, but it also constituted three levels of complexity within this same question we were asking ourselves, 'Whose fault is this?' The energy released by Tiananmen allowed an ancient civilisation to break through all these layers of historical chaos and finally relocate its root in humanity.

If we go back to the end of 1978, the streets in Beijing were at once both frozen and burning. At the Democracy Wall – a grey-brick wall, little longer than a hundred metres, near the crossroads of Xidan, covered by thousands of pages of hundreds of unofficial magazines – gathered a huge number of victims of the Cultural Revolution from all over the country.

On this wall I read *Jintian* for the first time: the brightness of Mang Ke, 'the sun rises / sky – that blood-drenched shield'; the cold, sharp words of Bei Dao, 'Disgrace is the disgraced person's travel pass / nobility is the noble person's epitaph.' I seemed to smell a fragrance

33

through its oily printed pages: poetry itself – a new language that had abandoned those big and hollow political words, and so shot directly into my heart.

Shortly after that, the underground literary circle floated up to the surface. There was the gloomy voice of Duo Duo, 'the beasts of burden wear the blinkers of cruelty / from their hindquarters black corpses hang like swollen drums'; the deep thought of Jiang He, 'Every fissure on the earth gradually / infests my face, wrinkles / raise weary waves on my brow' – and Gu Cheng, who whispered in 'Fantasia of Life,' written when he was thirteen years old, 'Sleep! I close both eyes / and the world is nothing to me.'

These poets were barely aware that, without consulting each other, they were creating and following a new poetics: they expressed their own feelings in their own language. Not only with respect to the themes of their poetry but also with regard to the language they were drawing on, they were breaking away from the political propaganda of the officially-sanctioned 'Non-Poetry' style. The early 80s debate about this writing was predicated on a complete misunderstanding – just like its name, Menglong Shi ('Misty Poetry'), which was given by officially-sanctioned reviewers and actually meant 'obscure, vague, incomprehensible'.

The officials called those poets 'anti-tradition', though poets will defend their right to oppose or revise the traditional. But calling them 'incomprehensible' was simply due to the limitations of lopsided and lazy reading. In contrast to official "poetry", filled with slogans containing neither feeling nor meaning – 'Socialism,' 'Capitalism' – 'Misty Poetry' returned to the images of Sun, Moon, Earth, River, Life, Death, Dream: how could this be called 'anti-tradition'? On the contrary, what this poetry precisely did was return to 'Tradition' – at least, to the pure words Classical poetry used.

Within Misty Poetry, there was a meeting between Li Bai and Du Fu on the one hand, whom we learned by heart when we grew up, and, on the other, the hand-copied poems of Baudelaire, Éluard, Lorca and Neruda. They all gathered together and enlightened us throughout the Chinese disaster. Since the inception of our writing, then, we have been inspired by nightmares, a bitter but bright formula that always stirs up poetry.

Jintian was without doubt the most important literary magazine in Chinese literature after 1949. With a total of just nine issues, and running for less than two years, it performed the Genesis-like act of formally naming contemporary Chinese poetry. It summed up two key points for Chinese writing: the significance of our generation's

34

experiences; and the conception and forms of a poetry which had developed from the linguistic nature of Chinese characters. I say 'experiences' meaning not only political life, because, since *Jintian*, the whole system of Chinese political language – its way of thinking, as well as its whole system of expression – has been totally abandoned. Both the aching void in our memory and the pain and numbness of life permeated our everyday life, and were therefore retrieved for the purposes of serious poetry. Our poems, published in *Jintian*, filled with shocking imagery, completed an aesthetic journey via Ezra Pound's 'Imagism' back to the soul of classical Chinese poetry: as though a modern import-export business, this strange literary journey unfolded like Marco Polo's, only in the opposite direction!

Simply by touching on the surfaces of imagery and sentence structure, Misty Poetry had already opened up the future of Chinese poetics: it had established a creative link enabling the rediscovery of the Chinese poetic tradition, making it a source of inspiration to the present. These ideas excited many young Chinese: the thousand copies of each issue of *Jintian* were passed a thousand times to still more people, who copied its blue and white cover by hand – wherever it touched, new poets, poetry salons, poetry magazines, and group after group of readers were created. *Jintian* ended forever the meaningless opposition between official 'Non-Poetry' and poetry: after it, the competition would only be between different kinds of poetry. A real, living tradition had been born.

But the shadow hadn't really moved away. In 1979, after a struggle for power within the central party apparatus, Deng Xiaoping established complete control, and the Democracy Wall was soon banned. *Jintian*, through pretending to be 'pure literature', lasted one more year, finally stopping when the police said, 'If the press turns one more time, everyone goes to jail.'

A popular subject at the turn of the 70s and 80s was 'Shanghen Wenxue' or 'Scar Literature', though blood is still leaking – when did we really recover from the wounds of the Cultural Revolution? In 1983, 'Anti-Spiritual Pollution', a centrally orchestrated mass movement began, and Chinese people watched the nightmare of the Cultural Revolution begin again. As one of the 'sources of pollution', my long poem 'Nuorilang' was criticised nationally, the charges running all the way from 'attacking reality' by stating that contemporary reality was 'dark and bloodied', to showing 'no hope in history'. I still remember today, how one older writer, who had experienced a lot of political troubles, looked at me then. In his eyes, I was someone who had been sentenced to death, or was already dead. Ironically, I had to admit to myself most of the charges were true – in fact, these critics should be called my best readers, because for exactly these reasons 'Nuorilang' became one of the most representative pieces of Roots Literature.

This term 'Roots' was used in the almost exactly opposite sense to the expression used by African Americans. Our root is not in other places, but under our very feet: in the depth of this land and its history. Cultural introspection in the 1980s forced us to question ourselves profoundly: within a political system of lies, is anyone merely a victim? Or are they also part of the persecution? At the very least, our silence was complicit in and subservient to that persecution. There was a crazy magic in this: our painful existence within history had secretly been turned into the pain of a kind of non-time.

We dreamt about moving forward, but woke up again and again in the deepest darkness of history. This was always called 'Revolution', but it had lost even the most basic virtues of humanity and common sense.

China in the 20th century could be called a nation of cultural nihilists, but was there any understanding we could base on that classical Chinese culture which the country had tried its best to abandon? We had failed to make a modern transformation of our own tradition, what we saw before us was something that could only be called 'Communist Culture' in the sense that it was the worst version of Chinese autocracy hidden beneath Western revolutionary language. With its multiple layers of internal splits, it was completely unqualified to be called 'traditional'. These issues were all being worked through in the depths of poetic thought and language. Our resistance had by now become a resistance to our own self-delusions and inhibitions. By the mid-80s, the energies driving poetry had reached a turning point: from relying on external and collective subjects as some sort of social intravenous drip, it turned to the individuality of the poet and of poetry itself.

Thinking of the 80s, we always feel a little homesick. We were lashed by waves of experience – some serious, some energising, some spiritual, some sexual. We counted time in months, even in days. Poetry had been opened up, and restlessly broke through the forbidden zones of politics, the economy, culture and sex. In 1986, a newspaper in Shenzhen – the first city in China to allow joint ventures with western firms – held an 'Exhibition of Modern Chinese Poetry Schools', a total of 84 Schools displayed their own manifestos with poems. They called themselves 'Third Generation', after the 'First Generation' of official Non-Poetry, and the 'Second Generation' of Menglong poets – and they are also known as 'Post-Menglong'.

This huge group of poets displayed very disparate qualities – their slogans were noisy and unclear, but together they outlined a period: contemporary Chinese poetry had transcended its ideological in-fighting, and had already built up aesthetic diversity. The original river of *Jintian* had created different tributaries which now ran toward different estuaries. The poets' individual thinking and aesthetic ideas were not only beyond official control, but also refused to be limited by the judgement of Misty Poetry. A synchronic period began, mixing up republished Chinese classics such as 'Songs of the South' ('Chu Ci'), and 'The Complete Tang Dynasty Poetry' ('Quan Tang Shi'), with the waves of translations that brought Homer, Dante, Yeats, Eliot, Plath, and Dylan Thomas. All this was hybridised, making up the genetic code of Chinese poetry today. Perhaps even we did not fully realise that, if you could take a bird's-eye view of the whole history of Chinese poetry, how colourful and interesting this period would seem.

When the Survivor Poets' Club met in 1988, China had a newly restored energy for political and cultural thinking. The second 'Survivors' poetry reading, held in the spring of 1989, could be called a group show of dissident stars, and therefore the 'Survivors' were banned immediately after the Massacre for being, allegedly, among the 'black hands' (party-speak for provocateurs) behind the student movement.

When I was in New Zealand and heard the news that *Huang* ('Yellow'), my new collection of poems, and my book-length essay, *Ren de Zijue* ('Awareness of Man'), had been banned and destroyed, I felt as though my poetry had died in my place, and another strange cycle of non-time began as a footnote to this period of poetry. It felt like the same situation had begun again, this time staring cruelly out from the lines I had written shortly before leaving China: 'Every non- person / only arrives home when they can no longer return.'

3

The Tiananmen Massacre was not a uniquely Chinese incident: within just four months, the Berlin Wall fell. Perhaps no one experienced more complex feelings than the Chinese did on seeing what was happening in Berlin. Before our very eyes, History was flowing in the opposite direction. The day when exiled Eastern European writers returned home was the day we truly began to be in exile. We were on a different and delayed train. But this delay perhaps also meant the issues went deeper. Those Chinese who had been exiled as political dissidents soon felt themselves to be the conscience of dissidents throughout the world. Today, on the one hand, ideological control in

China is getting even tighter, while, on the other, a selfish and cynical attitude floods the entire world. Money buys everything, even the principles of Good and Evil, in the mind of big companies' CEOs. The words I used in my poem '1989' – 'a perfectly ordinary year' – became, despite anything we could have done, true. Tears dried. The dead were forgotten. So, where could Chinese poetry go now?

The answer had to be back to Poetry itself. To be inspired by nightmares is still an effective formula. After 1989, a large group of Chinese poets went into exiled or stayed abroad. This meant a huge amount of Chinese poetry was now being written in exile. The exciting thing about this is that a cruel and painful experience made us write much better. Contemporary Chinese poetry reached a higher peak than ever before in the early 90s.

Bei Dao continued to smelt his cool images, 'The moon endlessly rubber-stamps black business.' Duo Duo's anger got stronger every day, 'I shut the window, and it's no use / the river flows backwards, and it's no use'. Gu Cheng's sudden death in 1993 cut down his unique, sharp, illuminating intuition, 'In fact   once the water is hot the horse has fallen over / the thinner   the legs the longer and the more fallen-over   is it possible not to fall over?' Zhang Zao's sweet-ness was mixed up with poison, 'The women take me to the edge of the universe / to eat ashes, ah, the unreal pasture'. Xiao Kaiyu quietly opened up the inside of things, 'Dozens of cows by the field lines, quietly growing meat.'

Exile, as a theme of life and the spirit, is complete now. It is not merely the result of events; it has become all poets' common form of existence – even an internal quest. Its place in poetry has become clear too. Exile does not provide poetry with an additional value. It has to be transformed into the depths of the language of poetry. Its literary value has to be based on how one writes. This is because a poetry-of-exile does not really exist: there is only poetry. This was what made us suddenly realise that all poets – crossing all places and times – are alive. A long list began with Qu Yuan, Du Fu, Ovid, Dante – but we all belong to the same state with no boundaries, we all have poetry as our 'Unique Mother Tongue'.

Poetry in China echoed the writing produced in exile. After Tian-anmen, China appeared to have lost its voice. Friends' letters were full of words like 'powerlessness,' and 'emptiness'. I was deeply moved by the fact that it was almost the same group of poets from *Jintian* and 'Surviving Poets Club' who broke the silence first. In 1990, Mang Ke, Tang Xiaodu and others published another unofficial magazine, *Xiandai Hanshi* ('Modern Chinese Poetry') – it even went back to printing with a Gestetner. In its first issue were new poems of mine, all written abroad.

Looking at the familiar names of the editorial committee, feeling the thin, rough paper, I knew there is a line that cannot be broken. It runs through time and space, linking us up no matter where we are. As we entered the present period of economic reform and 'opening to the world', this line became woven into a further network of writers, which in the internet era has become even bigger. Nowadays, the idea of contemporary Chinese poetry is without geographical limit, and private exchanges of our writing is – almost – beyond political control.

Among those remaining in China, Mang Ke continued directly from *Jintian* to complete a very rare case of self-renewal through his long philosophical poem, 'Timeless Time'. Yan Li deployed his powerful imagination to create a recognisable style based in metropolitan speech. The 'Post-Menglong' or 'Third Generation' of 1980s poets became the main force. Zhai Yongming, who had become known as the 'Chinese Plath' because of her famous early sequences, 'Woman', and 'Jing An Village', after two years of silence spent in New York, shone out in a series of new poems that deepened her work in the narrative mode, while maintaining the energy of her earlier writing. Xi Chuan, initially a representative figure among student poets, combined the roles of poet, scholar and translator, and let the perceptual strength of his poetry erupt within more philosophical reflections. Yu Jian has always been loyal to his 'poetry motherland and mother tongue' of Yunnan province, but with ' Zero File', a long political poem which has affiliations with conceptual art, threw out metaphor under the slogan of 'anti-metaphor'. Ouyang Jianghe, another talented poet who produces poems with his right hand and theories with his left, is always the brass in the poetic orchestra. Other outstanding figures include Bai Hua, Chen Dongdong, Zang Di, Yang Xiaobin, Sun Wenbo, Meng Lang, Wang Xiaoni, Zhong Ming – all post-Menglong poets who gained their followers and critics among the younger poets born in the 1970s and 80s.

Some claim poetry has been marginalised, submerged beneath the commercial China of the 21st century, but if you are a good diver, then you will find a huge population of poets, as well as hundreds of serious poetry websites – in fact, the ocean is bottomless, with countless hidden channels. What's important here is not the number of poets, but the depth of thought.

Today, "China" is a huge question mark. It no longer asks us about the choice between different ideologies as during the Cold War, but about what we should be and do in the choice-less situation individuals face under full-blown Capitalism. Shortly after the Tiananmen Massacre, Ouyang Jianghe pointed out that 'a profound break' had happened. Soon, this idea was developed by Tang Xiaodu, perhaps the most important critic of poetry in China since the 80s: he argued that contemporary Chinese poetry moved into a period of 'a poetics of the individual'.

This meant each poet had to construct his or her own individual system of philosophy and aesthetics, including their attitude toward the social and spiritual reality in which they found themselves, toward their mature concept of poetry, and toward the 'tradition' that had to be rewritten for each poet's work, leading ultimately to the form and language each poet settled on for every poem. Here, the term 'individual' was intended to point out the differences between poets, while 'poetics' indicated a complete system that could be challenged by others.

At this point, an argument I put forward comes into play: every Chinese poem must be both conceptual and experimental. Every collection of poems is a project of thinking and art. We must find the inner necessity linking our poetics to our choice of form, and push the writing until it becomes a journey. Therefore no one is permitted by that choice to repeat the same strategy, or, to put this more extremely, even when we think we are renewing the tradition, we are actually obliged to start again from zero. This is the only way to deal with the heavy political pressure, the complexity of language sources, and the incomplete cultural environment of recent and contemporary China. Seen from this point of view, the noisy debates which spring up among Chinese poets, like, for instance the one in 1999-2001 about the discourses of 'intellectual writing' and 'daily speech', all miss the point, because there is no forbidden zone in language, the only real question is how you use it.

Achieving a perspective from which we can look back on 20th Century poetics, with their emphasis on seeking new forms, is a painful experience for Chinese poets. Following a new fashion only to return to an inferior old mode is an often-repeated game. The aim of a poetics of the individual is to avoid this strategy, and build up instead the links between the ancient and the new: to seek so deep an understanding of the issues facing us that a new form of expression cannot help but be created. This is how poetry renews itself.

In recent years, we have been holding a series of deep one-to-one exchanges between Chinese and English-speaking poets, and also with Japanese, Arabic and Indian writers. Typically these take a form like the 'Yellow Mountain Poetry Festival,' the first poetry festival between

Chinese and English writers, which took place from 2007 to 2008. This was rooted in poet-to-poet translation, then went on to very intense discussions intended to establish shared grounds and concerns. Beyond these private discussions there were also public events, and the whole project was recorded, with this documentation providing a foundation for future dialogue. This is what I call an 'extreme exchange' – I think we should learn to love the word 'extreme': if the original is an extreme piece of writing, it challenges the translator to produce an extreme translation, and this leads on to truly exciting dialogues between the different cultures.

4

Jade Ladder is exactly this kind of extreme book. This selection of over 60 poets and more than 200 poems, including a number of long poems and sequences, is not only a gathering of the best of Chinese poetry in the last thirty years, but also a map of thought. It attempts to present a complete picture of the complex and exciting events which have been unfolding in contemporary China, and locate this in the depths of its poetry. To read it should be like taking a pulse in Chinese medicine, and the pulse of poetry is linked to every development in language, society, thought and culture in China. Every poem is like a leaf, growing from the branches of the poets' nervous systems, which in themselves touch a richer soil, right down to the depths of ore and magma. The Jade Ladder, then, is still Kunlun Mountain, standing at the centre of Universe; and whoever reads this book is climbing between earth and heaven.

This means that the works selected for this anthology were judged as poetry, and according to the quality of the language, without admitting any other standard, regardless of the fame any given poem may have accrued because it was banned or its author imprisoned, or because it dealt with a politically correct subject matter, whether that be exile, sexuality or political or other minorities. If it is indeed to be a project of thinking and art, poetry must embody its thought in its forms, not just discuss an idea. The particular concept, structure, form, language, sentence and words in a poem constitute its thought. I want to add to Mallarmé's concept of 'pure poetry', to say, pure poetry does not exist, but we must therefore write every poem as though it were pure poetry. Even the most private love poem, the sharpest political poem, are led to a deep understanding of existence by their individual expression. Therefore those works which were weaker as poems, but were once 'well-known' because of their social context, are not included here: between historic and poetic value, the editors of this anthology stand unambiguously on the side of the poem. Our motivation is simple: we are watched by Qu Yuan and Du Fu, and when did these great poets throw their works into the ring without great care? They would never attempt the kind of games with images that happen today, in which it becomes too easy to make the poem too obscure. In this anthology, we hope to rebuild the formal values of poetry. If Russian poets treat Pushkin as their point of origin, and if American poets need to sign a contract with Whitman, then contemporary Chinese poets must remember the thousands of great masters running all the way back to 2300 years ago when Qu Yuan appeared. They stand among us, outside time, staring at our pens.

This principle is demonstrated by the three stages of editing this book: the selection of the poems; the translation process; and its structural design. Three stages and one principle: to maintain high standards by taking no short cuts.

When selecting the poems, we didn't choose a work because of convenience, because it had already been translated or was easy to translate. We went back to the original Chinese, and selected what qualified from there. Both classical Chinese poetry and world poetry formed our standard, to judge whether or not the poem was unique. This was like a 'tower built downward': there was no existing model, we had to take a bird's-eye view on all these poets. The sheer quantity was the first difficulty. Luckily myself and Qin Xiaoyu, the Chinese assistant editor of the anthology, are both insiders and outsiders. He and I are two authors of contemporary Chinese poetry who, at the same time, also try to be its reviewers and examiners. Since 1989, I've been living aboard, and this distance is one necessary prerequisite for clear judgement. Qin Xiaoyu lives in China, in the eye of the whirlpool of contemporary poetry, and is one of the most exciting poetry critics born since the 1970s. Our map was therefore drawn up by both memory and reality.

This principle of editing is in itself a classical reference: *300 Tang Poems*, the best-known anthology of Tang poetry, edited around 1763 by Sun Zhu, selected only those poems written in the most exquisite forms, and no exception was made even for the great Du Fu. The difficulty of translation was rarely considered during this initial selection – sometimes, near-untranslatability was even seen by the editors as a proof of originality, and rather than a reason to exclude a piece, was taken as a good reason for it to be included.

We collectively agreed there must be creativity in the translation process. The poem in translation should reflect its original nature, making the original and the translation 'two trees grown from the same root.' Their differences are external, their cores identical, whether at the levels of concept, form or linguistic energy, or in the more difficult areas of music and rhythm, normally thought to be near-impossible to translate. Translation is, simultaneously, loss and gain within one process, and what is lost from the Chinese will, we hope, be balanced by gains in the English. Our target here was to bring Pound's profound power of discovery and invention into harmony with Arthur Waley's fluency of expression.

The structure of the book is one of its most distinctive aspects. We do not simply list all the poems by a given poet under her or his name, but separate them into different sections of the anthology as if into different territories of a map. There are six different 'provinces', almost six smaller anthologies, each based on a different mode. This separation into six modes makes each poet's different area of focus clear, and helps to locate him or her on the map of contemporary Chinese poetry.

Contemporary Chinese poetry can reasonably be called a miracle, because it illustrates the huge energy produced by a transformation of the whole of Chinese culture, an extremely complex blend of fission and growth. Even though poetry may be said to have cooled down now from the white heat of the 1980s, it's certainly the case that there is a bewildering diversity of choices in today's society. This pace of change and huge diversity means that the influences of both classical Chinese poetry and foreign literature can be described as the 'other', while at the same time they can also be seen as materials waiting to be selected in an act of self-creation. Contemporary Chinese poetry is, therefore, nothing other than a world poetry written in Chinese, and its effective-ness can only be assessed by a global readership.

This means there is no comparative standard of "Chinese-ness" that we can hide behind. The century-long debate about whether Chinese or Western culture should be the main source of modern Chinese thought has ended in this: our source can only be the individual who is capable of continually questioning more and more deeply. Based on this principle, anything, no matter which culture it comes from, can be selected and used. Was this the vision of Tang Dynasty poetry, or of Pound's Cantos? I would say it was and indeed it still is. The globalisation of poetry is the only opposition to that self-centredness, cynicism and unprincipled attitudinising which pollutes our nature and our hearts today.

Poetry functions like a central question-mark, it runs vertically through the axes of time and space, and poets create in concentric circles around it, their poetics constantly and necessarily expanded by recurrent acts of spiritual betrayal. One action is required of us all: to lay claim to the jade ladder standing in the vast depths of the human heart, and through writing poetry transcend ourselves.

YANG LIAN

PART ONE

LYRIC POEMS

QIN XIAOYU

Sword of the Universe: On Lyric Poetry

Since *The Book of Songs*, traditionally reputed to have been edited by Confucius in the 6th century BC, the lyric poem has always been the mainstay of classical Chinese poetry.[15] All the famous names from the classical tradition, such as Tao Yuanming (365-427 AD), Li Bai (701-762 AD), and Du Fu (712-770 AD) were, without exception, lyric poets. Many would argue that modern Chinese lyric poetry began with the May Fourth Movement. This completely changed classical poetry in terms of language and form, dismantling the traditional concept that poetry should be practically useful, a tool for teaching politics, and greatly subverting the Confucian 'Doctrine of the Mean' and its aesthetics. Contemporary Chinese poetry has largely continued in this direction. Recently, looking back on the ideas that drove himself and Mang Ke to start the underground literary magazine *Jintian* in 1978, Bei Dao said, 'People nowadays can hardly imagine what it meant to rename the sun in those days.'[16] This was the most valuable part of the Misty Poetry movement – its courage to break through conventions in extremely difficult times.

The relationship between modern lyric poetry and the classical lyric is still the subject of heated debate. One school of thought contends that the two share a continuity of values, and deny the independence of modern poetry, but have found this difficult to prove. Others consider the breaking point of 1919 to be the beginning of modern poetry, and therefore try to find within modern poetry itself its principles and aesthetic values.

We would argue that there has indeed been a profound change, deeper than many of the changes in poetic style that took place in the ancient dynasties, which has opened up a much wider aesthetic space – but without eliminating the structural unity between the two. Both classical and modern poetries share the goal of building up new phenomena by creating a poetic language that breaks away from what

15. See *The Book of Songs*, translated by Arthur Waley, edited with additional translations by Joseph R. Allen (New York: Grove Press, 1996), or *The Classic Anthology Defined by Confucius*, translated by Ezra Pound (Cambridge: Harvard University Press, 1954).

16. In these introductory essays, where Qin Xiaoyu is quoting from an untranslated text, as here, it has not been thought helpful or necessary to include a reference to the Chinese source.

Hegel termed the 'prosaic' nature of reality.[17] Lyric poetry doesn't paint the surface of daily experience, but builds an internal world through poetic expression.

For poets, this is a fate they have to face rather than a subject matter to talk about. Within this new historical context, how do we transform the classics and build up a strong connection with our tradition through individual creative energy, without falling into the arrogance of a historical nihilism? Different poets have taken different approaches to rediscovering and transforming the classics, or, 'smelting the old elements to make the new'.

One way of rediscovering the classics is that taken by Xiao Kaiyu: persona. Compared with classical writers, modern lyric poets tend to project ambiguous and complex self-images: prophets, revolutionaries, saints, madmen, thanatophiles, psychics, naughty kids, bystanders, ghosts. But Xiao Kaiyu created the persona of a Confucian bureaucrat for himself, and thereby his goal of rediscovering the classics acquired a counter-revolutionary aspect. He regards Du Fu, the great Tang Dynasty poet, as his model, and has tried to return poetry to the issues of ordinary life, as though he were an official who has to manage practical affairs. He rejects images of the Emperor and the people, because 'People often are just the faces of the Emperor,' but, equally, distances himself from what he calls 'professional intellectuals' who create purely linguistic wonders, arguing, 'this role of the Confucian official can help Chinese poets to mature…'

Zhang Zao tried from the beginning of his career to develop a poetic technique which would transform aspects of classical aesthetics and bring these into the depiction of contemporary life. His poem 'In the Mirror', which established his reputation at the age of 22, demonstrates this remarkable style. The poem echoes the methods of *Huajian Ji* (Among the Flowers), a well-known classical collection of decadent and erotic poems.[18] As often seen in classical poetry, Zhang Zao omitted the subject of his poem in order to create a sense of presence without anything seeming to be present, an illusion like the reflection in the mirror. From there, Zhang Zao began to develop his own musical language, skillfully creating a voice based on the natural rhythms of daily speech, in order to approach the musical beauty of the *ci*, a form of lyric poetry popular since the Song dynasty (8th–11th century).

Zhang Zao's experiment in transforming the classics is also shown

17. http://www.marxists.org/reference/archive/hegel/works/ae/ch02.htm accessed March 2012.

18. By Zhao Chongzuo (934–965 AD); see Lois Fusek, *Among the Flowers; The Hua-Chien Chi* (Columbia University Press, 1982).

in the way he turns classical symbols into the equivalent of Eliot's objective correlative. 'In the Mirror' begins with 'only if she recalls every regret in her life/will plum blossom fall and fall', and ends with similar but further developed images:

> only if she recalls every regret in her life
> will plum blossom fall and fall across Southern Mountain.

Plum blossom is a very common symbol in Classical Chinese culture. The young Zhang Zao brought a modern linguistic understanding to this image when he linked it with the Chinese character for 'regret', drawing on the visual similarity between 悔 ('hui', regret) and 梅 ('mei', plum blossom).

The literal meaning of 'lyric' in Chinese is 'poems which express feelings'. This was understood as a blending of emotion with reason, in contrast to the dissociation of sensibility that T.S. Eliot ascribed to poetry in English. Qu Yuan's anger, the hidden sadness of Ruan Ji (210-263 AD), the respect for nature of Tao Yuanming (365-427 AD), the deep concern for life of Du Fu (712-770 AD), and the great passion and will of Li Bai (701-762 AD), were all models of this expression of human feeling.[19]

This concept was explored after the end of the Cultural Revolution in 1976. During the 1980s, many poets, such as Haizi and Bai Hua, created slogans like 'the lyric is blood'. And after 1989, a number of lyric masterpieces were written by Chinese poets in lonely exile. At the same time, other poets who remained in China, such as Xiao Kaiyu, Sun Wenbo and Zhang Shuguang, began a difficult transformation based on what they called an 'ethics of responsibility'. They tried to advocate 'middle-aged writing' and narratives – poems of restrained feelings or even anti-feelings. They attempted to create a more or less dramatic distance between the subject (the lyrical self) and the world of the spiritual self.

Some younger poets, however, carried on the traditional lyric. Ma Hua was one of those born in the 1970s (called the 'Post-70s' poets). In 2003, he resigned from his job in Beijing and went to Mingyong

19. Qu Yuan, et al., tr. David Hawkes, *Songs of the South* (Penguin Classics, 1985); Ruan Ji, tr. Graham Hartill & Fusheng Wu, *Songs of my Heart (Yong Huai Shi): The Chinese Lyric Poetry of Ruan Ji* (Wellsweep, 1988); for Tao Yuanming, see James R. Hightower, *Poetry of T'ao Ch'ien* (OUP, 1970); David Hawkes, *A Little Primer of Tu Fu* (Penguin, 1967); and Burton Watson, *The Selected Poems of Du Fu* (Columbia University Press, 2002); Arthur Cooper, *Li Po and Tu Fu: Poems Selected and Translated with an Introduction and Notes* (Penguin Classics, 1973).

Village in Yunnan Province, and became a volunteer teacher for about 20 Tibetan kids. By Meili Snow Mountain, he threw himself into teaching, and passionately collected local Tibetan music and songs, recording traditional Buddhist ceremonies and rituals. He died in an accident in June 2004, when his jeep drove into the Lancang River.

'Snowy Mountain Canzonets' was the last group of poems composed by Ma Hua. It's made up of 45 poems of 5 lines each, with each poem containing 31 syllables. Ma Hua borrowed this form from Japanese poetry. His method contrasts with Zhang Zao's poems in that Zhang often uses symbols from classical texts while Ma Hua's 'Snowy Mountain' is simply the formidable 6000m mountain opposite his school.

Landscape Poetry is another great tradition in Classical Chinese poetry, pure landscape poetry being started by Xie Lingyun (*d.* 433 AD).[20] A good comparison here would be between Ma Hua and the great Tang Dynasty Buddhist poet, Wang Wei (699-759 AD).[21] Both built their understanding of existence through an engagement with landscape. Their poems are not, therefore, merely an attempt to paint a view, but rather to try and catch its soul.

Ma Hua's goal was to write things with crystal clarity. He hoped that his poetry would follow Wang Wei, achieving an inner beauty. He doesn't come to occupy the place, but to learn transcendence from the mountain, to be purified by it, the self opening like a worn-out wooden door. Here he clearly demonstrates the difference of his approach from the usual 'misty' image, which had almost become *de rigueur* for contemporary Chinese poetry. For Ma Hua, the image shouldn't be obscure. His poetics was grounded in simple concrete things, and by this means he hoped to rebuild clear links between those things and the poet's internal world.

The title of this essay comes from a famous Peking opera: *Sword of the Universe*. This was the name of the great sword used to kill a well-known bad emperor (the second emperor of the 3rd century BC Qin Dynasty). It is the central object which brings the story together. It could also stand as a metaphor for the relationship between lyric poetry and social reality.

In his essay, 'The Dangerous Journey towards the Landscape of

20. J.D. Frodsham, *The Murmuring Stream: The Life and Works of the Chinese Nature Poet Hsieh Ling-yun* (385-433), Duke of K'ang-Lo (University of Malaya Press, 1967).

21. Jerome Chen and Michael Bullock, *Poems of Solitude* (Abelard-Schuman, 1960); also Eliot Weinberger and Octavio Paz, *Nineteen Ways of Looking at Wang Wei* (Moyer Bell, 1987).

Language', Zhang Zao tried to mark poets' different attitudes to social reality as the main difference between Misty and Post-Misty poetry writing. In his mind, Misty poets like to join, while Post-Misty poets prefer to keep their distance and observe. Whether or not this is the case, there is still one thing all these poets have in common in: an uncompromising attitude toward preserving the independence of their writing.

This concept of literature keeping itself completely separate from official society almost never existed in traditional times. According to Zhang Zao, this was because the traditional bureaucrats and the poets were essentially the same people: intellectuals were therefore supporting the state in their work and as a result it would be very difficult for them to be critical of it.

The attitude and posture of poets changed markedly during 'The Democracy Wall' period that took place in Beijing in 1978-79 when the underground literary magazines built up another 'tradition' for Chinese poetry: in 'Answer' Bei Dao declared, 'I'm telling you, World / I—DON'T—BE—LIEVE.' A new posture of refusal was mixed with both social criticism and a romantic voice.

The same posture is shown by Post-Misty poets too. Meng Lang wrote the following lines:

> I despair too, so in my mouth is –
> Nuclear! Spoken from my mouth is –
> Not clear! Held in my mouth is –
> Nuclear! Swallowed from my mouth is –
> Not clear! The long-distance runner starving
> Just rushed out from a red corpuscle
>
> ('Confused in the Terminus')[22]

Here Meng Lang uses the character 钚 ('bu') for nuclear because it's made up of two parts: on the left, the metal radical and on the right, 不 ('bu' No). A degree of resistance is therefore already built into the character, which in this translation is brought out by alternating 'nuclear' with 'not clear'.

The hungry long-distance racer in this poem was a perfect image for a lyric poet under the control of a totalitarian state. In Zhou Lunyou's poem 'The Difficulty of Playing Chess against the Hand of the State Champion' his opponent is called 'the hand of the state'. Zhou Lunyou gives this poem (and the game) two endings: to be a

22. Where not otherwise indicated, all texts appearing in these essays are translated by BH and WNH.

recluse or a martyr – but as both endings are a kind of negation, the poet decides '...you must pretend nothing happened / and on a chessboard with no squares / keep on playing chess with that invisible hand'.

The underground literary magazines that began with *Jintian* and then proliferated continue to play an important role, as indicated by Xi Chuan: 'Today's way of publishing has opened up a small tradition for Chinese poetry. Because of it, a proportion of younger poets have lost interest in the official publications.' Based on these numerous unofficial publications, contemporary Chinese poetry managed to maintain its aesthetic independence and even its attitude of resistance. This became even more important when globalisation of the market became the new background to Chinese writing. Poetry, because of its uncommercial nature, naturally evades most attempts at control, whether political or commercial. Having endured going underground or into exile it can resist big business.

The very point of classical Chinese poetics, according to Confucius, was that 'poetry expresses the will'. If poets confine their will within their poetics, this is too restrictive, but, equally, if they connect their will too directly to social affairs they become shallow. Both are dangerous. In Duo Duo's words: 'A poet should maintain his or her own orbit in order to stay away from the revolution.' His writing has kept in a dazzling orbit for many years. Many of the Misty poets' well-known works which were based in their social situation have faded over time, but Duo Duo's surrealist poems of the early 1970s, which were full of the anger of resistance then, are still highly respected by younger poets now.

When Duo Duo demolished the surface of reality and built up something else, a pretended madness, he demonstrated his resistance to political reality at a deep level. He wrote 'In Weather Such As This No Meaning At All Is To Be Had From Weather' in 1992 when he was in exile in Europe, and the 'weather' is clearly political. Though he opposed writing directly about politics, he was still trying to open a little crack within this oppressive weather, and attempting to create 'another universe' from this.

Duo Duo could be seen as one of the best lyric poets of the Mao Zedong era. In the convex mirror of his poems, we recognise many of the principle elements which ran through Mao's time – autocracy, struggle, idealism, violence – all deeply rooted in the weather of Duo Duo's poems. As he wrote in 'Only Permit':

only permit one person
the person who causes your death has already died

wind causing you to be familiar with this death
only permit one death
each word, a bird whose head is crushed by a collision
ocean continues to leak from an earthen jar that stumbled...

Everyone knew who that one was. Within the long tradition of the autocratic system, there is always only one such individual: the imperial 'we'. But Duo Duo's resistance to autocratic power was also in its way autocratic. This was, to borrow an expression from Chinese medicine, 'opposing poison with poison'. Duo Duo employs equally cruel and ugly images. On the one hand he denies that reality is a nightmare, on the other he affirms like Baudelaire that something blossoms from sin. His poetics is different from Xiao Kaiyu's Confucian aesthetic, Zhang Zao's Taoist aesthetic, or Ma Hua's Buddhist aesthetic. He conveys an extremity of passion that can perhaps only be compared to the Red Guards of the Cultural Revolution itself. Perhaps this was why he said, 'Poetic taste is inhuman' – perhaps he wanted his readers to be both shocked and aroused by the aesthetic nature of the inhuman.

For Duo Duo, language becomes a further autocratic system that one must fight; he describes Chinese characters as 'in control / climbing over each other / to oppose their own significance'. His resistance to autocratic politics transferred that autocracy into his internal world. Poetry became a battle with itself, a fight against its own meaning. His best work was mainly written in two of the most difficult political periods: during the 1970s and just after the Cultural Revolution; and shortly after the Tiananmen massacre when he was in exile in Europe.

This may point to why many Misty Poets stopped writing in their fifties and sixties – otherwise a golden age for creativity. How could they continue to be angry when China's face appeared to have changed completely? Isn't contemporary China materially rich, culturally colour-ful, even internationally influential? Poetry is no longer a dangerous force for the regime at all. When the poets are no longer young men, where does their anger come from? Doesn't it get weaker and weaker, only to disappear finally into an ocean of pleasure, of selfish and cynical life. To many Chinese lyrical poets, the word 'poetry' only evokes the past.

For the Chinese, idealism was, initially, a lovely dream, which swiftly turned into a cruel nightmare, and now it has become a spiritual nostalgia for intellectuals. Looking back at the whole tradition of Chinese poetry, the gap between poets' ideals and reality provided the energy for their writing. The present global context has actually made this gap even wider. On this realisation is built the foundation for understanding all classical Chinese masterpieces – they become part of the world's canon not because of their antiquity, but because of this depth to their thought and aesthetics. Poetry faces this challenge all the time.

BEI DAO (*b.* 1949)

Accomplices

Many years have passed, mica
gleams in the mud
with a bright and evil light
like the sun in a viper's eyes
in a jungle of hands, roads branch off and disappear
where is the young deer
perhaps only a graveyard can change
this wilderness and assemble a town
freedom is nothing but the distance
between the hunter and the hunted
when we turn and look back
the arc drawn by bats
against the vast background of our fathers' portraits
fades with the dusk

we are not guiltless
long ago we became accomplices
of the history in the mirror, waiting for the day
to be deposited in lava
and turn into a cold spring
to meet the darkness once again

[Bonnie S. McDougall]

The Window on the Cliff

From a precarious position the wasp forces open the flower
the letter has been sent, one day in a year
matches, affected by damp, don't shed their light on me any more
wolf packs roam among people turning into trees
snowdrifts suddenly thaw; on the dial
winter's silence is intermittent
what bores through the rock is not clean water

chimney-smoke cut by an axe
stands straight up in the air
the sunlight's tiger-skin stripes slip down the wall
stones grow, dreams have no direction
life, scattered amid the undergrowth
ascends in search of language; stars
shatter; the river on heat
dashes rusty shrapnel towards the city
from sewer ditches hazardous bushes grow
in the markets women buy up spring

[Bonnie S. McDougall]

On Tradition

The mountain goat stands on the precipice
the arched bridge decrepit
from the day it was built
who can make out the horizon
through years as dense as porcupines
day and night, windchimes
as sombre
as tattooed men, do not hear ancestral voices
the long night silently enters the stone
the wish to move the stone
is a mountain range rising and falling in history books

[Bonnie S. McDougall]

It has always been so...

it has always been so
that fire is the centre of winter
when the woods are ablaze
only stones that don't want to come closer
keep up their furious howl

the bell hanging on the deer's antlers has stopped ringing
life is one opportunity
a single one only
whoever checks the time
will find himself suddenly old

[Bonnie S. McDougall]

The Art of Poetry

in the great house to which I belong
only a table remains, surrounded
by boundless marshland
the moon shines on me from different corners
the skeleton's fragile dream still stands
in the distance, like an undismantled scaffold
and there are muddy footprints on the blank paper
the fox which has been fed for many years
with a flick of his fiery brush flatters and wounds me

and there is you, of course, sitting facing me
the fair-weather lightning which gleams in your palm
turns into firewood turns into ash

[Bonnie S. McDougall]

Starting from Yesterday

I cannot enter the music
only lower myself to revolve on the black record
to revolve in a blurred moment of time
in the background fixed by lightning
yesterday a subtle fragrance drifted from each flower
yesterday the folding chairs were opened one by one
giving everyone a seat
the sick have been waiting too long

57

the winter shore in their eyes
stretches further and further away

I can only enter the winter shore
or else the hinterland
sending red leaves scattering in fright
I can only enter the dim school corridors
confronting specimens of every species of bird

[Bonnie S. McDougall]

SOS

rain beats against the dusk
the sharks of unclear nationality
have beached themselves, war bulletins
are still the news
you carry a measuring cup to the sea
grief lies on the sea

in the theatre, the lights dim
you sit among the
finely sculptured ears
you sit in the centre of the noise
and then you go deaf
you have heard the SOS

[Bonnie S. McDougall]

23. *(Opposite page.)* Tiantian, the nickname given to the poet's daughter, is written with repeated characters which look like a pair of windows. The same character also forms a part of the character for the word 'picture'.

A Picture [23]
(for Tiantian's fifth birthday)

Morning arrives in a sleeveless dress
apples tumble all over the earth
my daughter is drawing a picture
how vast is a five-year-old sky
your name has two windows
one opens towards a sun with no clock-hands
the other opens towards your father
who has become a hedgehog in exile
taking with him a few unintelligible characters
and a bright red apple
he has left your painting
how vast is a five-year-old sky

[Bonnie S. McDougall & Chen Maiping]

For T. Tranströmer

you take the poem's last line and
lock it centre heart – it's your centre of gravity
centre of gravity in a church swinging among tolling bells
dancing with headless angels
you kept your balance

your grand piano's on clifftops
the audience grabbing it and holding tight
a crash of thunder strikes, a flight of keys
you wonder how that night train
caught up with tomorrow's darkness

leaving your blue train-station house
you brave rain to check mushrooms
sun and moon, forest signal-lights
behind the seven-year-old rainbow
a capacity crowd's wearing automobiles as masks

[David Hinton]

A Guide to Summer

as if beaten into gold foil by invisible artisans
the sea suddenly breaks into light –
fleets chasing night set out in all directions
carrying lights, those crystals of angels

flocks of gulls perform mystical calculations
and the result is forever one casualty
wind raising its limp feathers
making more of this one dying fact

sheer accordion-spread canyons
echo, driving naked lovers into hysterics
an old castle on the coast
maintains symmetry with its image at sea

[David Hinton]

Landscape Over Zero

it's hawk teaching song to swim
it's song tracing back to the first wind

we trade scraps of joy
enter family from different directions

it's a father confirming darkness
it's darkness leading to that lightning of the classics

a door of weeping slams shut
echoes chasing its cry

it's a pen blossoming its lost hope
it's a blossom resisting the inevitable route

it's love's gleam waking to
light up landscape over zero

[David Hinton]

Moon Festival

Lovers holding pits in their mouths
make vows and delight in each other
till the underwater infant
periscopes his parents
and is born

an uninvited guest knocks at my
door, determined to go deep
into the interior of things

the trees applaud

wait a minute, the full moon
and this plan are making me nervous
my hand fluttering
over the obscure implications of the letter
let me sit in the dark
a while longer, like
sitting on a friend's heart

the city a burning deck
on the frozen sea
can it be saved? it must be saved
the faucet drip-drop drip-drop
mourns the reservoir

[Eliot Weinberger & Iona Man-Cheong]

Black Map

in the end, cold crows piece together
the night: a black map
I've come home – the way back
longer than the wrong road
long as life

bring the heart of winter
when spring water and horse pills
become the words of night
when memory barks
a rainbow haunts the black market

my father's life-spark small as a pea
I am his echo
turning the corner of encounters
a former lover hides in a wind
swirling with letters

Beijing, let me
toast your lamplights
let my white hair lead
the way through the black map
as though a storm were taking you to fly

I wait in line until the small window
shuts: O the bright moon
I go home – reunions
are one less
fewer than goodbyes

[Eliot Weinberger]

To My Father

on a cold February morning
oaks in the end are the size of sadness
father, in front of your photo
the eight-fold wind keeps the round table calm

from the direction of childhood
I always saw your back
as you herded black clouds and sheep
along the road to emperors

an eloquent wind brings floods
the logic of the alleyways runs deep in the hearts of the people
you sending for me become the son
I following you become the father

fate coursing on the palm of a hand
moves the sun the moon the stars to revolve
beneath a single male lamp
everything has double shadows

the clockhand brothers contend to form
an acute angle, then become one
sick thunder rolls into the hospital of night
pounding on your door

dawn comes up like a clown
flames change the bedsheets for you
where the clock stops
time's dart whistles by

let's catch up to that death-carriage
spring path, a thief
explores for treasure in the mountains
a river circles the song's grief

[Eliot Weinberger]

MANG KE (*b.* 1950)

The Moon on the Road

1

The moon walks me home.
I want to carry her into tomorrow.
All the way in this silent calm...

2

Miaow, miaow, miaow...
Please do not disturb.
Are you human,
or something more reliable, perhaps?

3

Certainly,
There's nothing better to take pride in than being human.
But you?
You're a cat.
And a mouser may look at a Mao.

4

I want to carry her into tomorrow!
However, whatever –
A little thought is better than no thought at all.

5

Life really is this wonderful.
Sleep!

6

The moon floats alone above the waste.
Exactly when she wandered off,
I haven't the slightest.

[BH, LMK, WNH]

Sunflower in the Sun

have you seen
have you seen that sunflower in the sun
look at it, it hasn't bowed its head
but bends its head back
as though to bite off in one
the noose on its neck
held in the sun's hand

have you seen it
have you seen the swaggering
sunflower glowering at the sun
its head almost blocks the sun's light
and its head, even when there's none
still gleams bright

have you seen that sunflower
you should get close to it
get close then you'll see
the earth beneath its feet
every fistful you grab
will surely squeeze out blood

[BH, LMK, WNH]

Spring

The sun gives its blood
To the dying earth.
It sets the sunlight flowing
Into the body of the earth
And makes green leaves and branches
Grow from the bones of the dead.
Can you hear it?
The offshoots of dead bones
Are the clinking winecups of flowers.

[Michelle Yeh]

DUO DUO (*b.* 1951)

A Single Story Tells His Entire Past

When he opens up the windows of his body which give onto the ocean
And leaps towards the sound of thousands of clashing knives
A single story tells his entire past
When all tongues stretch towards this sound
And bite back the thousands of knives of this clashing sound
All days will squeeze into one day
Thus, each year will have an extra day

The last year flips over under the great oak
His memory comes from a cattle pen, overhead is a pillar of lingering smoke
Some children on fire holding hands sing and dance in a circle round the
            kitchen knife
Before the flames die down
They persistently rage round the tree
The flames finally injuring his lungs

And his eyes are the festival days of two hostile towns
His nostrils two enormous tobacco pipes pointed at the sky
Women wildly shoot love at his face
Forcing his lips agape
Any moment, a train traveling in the opposite direction to death will pass by
Forcing a morning between his outstretched arms
Pressing down the sun's head

A silent revolver announces the approach of this morning
A morning more cheerless than an empty basin thrown to the ground
A sound of branches breaking in the forest
A broken pendulum on an old door shutter lifted
            down from the funereal street
A single story tells his entire past
Death has become a superfluous beat of the heart

When stars dive towards the snake venom-seeking earth
Time rots beyond the tick-tocking of the clock
Rats shed their milk teeth on the rust spots of the copper coffin

Fungi stamp their feet on decaying lichen
The son of the cricket does laborious needlework on his body
And then there is evil, tearing apart his face on a drum
His body now entirely filled with death's glory
Entirely, a single story tells his entire past

A single story tells his entire past
A thin lanky man sits resting on a tree stump
The first time the sun reads his eyes closely
And closer still it sits on his knees
The sun makes smoke between his fingers
Every night I fix my telescope on that spot
Until the moment the sun dies out
A tree stump takes its rest where he sat

More silent than a cabbage patch in May
The horse the road walks past in the early morning
Death has fragmented into a mound of pure glass
The sun has become the thunder rolling down the road
          of the mourners returning home
And the children's slender feet tiptoe onto evergreen olive branches
And my head swells up, like millions of horse hooves stamping on drums
Compared to big, crude, curved knives, death is but a grain of sand
So a single story tells his entire life
So a thousand years turn away their face – look

1983   [Gregory B. Lee]

Farewell

Forever embracing the white birch
Is just like embracing myself:
    a whole mountainful of red peppers stirring me
    a whole handful of pebbles scattered on the ground
    a whole tree, all of these are my memories…

Autumn is the most desolate of lutes
Things from the past, vigorously strumming:

fields harvested
ah, fields with no home to return to
should you wish to cry, don't miss this big opportunity!

1983   [Gregory B. Lee]

Looking Out from Death

Looking out from death you will always see
Those whom all your life you ought not to see
You can always be buried somewhere as you please
Sniff around as you please, then bury yourself there
In a place that makes them hate

They shovel dirt in your face
You should thank them. And thank them again
Your eyes will never again see your enemy
Then from death will come
When they are consumed by enmity, a scream
Although you will never be able to hear again
Now that is the absolute scream of anguish!

1983   [Gregory B. Lee]

Milestones

A main road attracts the very first direction that makes you dizzy
That is your starting point. Clouds envelop your head
Preparing to give you a job
That is your starting point
That is your starting point
When the jail squeezes its temperament into a city
Bricks and stones in the middle of the road hold you tight
Every year's snowfall is your old jacket
The sky, however, is always a blue university

The sky, that miserably pale sky
Sky whose face has just been pinched
Agrees to your smile, your beard
Hastily eating
When you pursue the big tree that penetrates time
Golden rats, having crossed the water, dream of you:
You are a crinkled bean in a fierce storm
You are a chair, belonging to the ocean
Wanting you on the shore of humanity, to study all over again

To seek yourself, on the journey when you know yourself
Northern snow, that's your road
Flesh on shoulders, that's your food
Oh traveller you who do not even look back
Of everything you hold in contempt, nothing will ever vanish

1985 [Gregory B. Lee]

Shrubs

What we've said over and over they can't hear
They see each other but do not see
On the surface see but do not see
Roots

However seek each other in the mud
Once found they twist each other to death
Amongst us there are people who
Call this behaviour:
Love

Lovers who have just climbed trees
Are also thinking this over
They call it:
Making love.

1985 [Gregory B. Lee]

Stupid Girl

In the pitch black night dyeing mother's hair, the sound of horseshoes
Approaches. Mother's coffin
Starting to put on clothing for mother.
Mother's shoes climb up the tree alone
Wind left for mother, like iron refuses to disperse
Mother's end
Means winter
Out of enmity disintegrates

Winter has already completed its oppression
The sound of horse hooves blossoms on the clanging iron plate
On the earth swept to glinting by the snow, the wind
Says the wind is cruel,
Meaning a different sort of cruelty: says
Things which escape into the sky
Are paralysed in mid-air,
Meaning mother's whole life
Is just ten toes simultaneously broken
Says mother throwing charcoal in the fire
Is throwing a child, meaning a stupid girl
Sympathising with the ashes in the fire
Says this is wrong, meaning:
'I will offend again!'

1988   [Gregory B. Lee]

Walking into Winter

Sounds emitted by the leaves have changed
Rotting fruit and kernels sting the eyes of the passer-by

On the red roofs where the grain was sunned
Shimmering skulls of tiny insects, piled up as autumn's substance

A touch of autumn is brushed from a woollen overcoat preparing for winter
Fungi from decaying coffin wood have already walked into winter

70

Youngsters in sunlight have become ugly
Marble parents sob noisily:

When water at the well-bottom is gone
Ploughs are dead in the ground

When the iron is bent in the smithy's hands
The harvesters hold bent blades to their breasts

Those in the funeral procession are rolling drunk
The translated sounds of the wheat waves of May are already so remote

Trees contemplate the far away places preparing to marry them off
Cows, in bowel-tightening dung-retaining posture, defy the movement
          of the heavens...

1989   [Gregory B. Lee]

In England

After the church spires and the city chimneys sink beneath the horizon
England's sky is darker than lovers' whispers
Two blind accordion players, heads bowed, pass by

There are no farmers, so there are no vespers
There are no tombstones, so there are no declaimers
Two rows of newly planted apple trees stab my heart

It was my wings that brought me fame, it was England
Brought me to the place where I was lost
Memories, but no longer leaving furrows

Shame, that's my address
The whole of England does not possess a woman who cannot kiss
The whole of England cannot contain my pride

From the mud hidden in the cracks of my nails, I
Recognise my homeland – mother
Stuffed into a parcel, and posted far away...

1989-90   [Gregory B. Lee]

Watching the Sea

Having watched the winter sea, what flows in the veins is surely blood
      no more
So when making love one should surely gaze on the ocean
Surely you are still waiting
Waiting for the sea breeze to blow on you once more
That breeze will surely arise from the bed

That remembrance is also, surely is
False images of the ocean preserved in the eyes of dead fish
Fishermen are surely engineers and doctors on vacation
June cotton in the earth is surely cotton swabs
Surely you're all still in the fields seeking vexation
Trees you brush by are surely bruised and swollen
Huge rage surely makes you have a future different from the crowd
Because you are too fond of saying surely
As Indian women will surely reveal their flesh at the waist

The distance to the place you live together is surely not far
The distance to Chinatown is likewise surely not far
Surely there will be a moon shining like a mouthful of spit
Surely there will be people who say that is your health
No longer important, or even more important, surely
Surely it stays in your mind
Just like that arrogant bomb-casing on England's face

Watching the sea surely uses up your lives
Stars preserved in the eyes have surely become cinders
The ocean's shadow surely seeped from the seabed to another world
In a night when somebody anyhow must die someone surely must die
Although the ring surely does not wish to be long dead on the flesh
Shooting hormones into a horse's ass will surely stir it up
So to arrange tidily is then surely to create disorder
When a bicycle chain falls off peddling surely gets faster
The spring wind surely resembles the kidney stone sufferer's fastened
      green belt
The taxi driver's face surely resembles stewed fruit
When you go home that old chair will surely be young, surely

1989-90 [Gregory B. Lee]

I'm Reading

In the November wheat field I'm reading my father
I'm reading his hair
The colour of his tie, the crease of his trousers
And his hooves, tripped up by shoelaces
Now skating on ice, now playing the violin
The scrotum shrinks, the neck, knowing too well, stretches toward
     the sky
I read as far as my father's being a large-eyed horse

I read as far as his having temporarily left the herd
His coat hanging from a small tree
And his socks, and appearing indistinctly in the herd
Those pallid buttocks, like a meat-stripped
Oyster shell containing a woman's toilet soap
I read as far as the scent of my father' s hair oil
The smell of tobacco on his body
And his tuberculosis, illuminating the left lung of a horse
I read as far as a boy's doubts
Rising out of a patch of golden corn
I read as far as when I was old enough to understand
The red house roofs where grain is dried start to rain
The wheat sowing season's plough drags four dead horse legs
Horse skin like an opened umbrella, and horse teeth scattered
     everywhere
I read as far as one face after another is carried off by time
I read as far as my father's history silently rotting in the ground
Locusts on my father's body, just continuing to exist alone
Like a white-haired barber embracing an aging persimmon tree
I read as far as my father's returning me again to a horse's belly
When I just want to turn into a stone bench in the London fog
When my glance passes over the men strolling down the bank-lined
     street...

1991 [Gregory B. Lee]

They

Fingers stuck into pants pockets jingling coins and genitals
They're playing at another way of growing up

Between the striptease artist's elevated buttocks
There is a tiny church, starting to walk on three white horse legs

They use noses to see it
But their fingernails will sprout in the May soil

The yellow earth of May is mound upon mound of flat explosives
Imitated by death, and the reason for death is also

In the very last jolt to the soil of the ironware in heat
They will become a part of the sacrificed wilderness

The silence of the long dead dead before dying
Made all they understood change no more

Their stubborn way of thinking, their doing
Their giving away childhood

Kept death intact
They made reckless use of our experience.

1991   [Gregory B. Lee]

Instant

The instant the sound of the street cellist recollects
In the sky at dusk the last brilliant fleck of sunlight is dying out
Dying over an old railroad station

A grey intestine opens wide in the sky
Outside it there is nothing
Except for a weight, still sitting atop the river's surface
That was the weight of the church shimmering
Now, it seems there is only silence

After the sound of the cello there is only silence
Trees quietly change colour
Children quietly drink their milk
The sand freighter quietly sails by
We watch, like tiles quietly watching a roof
We sniff the air of when whoever and we were together
It's already quietly died out

Whoever existed, it was only light displayed no more
Whoever left themselves, it was only an instant
Whoever said that instant was our whole life
And this instant, the sound of Scottish rain
Suddenly pattering on a basin –

1992   [Gregory B. Lee]

In Weather Such As This No Meaning At All Is To Be Had From Weather

Land has no boundary, railroad tracks no direction
Rejected by a dreamed-out dream
Stuffed into a shoebox
Controlled by a sort of lack of means of denouncing
In the time an insect takes to walk by
Those fearful of death increase their dependence on fear

>   In weather such as this
>   You are an interval in the weather

Whatever you stare at you are forgotten by
Inhaling what it exhales, it bores into your smell
Staring upon the change before daybreak
You find the opportunity to turn into grass
Passing by trees grown by people
You forget everything

>   In weather such as this
>   You won't stand by weather's side

Nor will you stand by faith, only by the side of fabrication
When horses' hooves no longer fabricate dictionaries
Ask your tongue to fabricate hornets no more
When wheat in fabrication matures, afterwards rots away
Would you please eat up that last plum in the nightingale's song
Eat it up, then leave the sound of winter on the branch

      In weather such as this
      Only fabrication advances

1992 [Gregory B. Lee]

The Time I Knew the Bell-sound Was Green

From whichever way the tree faces I accept the sky
In the trees hide olive green words
Like light hiding in a dictionary

Recorded by stars that have passed on
Balanced by flocks of blinded birds, light
And its shadow, death and death to come

Two pears swaying, on the tree
Fruit has the earliest shadow
Like the bell-sound hiding in the trees

On the trees, December wind resists yet fiercer wine
There is a gust of wind, hastening the arrival of discourse
Blocked by the upright post of the granary, blocked off

Dreamt by the marble stone's bad dream, dreaming of
Being startled by the sound of the wind going down to the tombstone,
      startled awake
The last leaf flees to the sky

Autumn's writing bursts from the tree's death
Just then, the bell-sound illuminates my face
For the last time delivering a golden sky –

1992 [Gregory B. Lee]

Locked Direction

It was the unemployed locksmiths who were the very first to direct your gaze
When your hovering buttocks passed through the shadow of the apple tree
To the glum face of a cook, turning towards the fields

When tongues kneel down, gradually kneel in the same direction
They cannot find the mouth that can say you
They want to say something but cannot manage to

      Say: There are still two olives

When kissing you can become robust
And there is another tongue, which can be a wine bottle corkscrew
And there are two clouds on a clear day, embracing on the river bank
There's the kiss you shared with another right now becoming the
wild strawberries that grow in the borderlands

      What's it matter that tongues are agreed

It's in the midst of corn that there are riddles! History's decayed
And marble bites your neck
Two olives, riddles within riddles
Control the magnet in the bird's head, shaking ancient scenery
Maybe making people's nothingness vacillate between two pillars of cement

      Only then will the dead have souls

On a street of black umbrellas
There's a heavy bag of oranges about to be picked up
From within a poisonous oyster another sky is about to open up
In the horse's head, a marble bathtub cracks:

      Green time approaches

A frozen chicken in the refrigerator earnestly hopes
Two raisins dependent on the roast leg of lamb earnestly hope
From within unforecastable weather
From within the dripping sound of coaxing a boy to pee
From within the skimmed milk
From within the last operation

Earnestly hope, together with golden sand to blaze once again into the storm

A storm rises from within the sweat glands of smoked meat
and the armpits of violence

When ice floes deploy the posture of pregnant women to stay afloat
Earnestly hope are the only words they leave behind
When your hovering buttocks break open locked direction
Obstruct with naked flesh the passing of the long night
The words they leave are the sperm that pierce through cement –

1994   [Gregory B. Lee]

Unlockable Direction

It was the unemployed locksmiths who were the last to direct your gaze
When your hovering buttocks pierced through the roast chestnut man's coma
To a cook's covered-up face, kneeling towards the fields

When tongues kneel down, gradually kneel in different directions
They find the mouth that can say you
But say no more. Say, they abolish it

Hear say: There are still two olives

When kissing you may become robust
Hear say there is a tongue may replace a wine bottle corkscrew
Who says there are two clouds on a clear day, embracing on a river bank
Whose kiss was shared with whom became the wild strawberries that grow
in the borderlands

It doesn't matter that the corn agreed

It's in the midst of the shadow that there's corn. History's decayed
There are shadows of marble biting your neck
The shadows of two olives, shadow within shadows
Break open the magnet in the bird's head controlling the salad in the bird's crop
Maybe making people's nothingness stagnate between two pillars of cement

The dead will never again have souls

On a street once filled with black umbrellas
There's a heavy bag of oranges that has finally been picked up
Grey skies from within a poisonous oyster flick open a big stage prop
The thought in the horse's head, as clear as a light bulb filament:

In a performance green time approaches

A frozen chicken in a refrigerator wakes up
Two raisins dependent on a roast leg of lamb wake up
From within already-forecast weather
From the dripping sound of inhibiting a boy's peeing
From within skimmed sperm
From within an operation there wasn't strength to complete
Wake up, together with golden sand once again blaze into the storm

A storm that bursts out from within the shower head

When pregnant women deploy the posture of ice floes to stay afloat
Floating is the only word they leave behind
When your hovering buttocks lock up that unlockable direction
Confess with naked candour the passing of the long night
The sperm they leave behind are words built to death by cement.

1994 [Gregory B. Lee]

ZHONG MING (*b.* 1953)

Devil in the Well

> 'Fragrant angelica drowned in a stinking pool'
> – Liu Xiang, *Embittered Thoughts* from *Nine Laments*[24]

'Then I'm the one playing the whistle under the peach blossom!'
Paper Embroidery Boy, have you changed your silky heart?
When I'm about to drill your muff
can you turn into *Rain on the Parasol Trees*?[25]

A dream so very unjust:
a foam-spurting toppling swing,
bedding made of silver
a curtain of water washed by a crescent moon.

Tiny tiny devil in the well, so very bent your eyebrow-ends;
eh, two slanting breasts,
an arse so very wet.

Oh, a bronze man would die at the sight of it,
straight into the bush to bust his bowl, see!
Innocent boy, can your eyesight
penetrate that half-rumpled red dress?

A demobilised emperor, with willow fingers
he loaded me into the little Red Chamber.
His stiff cicada snout,
it took my ring off in the curtain's shade.

Between the legs, a lawn of weeping and wailing,
an embroidered quilt of clouds, of death.
With an opposite-sex Tang Minghuang grinding away all night,
until the west wind brings the news of parting.

24. See David Hawkes, tr. *Songs of the South* (Penguin Classics, 1985).
25. A play by Mongol dynasty dramatist Bai Pu (1227-1306), telling the story of the affair between Tang dynasty Emperor Minghuang (685-762) and the dancer who became his consort, Lady Yang. It ended in civil war, Lady Yang's death at the hands of the Imperial guards, and the emperor's abdication.

The horse on top of the wall, I rolled off its back
I maddened his cruel heart,
pushed him into bloodshed and horror,
turned an aristocratic embryo into a hooker from Hangzhou.

Cherry-lipped little devil, poking the world's bones,
the well-bottom is so very big, there are perfume-gatherers stepping
        on the scenery,
there is a spine pressing on the sisters' black-painted eyebrows,
how much of hate is water, and how much is tears?

Even more Chinese scholars and emperors in the crowd,
twining with dead hair the ropes that will hang them,
substituting lonely night-time tears for these terrible times,
oh, in the end it's still an open well of beauty!

I'm cuddling a carved bronze vase of bitter bile,
hugging a bottle of West Lake water from Hangzhou, a handful of rice straw,
sunk in a puddle of tears for ever and aye,
under the touch of the uncertain moon.

Little god of fallen flowers, hidden three-inch lotus shoes,
who planned this inexpressible dimension?
A haggard silver bed full of the nightingale songs of women –
for whom am I playing my whistle with such loving care?

11 May 1993   [BH, WNH]

Dried Fish

Left behind in unweeping treetops, the secret mark.
Flowery coat, bulging with two fish, lets the wind look:
is it the one tail that churns the river, swallowing smoke and spitting out the moon,
or is it the other soaring to the skies to erect a horoscope, sealed in lacquer skin?

Washerwoman, southern washerwoman, see
two gleaming eyes of gold coin, shining on a crow-black intelligence,
hold it in both hands, lover, oh tell me all the lies,
sweetheart, gentle, but nearly nothing at all.

Is that spring suit still enough to cover my carcass,
to make these snow-spinners cast away their armour and come again,
at play among the lotus leaves, are they east or are they north?
In the weeds a brouhaha of voices, oh, splendidly shod in leather,

a flock of birds fluttering on the flowering branches, a dream of angels,
      don't know
how to endure the cold, don't know the bitter tree in the archive of
      itinerant letters,
the pretty sandstone turned, too, into a peach in a dream,
arousing these cheeks and chins. Someone wearing gold and silver

bouncing among the leaves on the tree, frothing at the mouth,
the little silver pub, perfumed teeth matching lovely legs,
why is my heart so low, so melancholy,
my much-caressed face still not sure how to behave?

Are separate nails better, or is their total handier for
floating through the air? Is an overcoat that reveals the fish tail better,
or is a naked couple entwined around each other,
painting their single pale line by day and by night?

The river flows past this stone and not a trace of it is ever seen,
but fish are telling us of things slowly accumulated,
all this still moving train of thought, northerner's and southerner's
mutually mocking voices, vague white splinters.

Weaver Girl, the silk-weaving Weaver Girl, makes me think of
those hunters who are afraid of something, and so venerate that something
as an ancestor: for example, wild boar, skulls, the sun's
beard, woman's organs of generation. They annotate straws in the wind,

finally gulped down by the fish in the straw. The easiest things for them to
break are cotton shirts, not hearts, so they
listen unmoved to the music of the Weaver Girl's strings,
eyeballs of dead fish turning in blank spaces to face upward.

The little breeze blows evenly through the trees, forest tips hung with old
      clothes,
the path, oh, the path, it's always full of fallen leaves!
What's least visible is the gentlest, distinct and gentle as a streamer,
when fish and fish trickle across the river, there will always be weeping!

1992 [BH, WNH]

Eating with the Lamas, Zhao Jue Temple, Chengdu

'All I smell is humans becoming ghosts'
Han Shan (*fl.* 9th century AD)

I don't want to see white clouds – day and daily
the pitter-patter of chewed pine kernels in the thicket,
never for an instant forgetting the magic of food and
drink or the people's rough coarseness.

In the face of holy foresight I swear I'll be more focused,
like the court's most cautious oil lamp or yellow streamer,
more controlled by heat and cold, feeling the look beneath the cassock.
There's no one slaughtering live fish on the flagstones,

there's only straw sandals carelessly kicking tyrants.
Hiding their faces as they furtively eat, talking of mysteries and demons,
but they don't get any pity; in the House of the Senses
the monks are mixing the rice in their begging bowls,

every grain pure white, instant enlightenment in one thought.
Whoever is able to live in solitude and keep away from downtown crows,
can then be too idle to deal with these dozy dopes.
And those grudges too, coming from that rough coarseness.

Not knowing to take the shoes off, not knowing to bow down,
knowing even less about that abstraction of language, how to be
sweet, how to be grown-up, how to be disciplined;
pain, the shame and pain discovered in the night,

torments those actions lacking in ceremony,
inside only rice stalks and the depressing nature of poverty,
only mosquitoes and flies tumbling inside,
one speck of Buddha's swarf would calm those things down.

I can't bear those tearful palenesses,
I'd rather totter on crane's knees and examine my conscience; [26]
in this life can I still see that idleness comes from the empty skeleton,
and still inhabit and observe the sweet heartbeats?

13 January 1999   [BH, WNH]

26. 'Crane's knees' is one of the Eight Faults in both versification and calligraphy: Zhong Ming is admitting to fallibility.

YU JIAN (*b.* 1954)

Beer Bottle Top

no idea what to call it   just now it was still at the banquet's top table
the guardian of a bottle of stout   indispensable   it had its own identity
signifying twilight contentment   and the depth of a frothy glass
it jumped away with a bang as dinner began   a motion much like a bullfrog
the waiter almost believed it was a real frog   he even thought something
actually came back to life on the food–filled dining table
he rued his illusion   focusing straight away on a toothpick
he was the last   after this   the world wouldn't think of it ever again
there would never again be a dictionary entry about it   never again its
denotation   never again its connotation or figurative sense
while the china plate originally placed below it   would have signified the
flavours of Sichuan
the napkin was being used by a general's hands   roses in full bloom
          a metaphor of nobility
on its peculiar curve it left this event   this wasn't its curve
breweries   never designed a line like this for a bottle of beer
now, it lies together with orts like cigarette butts   footprints   bones and
          floorboards
none having anything to do with any other   an impromptu pattern   nobody
useful to anybody else
and it's even worse   a butt can make the world think of a dirty tramp
a bone signifies a cat or a dog   footprints surely hint at somebody's whole lif
it's junk   its white is only its white   its shape is only its shape
it's beyond everything our adjectives can touch
at that time I hadn't started drinking   it was me who opened this beer
that's why I got to see it jump so oddly   gone, as simple as that
I suddenly wanted to jump out like it did with a BANG, too   but I couldn'
being the author of an anthology and a sixty-kilo body
I merely bent over   picked up this rare little white beauty
its hard   crimped edge   scratched my finger
making me feel a kind of sharpness nothing to do with knives

[BH, LMK]

The Nail That Skewered the Sky

my daughter is memorising a chapter of her English textbook
she always gets stuck at the word nail
the mirror is hanging on a nail
my wife is admiring herself in the mirror
but she always bumps into the nail
the eerie sound from the TV next door
is also sucked back into the wall by the nail
with the water in the kettle whistling at boiling point
the nail has nailed the night down even deeper

I've found the nail that skewered the sky
I nail it into the wall inch by inch
nail it into a black dot
like a fly crawling on the wall

[BH, LMK]

YAN LI (*b.* 1954)

Unstoppable

can't stop
whiplashed broken-necked thought from looking around
can't stop either
sunlight from waving neckties nothing to do with office workers
can't even stop
the clang of cracking eggshells in birdsong from soaring on
can't stop
the water surface from rusting out sunken ships soon or late
can't stop either

moistly aroused nipples from firming up in milk powder
can't even stop
life growing computerised then going on ageing
can't stop
beasts from appearing and disappearing in the forest of buildings
can't stop either
frogs from jumping out of the pond trodden by lotuses
can't even stop
frogs from going on stuffing lotus seed songs into their roots

can't stop the kitchen smoke
can't even stop the village from going on heat

[BH, LMK]

Lift Inside the Body

Romance really can resist mediocrity
Humour, even more, can make knowledge start dancing
Not many people still want to use the endless steppes of the distant past
To gallop inside a body where there are no skyscrapers
Primitivity doesn't mean much
Ancient history too stupid too fatuous
Modern people have long dug for oil and ore beneath the ruins
Archaeology has actually lost its past mystery
Modern people, in their hearts, even
Make tall buildings raise the ruins of the future
That's why we in the modern age
To climb the brain and look out over the scenery of thoughts
Have to go the length of being tourists
Inside our own bodies
And waiting for the lift

[BH, LMK]

The Acupuncture Point for Liberty

I want to give Lady Liberty a massage
she's been on an island so tiny it couldn't get tinier
standing for so many years
her back and legs must be aching like no one else's
I want to negotiate with the new century
to give her a chair to take a little seat

thinking of the way she would sit down
it makes me think of giving her a glass of something
and so I think of Coca-Cola, ever-popular
and of the hamburger that goes with it
I've thought of the torch in her hand
and even of changing it into an ice-cream cone

but, oh, Lady Liberty!
in the end what kind of liberated life
does your lack of hunger and thirst symbolise?
and who is it
chose for you this gender to delight men with?
though I know better the orgasm liberty gives
only those who see life as a prison
can come to any deeper understanding

Lady, oh Lady
instead of giving you a chair
and those who press you to take the big step into the Atlantic
I want even more to give you a massage
but liberty, oh liberty
up to now I haven't found
the real acupuncture point for you

November 1999 [BH, LMK]

'Lost'

is a wonderful word
I put a bet on poverty and I lost
I put a bet on pain and lost
I bet on sickness and lost
the problem is who I lost to –
which gambling house
which government
even which god
can take all that on board
the next problem is
my tolerance seems even greater –
I keep winning

[WNH & Yan Li]

WANG XIAONI (*b.* 1955)

White Moon

The midnight moon exposes every bone.

I breathe ice-blue air.
All the world's follies
are falling like fireflies.
The city is a carcass.

No living thing
can match this pure light.
I open the curtains to watch earth
hold such pouring silver
until I forget I'm human.

Life's last act
is silently rehearsed under a bleak spotlight.
The moon lands on my floor
to reveal my blanched feet.

[Pascale Petit & Wang Xiaoni]

Four Typhoon Poems

1 *Today the Wind Invaded the Sky*

The island stood up –
all its body feathers were excited.
The cyclone leaned forward and danced from the other side of the sea.
The windowpanes gnashed their teeth.

I stood and stood –
I could not do anything.
I stood looking at today's wind,
watched the rampaging bandits carry their few pathetic grey heroes.

2 *A Line of Jackets Airing in the Gale*

Whose son do these belong to? Whose west wind
is quick-marching that troop of soldiers on the washing-line,
coconut trees blasting all around them, red coconuts crashing every
         few seconds?

Nobody knows why the rude wind rushed onto our island
on such an urgent afternoon and drove these innocent soldiers
between two old bauhinia trees,
beating their torsos –

the fronts of their jackets sticking to the backs.
In the gale's army, every uniform was empty.

3 *The Evening the Typhoon Arrived*

On the evening of the typhoon, the sky filled up, the human world
      was wiped clean.

From west to east, herds of black bulls stampeded overhead.
The gale's hooves kept knocking against the windows.
Everything on earth rose up to heaven.

Humans were enclosed by the evening,
the evening was enclosed in a blasting drum.
Arrogant gusts

rolled out chariots from the otherworld
and didn't meet any resistance.
This is how these things happened.

4 *The Aftermath*

Plants had their long hair sheared,
any nerves that had not yet died writhed over the ground.
Lunatics smashed their asylums –
at last it was their turn to party.

I sat safe in a fish's belly.
My heart heaved with huge dark yellow clouds.

Heaven unleashed whips of lightning.
Wind and rain crushed the city,
scratched off its newly painted gold scales.
The swollen lotus pond in front of the window suddenly shrivelled.
The puffed-up were ruined in an instant.

[Pascale Petit & Wang Xiaoni]

YANG LIAN (*b*. 1955)

The Winter Garden 1

trees frozen red in the snow   as if wearing worn-out windcheaters
snow crunching underfoot
the hurried night always wears brand-new soles

goats fear loneliness   for every ear
cries become bitter weeping

the path   a cow, just dropped a calf
scarred head to tail by the whip, panting paralysed in bloody mud

streetlamps come on still earlier   lovers dim as stones
stand, faces blurred, by a metal bier
the vole is an exhausted nurse   stealthily
slinking into the garden's wounds to dream
flowers   are preserving their pink flesh below ground
like dead children   straightaway, fresh tender ghosts

underdeveloped stars   lock us up with iron railings

The Winter Garden 2

in this world the ones who trust writing least   are poets
in the blank snow   roses have been withering since birth
the flame is far away from two cold hands
winter bustles about   like an industrious editor
I   become something spiked by the sunlight
bending to sniff at my death-stench which grows daily stronger
in one man's north wind   the garden long ago ceased to be

existing for the imagination   in the end, as always, returning to the
imagination
the blue music of tree and tree   is played only on silence

so the same heavy snow has twice fallen on my shoulders
when it covers the garden   I am forgotten
stepping on an intersection   I am mistaken
under the lamps the empty street is like a hoarse throat
declaiming   and for years the withered and fallen words look on

The Winter Garden 3

some people, addicted to corpses   love to stroll in winter gardens
people who salute ruins   can appreciate
a plot to drown a kitten in a ditch
pressing its head down like crushing a walnut
it's definitely children   children running into the garden

children know better than anyone how to trample flowers

even our dying day is unreal   a piece of a charred pole
poking slantwise from the ground like the crocodile's long snout
the sky is so gloomy it seems like daylight sleep
fishbones vomited by the ocean   stab us too
in dreams live fish, scraped clean of scales, are stabbed one by one
alive beneath the travelling knife

all flesh is reduced to a place with no power to look back

touch   all that is touched is non-existent
and cancer swells impalpably in the depths
a black pregnant woman   enwrapping a raped springtime
a treetrunk sliced by sight
swans' necks become pale underwater snares
once we have divided the world with fractured compound eyes
we are all blind   each spectre sets the white snow off
exposed in the dry ice-hard wind
endures the pain of bones budding

until   the garden is shamed into colour
lashed all its life by an unidentifiable season

[BH]

92

The Lying Game

when we lie   tiger stripes mark the night
   on the roads   since they were shamelessly sold by the lamplight
          lies   replace travellers

we go strolling   yet an ant rushing into the forbidden zone of sleep-talk
         has to understand   fingers
      the mortal weight of the moon at each setting
    and   idiotic cries for help in certain tiny throats

     no   no one has ever lied to himself
     it was just the words playing with him
     playing at sleep   we dream of oceans
   playing at oceans   we drift toward another islet
      disembark there   we are hungry
      rear or butcher monkey and parrot
      are turned afresh into savage stones

   but we don't speak   when we don't speak
our hands become crocodiles biting each other's tails in dead water

    we think the speech which deceives us   is only
    truth   the dying day of every line of poetry
    is a mirror, smashed years ago, preserving a face
         drooping earlobes
      hang from a boy's trundling hoop

a lifetime's suns are trundling down night's steep slope

   when words come trundling down   mutes are born
     the mad silence in the heart of a mute
  is the silence in the tiger's heart as it springs on the gazelle
   flesh is ripped   can't even make the noise of paper
      we have always been mutes
    and so   we are playthings for lies

[BH]

The Foundations of Terror

with carnivorous greed terror digs upwards
the breath it buried below ground   simultaneously buried in the sky
a child smothered by a teat of stone
skeleton split open   like scattered stars
pallidly glittering after a storm
in a paralysed body   only hatred can be reborn

live again   take the ugly organs
and expose them again to the saturation bombing of spring
blueprints   soak into the bloodstains
develop the first aerial photo of our ruins
we are destroyed   and you appear

you are all destroyed   and he appears

they are all destroyed   we squat at the foot of the wall, digging
with the precision of a timepiece a thousand gloamings create the next
child   when parents are dug out of the childbed of the sky
everyone is born to commemorate their own disappearance

live   living stones still must carry on
collapsing inside   warrior in a secret battle
thighs embracing his horse
time and again galloping the length of the rooftops of green grass
he hears behind him   mother earth healing like the surface of the sea
that smothered child already a thousand years old
long ago turned blue   walking in the dense fog that shrouds birthdays

with our bodies   dying
we build a village which covers the world from below

[BH]

Incident

you're still that way   calmly walking away from an incident
one incident among so many
one day among so many neglected months and years
as rotten fields remove your shoes once again
snow   sustains you on frostbitten toes

the day's overcast, grey, but doesn't look like snow
only your coldness moves from life towards death
past events are silent   can't leave footprints in the snow

old clothes are always modest   just the way the wooden cots of the dead
slip to the sea from below another pair of bodies making love
no other incident can happen in a past one
a lifetime of mistakes   stand like towering trees on a mountain
more distantly white than snow
that bone walks out of you
the days walk out of the bone   you
are thrown away, one behind the other

seeing each other as so many uninhabited moonbeams

[BH]

Darknesses

1

green leaves always forgotten when   windows are too green
like every pebble roughly thrown by spring
hitting spring itself

birds   still wearing arid skates of blue
though old dog eyes are tired out

no need to translate the riverbank's slapping
the aesthetics of death   incite the swarming of the flowers

95

fields alone   can tolerate the furious heart
fleeing still further   April sniffs out blood
in sunlight the wood crouches behind us
knowledge that can't be taken away   it takes away the dead
reciting a poem   a deepened stillness

the other world is still this world   darkness would say

2

a storyless person   escapes into a day
with a gesture of escaping from the day

a pastless person   has passed away
seagulls worked into an abstract book by the evening

locked in the isolation ward   who isn't crazy
delusions   more like fragments than flesh
fragments of glass   shattering skeleton heard on the periphery
fragments of rotting tongue   twilight washes away, just washes away

rats squeal   shrill squeals as light stamps on itself
each day startled awake by each day

with one black night   a personless story
still won't come true told twice   darkness would say

3

each shower of rain makes you sit at your end
rain rapping on the roof   tiny animal steps
move you motionlessly into the darkness
in motionless weather you need others to sleep
to sleep is to leave   the world of the rainy season leaves
once darkness has passed through you like a thoroughbred through the fire
hear inside you   silvery white stitches everywhere
stitching a worn-out windcheater of flesh

every shower falls only on this bare ground
when you begin reading from your end   a page of black explanation
unweariedly swaps someone else for next day
forges an address   the graveyard street still muddier
finds fault with this hand   beggars huddle together in mutual hatred

making a city with nowhere to shelter from the rain
a flock of soaking crows collides inside you
breeds different crimes with identical faces   darkness would say

4

but darkness didn't say a thing   between dark and dark
only this spring

kite's bones hang in the treetops
bark shines   lovers pass kissing under the tree
pollen in the lungs beating last year's gong
a bright red clown   always makes children run wild

greener and greener the teeth that chew little hands
old newspaper lawn   hands over scissors of flame
so April   sees the river flow like a mirage
the current's forgotten colours   see us as mirages
once the dove's call is burned black   all the stars
are   broken toys stuffed in a pitch-black floodgate

in darkness there's always a body drifting back to the place of no dreaming

even we fear   only fear our own terror
darkness doesn't say a thing   every walker on the streets
starts muttering to himself
darkness   is listening to the orange-red darkness of lipstick

a spring school always makes us ignorant
memory   who lives in it is a ghost
but sickness attenuates the look
when a mirror's worn on the face   the ocean digests a dead fish
being vomited is still endless chatter

darknesses are too many   for life ever to have got there
spring walks out of us   only then   is spring silent at last

[BH]

Violence in the Forest

tangled on broken necks   sky turns its collar up
slogans still smoking   sky has begun eating meat
woods bend their heads   and sky laughs far away
tree stumps piling up   sky has forgotten

this is the violence you see every day

gregarious green feet
running to death in a more and more deathly silence
hear sky   contentedly fill in earth behind them

thunderstorm   turns you to a soaking wet chopping board
how sweet to the ear a knife hacking at the back
sunlight's stylus scratches the growth-rings   they'll never grate again
tree trunks   have come with an effort to the truth of their disposal

this is everyday violence

sky   fells the forest because it's turning human
because people don't bleed every day
just as you enjoy   in peace and quiet   your endless twitching

this is every day

[BH]

A Zürich Swan

as he says   happiness takes the form of a dirge
hanging on to a beauty it doesn't know
the dancing waters   have feigned sleep for seven hundred years
shooting a hurried glance at the person on the bridge's arch
 as she says   if you can't retrieve it then chew it bit by bit
another snowstorm plunging into the armpit
orange-red beaks stretch one by one toward a familiar-seeming shore
the ardour of the flesh   craves discarding

98

a twitching quill pen   had it signed more deathbeds
would still be singular   as he said when he stood on the water
as she   recognising in its reflections the only coldly overlapped swan
flapping broken wings on the riverbed   says   sunlight is cud-chewed
the beauty of fingers lies in holding tightly on to obscurity
leaking the blue of the inner self   a more dazzling setting for a sliver chain
bent into its own blood-fouled ornament
confirming the great bird's frenzy   dirge-like serenity

[BH]

Shadow Play

pain is like beauty   with the self as the aim
the wall is an arena for a walking cat
and the dance   is third-person kitschy red & green
backstage a hand is lowering the setting sun   between the shadows
organs in love   hold the bat-squeaks tight
breaking up   dusk dances on the fleshy mat of a palm
in the cat's eye each instant is leaping
skin   bearing the weight of the cut-out hometown

captured in the tattoo's bud
a role is endlessly skinned into theatre
lamplight skinning the gloaming   catching reality turn itself half over
shadows raggedly wear personalities
laugh the laugh sewn together daily   backstage
the murderous hand responds   under the cat's claw
all setting suns lapping their own bloodlessness
supporting each other into the blackness of applause, asleep cuddling gifts

[BH]

Father's Blue & White Porcelain

a small jar of night   a thousand frontiers carrying him
the sky of old age continues the firing in the kiln
continues arranging this pot plant   lamplight
a glazed hand   refines a blue cough
in his flesh he embroiders the fragile whiteness of posterity
turns around a thousand times   the little
room a snake's stomach swallows the longest diameter of life
his night-long waking   like the sleep-talk of the whole world

awake and not looking at humans   not even waiting for
a cup of darkness tea   four walls softly slide up
a small iron table sinks in to a venom-coated shaft
another red-hot circle sealing
his book   its unread wings tightly closed
how many bloomings and fadings of seventieth birthdays have been fondled
startling a container with petals that cannot be rubbed away
lying down   revealing again the birthmark of day

[BH]

Stroller

Whether the golden fish sing about the rise and fall of the city or not
a line of swans on the riverbank study the book of their feathers
whether they model girls with mirrors or not
the stroller's self is filled completely by the sound of the wind
        led by a pitch-dark street
towards this stretch of marshland   where feet sink in an inch
the banks overflow with green which knows winter's weakness only too well
after the rain   the grassblades kneel on broken knees
one cloud invents an eclipse
the horizon watches him abruptly change between light and dark
        breeding a night in which a wild goose calls him continuously
towards this act of forgetting
feeling softly swallowed by the valley
feeling he has already become the valley   an empty willow

100

whose golden explosion throws out a womb endlessly giving birth to the sky
      listening to the wooden fence shout in the wind
      so nailed to death it stops the days
he arrives at the shared wetness of water and blood
where drowning waits   the chattering future a little bar
with a locked door   he is the entire city holding a stone cold cup
      as though planted, panting
walking further   to be buried in the skeleton of an old iron bridge
walking impossibly further   rusty blood-red bushes
burst through his window   ghost-like sunlight appears once
revealing the swollen dark water-level settled over his head
      the drowned landscape is here
      in the dark the separated
          lonely hanging step is here

[WNH & Yang Lian]

A Night in the Purple Palace
(Adagio)

In this seraglio night always consists of   moonlight, jade steps and a
      curtain of pearls
all imaginary   a bunch of flowers against blue wallpaper
imagine   caving in under the concubine's clothes a mound of snow
snow waiting impatiently to be possessed its crystalline body slowly
turning   constantly curling in on itself in a slow dance
a bunch of tulips divesting itself of the love of self as it brightly declines
a kind of purple whisper   which must be spoken breathily
addressing only him   as he crushes the petals heavily
a drop of purple milk   like a concubine impatiently waiting to be sucked
concentrating   the entire world into one burning duct

In this seraglio   fire always has the rude playfulness of tongues
a pointed tip   licks the emptiness of skin   midnight's cling
green like leaves gathered at the concubine's ankles
his preference for her   a shower coming from every angle
watering the flower the little purple bowl of her nipple fills
in revenge against time   the pigment holds ocean's deepest spoils
a bunch of tulips slips in a single night from soprano to mezzo

tonight   tyrannous beauty is balanced by this aesthetic of erosion
this evasive scent which the concubine keeps for him alone   and only
        lets him savour
when the silky light can't stop   purple very gently splays open

In this seraglio there's always this dead bone phosphor light becoming a
        pistil's gleam
conducting the body's desire   to be played for all four seasons
carving out this hole cut through   the concubine's sculpted days
the wallpaper is blue like a crazy mind sewing up all past pains
only once   the hours' bitemarks into each flower
darken endlessly   the night is stitched onto flesh   endlessly fresh and
        tender
once in the beginning   purple   gradually spread like a drop of milk
slowly absorbed by the universe   which sees his lasciviousness   and winks
by staring he bestows on the concubine a totally dark grammar
the vase is like a word resting between the hands

[WNH & Yang Lian]

ZHAI YONGMING (*b.* 1955)

The Sorrow of Submarines

9:00 a.m. at work
I get coffee and pen and ink ready
then crane my neck to check how high the typhoon signal is
coming in from far away
whether it's in or out of use
my submarine is always on watch
its lead-grey body
hides in a shallow windless pond

at first I wanted to write that way –
now that wars aren't quite coming
now that cursing   has changed its form
when I listen in   I can hear
the clatter of silver spilling out

I still lose my heart   scarlet seafood
in amongst all life's hardships   gets redder and redder
we eat it   shuffling hands process information
as I begin to write   I see
lovely fish   have surrounded the shipyard

state-run enterprises' bad debts   and also
neighbouring countries' slack economies   as well as
young girls' make-up trends
these erratic receipts   have surrounded
my shallow pond

so, this is how I'm writing it:
better check out
my submarine   where it last set sail
inside whose blood vessel did it anchor
the star stalkers, the hip, the heavy metal disco crew
have analysed the periscope of writing

alcohol, nutrients, high calories
like prepositions, pronouns, interjections
lock the composition of my skin
submarine   it has to dive on down to the ocean floor
urgently   yet uselessly diving down
no single code will ever control it again

I've written it before   I'm still writing it like this:
it's all already so irrelevant
but you're still building your submarine
it will be a war memorial
it will be a war grave   it will take its long sleep on the ocean floor
yet it will also be so much further and further away from us
a state of mind suitable for solitary confinement

just what you see:
now   I've got my submarine built
but   where is the water?
the water is slapping on the world
so right now   I must invent water
and for the sorrow and sadness in every single thing
contrive a rarely-found perfection

[BH, LMK, WNH]

By Sickness Turned Doctor

looking at those poached, cloud-steamed people
looking at those bloodsucking, malignant people
some pan-fried...some stewed...
some plucked...some mended...
German doctors never understand
the coordination of the Chinese Five Elements
neither do they understand
Chinese lungs, Chinese stomachs and other organs
why they need no anaesthesia

as I was broken-heartedly watching
200cc of fresh blood
being drawn through the syringe
in the end the blameless began to whimper
faced with the doctors' do-gooder eyes
I could only submit to their whiteness
That global conviction it saves the dying and serves the suffering

in the end they had to pour a whole bottle of red
into this violently bloated blood vessel
in the end they had to observe   smell   listen   diagnose
so they could see through my heart
so they could constrict my days and nights
(German doctors specialise in only one discipline
how inconvenient for them)

this is an era for applying the emetic method
this is an era of collective apoplexy
this is also a world of learnt imbalance
doctors too late for dialectics
prescriptions flown and gone
patients panicky and short of breath
their pulses chaotic with terror

unavoidably there will be vomiting   before a blood
transfusion   new blood flowing toward the ecosystem
unavoidably there will be the bone-chilling touch of a scalpel
so they can penetrate   so they can x-ray the marrow
and directly take the life away from germs

was there any proof I was surrounded by fevers and comas?
they dined on germs   eliminated cells
while racing and flying   with the wind underfoot
pulsing and passing away like dawn bells and twilight drums [27]
they were truly addicted

were the symptoms of seasonal illness simply a pretence?
they recounted to me the small fevers of the *fin-de-siècle*
they despaired of each and every heartbeat in the world
and the rises and falls in tribulations
they either lacked certainty in the steps they took
or suffered from long-term sleep deprivation

and I   by sickness turned doctor
both assailant and defender   in order to
preserve a sensibility
like keeping a newborn alive in an incubator
I stir up her heart's energy
to make her complexion rosy
rouse her channels and meridians   until
warm as toast   I hold her in my arms

2 April 2000   [BH, LMK, WNH]

The Chrysanthemum Lantern Is Floating Over Me

A chrysanthemum lantern is floating towards me.
In the enveloping silence of pitch darkness –
a low murmur of children on the riverbank.
The lantern is so sheer a bird's shadow shows through it.

The children's chorus floats over with the lantern.
There's no fear, no pain,
only the lantern, the lightness of chrysanthemums
and the red glow of its candle.

---

27. The denotative sense here relates to old China, where bells announced
the opening of the city gate, and drums its closing. The connotation is the
passing of time; or a timely exhortation to virtue and purity.

A young girl also floats over –
a girl and her maids,
their hair up,
their luxurious clothes nothing but
silk, ribbons and buttons,
nothing but tinkling tassels when they walk –
tassels, earrings, phoenix hairpins.

The young girl and her wet nurse
have known death.
They are both searching for something leisuredly.
They face the midnight moon.
The girl is gentle and the light soft.
They float towards me
transforming the ordinary night
into a somnambulist trance.

Every night
the lantern floats over me.
Its owner wanders to the end of heaven,
his pace sometimes fast, sometimes slow.
No one can catch up with him,
the children grow up with him.

This is the story of the changing world and of the lantern.

If I sit on the floor
the chrysanthemum's shadow, the light's shadow and the shadows of people
frighten me
and I sometimes slowly, sometimes quickly
make a silvery sound in my room.

If I sit on the bed
I can enjoy this sensation
while I gradually turn transparent,
gradually change colour.
All night I merge into mist
then rise into the air.

[Pascale Petit & Zhai Yongming]

106

Fledgling Tart

the fledgling tart was also called Pretty Babe
she was wearing a ruffled lace mini-blouse
her thighs were already appetising
but her mother was more beautiful
they were like sisters   'one of them is like a gazelle...'

this is the kind of babe that every man likes
and the babe likes the feeling of looking into the lens

the fledgling tart I saw wasn't like this though
she was twelve   skinny, her clothes weren't clean
with eyes that could contain a whole world
or maybe   they couldn't even hold a single tear

her father was a farm worker   young
but his hair was already grey
her father spent three months
step by step, looking for
his missing babe

three months for a fledgling tart
would be close to a hundred-odd days
three hundred-odd men
but this was not simple maths
she never could understand why
so many old, ugly and dirty men
wanted to sprawl on her belly
neither could she understand what all this really was
only knew that her body
turned light, turned empty   had something taken away

fledgling tarts were also known to be beautiful and brainless
of this she knew nothing at all
only at night she counted it up
in her maths jotter there were three hundred-odd
nameless   addressless   shapes and bodies
together they were called consumers
those numbers were like ancient symbols in a graveyard
before the sun rose   they were consumed

reading the newspapers, I'd been thinking:
can't write poems for this
can't turn out poems like this
can't chew poetry and creak away
can't knock words into teeth   to worry at it
those illnesses   those operations
those statistics added to twelve years old

poetry, bandages, photos, memories
abraded my eyeballs
(this is the zone where light and shade connect in the retina)
everything states this: it's all useless
all harm that nobody cares about
the everyday data
creating a whole life of sorrow for some

in part she was just a news photo
twelve years old   standing with the other girls
you couldn't tell   she had an ovary missing
generally speaking   that was just a news report
every day   our eyes collect thousands and millions of images
these control the consumers' pleasures
they're gone in a flash   'it' is just like that too
the volume of information   hotlines   and the international viewpoint
like giant linen   wipe away one person's lowly pain

people like us   to have seen is to have seen
it was crumpled   stuffed into the black iron bin

21 April 2002   [BH, LMK]

28. (*See opposite page.*) This line references *Zuo Zhuan*, 4th year of Duke Xi. See Legge's translation, *Tso Chuan, Duke Hsi* in *The Chinese Classics*. One metaphoric interpretation of this line is 'Even if my herds wander far away, they'll never come into contact with yours', i.e. why do you make war on me when we are so far apart we can do no harm to each other.

29. The Grand Historian is Sima Qian (ca. 145 or 135 BC–86 BC), author of the *Historical Records*.

BAI HUA (*b.* 1956)

In the Qing Dynasty

in the Qing Dynasty
idleness and the ideal went deeper and deeper
cows and sheep were at peace, the people played chess
and imperial exams were just and fair
currencies were different in different places
sometimes even grain was exchanged for
tea leaves, silk, porcelain

in the Qing Dynasty
landscape painting had attained perfection
papers were overflowing, kites everywhere
lanterns were well-proportioned
temple after temple faced south
there seemed an excess of wealth and fortune

in the Qing Dynasty
poets cared nothing for a living, only for reputation
drank wine as petals fell, the wind gentle and the sun warm
even the pond-water was fertile
ducks swam in pairs before the wind
– just so horses in heat do not couple with cattle [28]

in the Qing Dynasty
someone dreamed about someone
reading the Grand Historian in the night, [29] sweeping the floor at dawn
and the Court established the Council of State
every year promoted long-nailed mandarins

in the Qing Dynasty
men both bewhiskered and clean-shaven
were strict on teaching by example, solemn in speech and manners
country folk were reluctant to learn their letters
children respected their elders
mothers ceded power to their sons

in the Qing Dynasty
with taxes and with dues the people were heartened
irrigation works were built, schools managed, ancestral halls
maintained
books were printed, local gazetteers assembled
habitations decked out in the antique style

in the Qing Dynasty
philosophy poured down like rain, science couldn't keep up
someone was playing six and two threes[30]
gratuitously anxious
rage became his life-long career
until, in 1840, he died

[BH, LMK, WNH]

Autumn's Weapons

struggle moves to extremes
slogans move to extremes
the stone-eating bayonet moves to extremes
I hear the degeneration of the air

this suits you perfectly
in ancient autumns
a man would die for this
swallowing ennui
swallowing paper tigers
the voice of the people never in the ear

today I want to start again
investigate each kind of sacrifice
the radiance of charging extortionate prices
sharp revolutionary bones

30. Literally '3 in the morning and 4 at night' – a quotation from the
Zhuangzi story about the monkeys dissatisfied with their 3 nuts in the
morning and 4 nuts at night, who were pacified with the offer of 4 in the
morning and 3 at night.

at this time, in Chengdu
everybody's in my face
giving me cars
giving me extremes
giving me violence and the market

Autumn 1986   [BH]

For Mandelstam

He who lived on his nerves
what did he fear?
did he fear the pure state of nudity?
No: he feared the voice
the voice that threw away thought

the poet in my dream
passed through a north too heavy
passed through a childhood thin, feeble, hallucinatory
inevitably you came to the mortal world

today is the day I shoulder your eccentricity
today, the day I shoulder your naiveté
today I shout out your tragedy

silence makes clear
poetry's heart beats, poetry shows mercy,
a guiltless tongue infects language
and this too is one day in my memory

the oxen have stopped the plough
the sickle has given up running for its life
the autumn wind is holding its breath –
Cold, you've pushed Moscow's anxiety

on to the bringing in of winter
you've got a grip on bowels, hearts and wordless throats
you face a skyful of snow, craning your neck, expectant –
look, he's coming
of all our poets the most exasperating ghost!
he's heading toward me

111

I've begun to belong here
I've begun to squeeze myself into your shape
I've begun to take the place of your brutal heaven
I, this child from outside who can never grow up
faced with all this –
the masses on the roadside – can only be more alone

November 1987   [BH, LMK, WNH]

Jonestown

children, you may begin
this one night of revolution
one night of the life to come
one night of the People's Temple
the shaking eye of the storm
weary of those invincibles
desperate to bring us there

the enemies in our hallucinations
shower us with attacks
our commune the same as Stalingrad
the air heavy with the smell of Nazis

the time of the hot-blooded vortex is come
emotions breaking through
fingertips stabbing
glue unconditionally surrenders to class
the patience of vain hope struggles with reaction

from spring to autumn
impatience and disappointment spreading everywhere
marching teeth gnaw at an unbearable time
the ammunition in boys' chests longs to explode
eccentric taboos worry at tears
watch the left-over masses already launched

a girl is rehearsing suicide
her lovely hair tending to intensity because she's crazy
hanging so kindly on her helpless shoulders

the mark of her seventeen years
the one and only mark

but the token of first love in our spirit
our dazzlingly white father
the bullets of bliss bang into his temples
his naïve dead soul still pouring forth:
a faith-healing, bushido religion
his body beautiful in its coup d'état

the mountains of corpses are no longer rehearsing
the unprecedented silence swears oaths aloud:
GET THROUGH THE CRISIS
DRILL THE MIND
PURE SACRIFICE

confronting this White Night gathers in the betrayal of the flesh
this last White Night of humanity
I know this is the night for me to harvest my pain too.

December 1987   [BH, LMK]

Spring Jaunt

the character inside the red walls wants to go home
the frog lying prone under the poplar trees
is which flower, insisting on *tendresse*?
jasmine? oh, no – a flower that is nameless

I see a girl throwing a leather ball from her little hand
I see a vegetarian holding a fistful of fine sand
old age is a command, heartbreak the ends of the earth
everywhere gardens of flowers cover the land
everywhere tender pity is pouring forth

yet, my one and only dear companion and friend
my one and only dancer at springtime's end
I want, I want
I want to share my joy in your brow, so cool, so radiant

7 March 1989   [BH]

Summer 1966

to grow up, oh, to grow up
only three days, three days!

a heart turned red
a motherland trumpeting on the streets

blow, oh, blow, oh youth come early
blow green love, blow the whole world's thoughts green too

see how lovely politics is
army uniforms worn in summer

oh, life! oh, joy!
that very last badge
that song of homesickness and freedom
oh, no, that ten-year-old's flawless heaven

26 December 1989   [BH]

The Suzhou Year

First Lunar Month, first day: the Rising of the Year
farmers wake at dawn to watch the water
open the doors, set off firecrackers three times
carrying in the morning, the younger generations kowtow
the neighbourhood offers New Year greetings
farmers are busy with their own affairs

fifth day: birthday of the God of Wealth
farmers greet visitors one after the other
buy cloth

fifteenth day: hang stove lanterns beneath the kitchen cabinet
for five successive nights
hang up tree-lanterns, set out a grand lantern market
in the countryside, crowds blot out the sun

women cross three stone bridges to drive away disease
the public beat drums and gongs, bring the festival to life

Second Month eighth day: the Great King crosses the river, monks eat meat
in the holiday week, storms will come
some people are named as deacons, some swallow dirt
farming families will get ready with this weather
for good or bad luck, look at Second Month twentieth day

Third Month third day: ants move rice-grains uphill
farm wives wash their hair, clear their vision
and eat deep-fried food

Qingming Festival: wheat straw cut, early Spring picnics
shafts of deep blue and light green in the water
women go in groups
to pray for everlasting youth

Fourth Month first day: loafers shoulder big gongs and tea chests
in *The Night the Squire Joined the Western Army*
the russet-clad cast play headsmen
(the actors are butchers, greengrocers, bean curd sellers)

Summer Solstice: three new things are seen – cherry, green plum, barley
on this day, no need for doctors
broad beans are waiting to come into season

Fourth Month fourteenth day: befriend immortals
Master Lü the Progenitor passes by
no need to hide from him
his shadow falling on the crowd saves the world

Fifth Month fifth day: Dragon Boat Festival comes with swords of rushes
comes out of the stand-in for Summer Solstice
kids write *KING* in stripes upon their foreheads
drape themselves in tiger skins, grab garlic
while the city god is Boss of Bosses

Sixth Month sixth day: monasteries and temples sun the scriptures
every household airs books, paintings, clothes and blankets
stray dogs roll on their backs in puddles
old folk play chess, listen to the storyteller or do nothing

children take tea in seven homes
surfaces seem to shimmer and break up

Autumn Equinox: offer watermelons
make fritters and butterfly-cakes
for a hundred heaven-sent years

Eighth Month fifteenth day: Mid-Autumn Festival
dried persimmons, moon cakes under the moon
when the greens are eaten
serve up the carp
jinxes are not allowed to join in

Ninth Month ninth day: visit the heights outside town
watch clouds, watch trees, watch birds
hawkers will roam the foot of the hill

Eleventh Month: short days and long nights, markets prosper
the rich collect their rents, call in debts, add salt to our wounds
and Winter Solstice is as big as the New Year
farmers respect this day

Winter Solstice: the family share New Year's Eve dinner
bean sprouts for all you desire, cabbage for happiness
sticky rice cake and sweet rice balls mean union and unity
sons are not allowed to leave town
married daughters bring bad luck to their own families
leave pumpkins outside the door all night

Twelfth Month: bring the year in, see the Kitchen God off
many hand-made lanterns and lamps
the bustle, the buzz and the genteel excuse me

New Year's Eve: more chicken and duck and fish and pork
beggars with lanterns after luck-pennies
endless coming and going, up till dawn

End of New Year's Eve: boys talk of absent friends
with melon seeds comes a new year and good luck
mice are young girls' enemies
only the great don't grow old: set off firecrackers three times

[BH, LMK, WNH]

116

GU CHENG (1956-93)

The End

In the wink of an eye
The avalanche stopped
On the riverbank, giants' skulls piled high

The junk in mourning clothes
Slowly passes by
Spreading a yellowed shroud behind it

Many handsome green trees
Their trunks twisted in pain
Are consoling the brave with tears

God has buried the hacked moon
In thick fog
All has come to an end

The gloomy contours of the hills
Represent a vague history
Still being recorded

[Michelle Yeh]

We Write Things

we write things:
insects   looking for paths in a pine-cone
or moving pieces pawn by pawn
sometimes   all for nothing.
chewing over some gleaned word
malchosen
within it, mould and mildew
so chew another

impossible to drive the cart –
on time – into the pine
seeds fall to an earth
covered over with pine-cones

[John Cayley]

Truly, This Is the World

Truly, this is the world,
a festival of lilac.
She is there, talking with a friend,
she is nineteen,
behind her, April and May.

I can see her clearly –
with a field between us –
I can clearly see the finest wisp of your hair.
A dark inky rainstorm is sweeping across the field –
what a fine storm.

Do lakes please you?
How many do you wish for? In the veins
of this gem there is scrolling of thin gold.
How many do you wish for? Is it enough?
Flower garlands scattered over russet clay.

I answered. No, I didn't. I answered
May, June, July.
The breath of dawn has turned a shade warmer,
the flowers are slightly farther away:
I have never lived in the world

August 1983   [Seán Golden & Chu Chiyu]

Distribution

at the place where the highway turns into small paths
grass turns into forests

my heart is most bleak
there is a waterlogged hollow under my tongue

bodies shed shadows
I come from a lamp

I put cricket grass in the window
eyes behind, hands in the streets

November 1983   [Seán Golden & Chu Chiyu]

Nature

I'm fond of that once-thrown spear
the ten thousand leaves in the tree
military troops crowding the earth
They show just their faces along the long, narrow road
ponderously waving their bird-nest banners
this is the subtle place where life fails

[Joseph R. Allen]

Source

the steps up to the fountain
a horse of the forest steps lightly over the iron chain

all of my flowers are dream flowers

my flame
the blue hue of the ocean
the strongest soldiers of the clear sky

all of my dreams are water dreams

link after link of the chain of sunlight
the air delivered in a small wooden box
the postures of the fish and the birds

softly, I call your name

[Seán Golden & Chu Chiyu]

Horned Toad

I'll not tell anyone
not any sniper lying in wait
what happened out there on the dam

Women look at us
or don't
and they starch their clothes
swaying wolfberry trees

Red, white, and screaming prickly beards
fill the women nearby with unease

[Joseph R. Allen]

120

Blood Relatives

She jumps up
and spits out a splinter
spits out the necklace of bones
above hangs a salad fork
and my wedding veil of days to come
Everyone sets their coffee on the floor
the nurse holds the boy

[Joseph R. Allen]

Wolf Pack

Light
inside the easy-to-open jar
traces of light along its inner wall

Someone covered with hair
in the flickering corridor

[Joseph R. Allen]

SUN WENBO (*b.* 1956)

Nothing to Do with Pagoda Trees

Treefuls of pagoda flowers float up like clouds, bowing to
flawless white – at this moment my youthful heart goes wild
standing one foot higher than the birds – there's winds madly whirling,
but still no way to stop me. I say, *Thank you.*
Meaning I've seen the beauty of solitude
– those judgements from experience, they're no use now;
their beauty is beyond words – it's just what I think of, once a year,
how reincarnation is real to them, but not to me.
To this I'm witness, and it grieves me. I say: ah, flawless white!
thinking cloud formation and dispersal are seen more clearly higher up:
scene of the void, scene after scene of the void – thinking my elders the sam
as me, them saying self and other are aggregate while a person is has no stab
       form; with them, I can only
congregate in my dreams. What a congregation it is
– I, shaping my forms with what I see, am comrade to the pagoda flowers.

[BH, LMK]

OUYANG JIANGHE (*b.* 1956)

from Thanksgiving Day

1

From the Martian's window it's not possible to make out whether snow
is really falling or if it's a paper backdrop hanging behind
a honeymoon trip. This is Thanksgiving
when the dead bestir themselves to leave for dyspeptic Mars
and their pre-mortem turkey marriage. According to the theory of relativity

time flutters in the wind at two speeds, frozen and salted.

God is a telephone operator: from the local telephone counter
you can call aliens. The police car, quick as an executioner,
has almost caught up with the bullet when it turns
everything within range of a toy gun into an oxymoron. The thief
　　　　has stolen
the wheels from the crash, but with the feet of a sparrow
you can bundle up your metrics, step over the vote of a scarecrow

and see the Catapult King directly. For the whole thing
simply multiply any majority including the ghosts' majority
by the zero of the minority. Handcuffs will be worn two times
once as zero, twice as infinity.
But both hands can always work free: you've given the dead
a stage but left the house seats empty.

The locals have taken those seats out. The football park
flies toward the sky, which is paid monthly, and there's no goalkeeper.
What a weird game: birds whack into the net
and the nature of soaring is changed. Fish fling themselves from water,
take rhetoric's bait. You really are going to Mars
but stop off to go fishing. Oh transforming scene,

one female body becoming so many mermaids
who have never in their lives worn a dress
preferring to be seen from a distance by clouds in trousers
as dancing waters: a kind of gaze on tiptoe
above an understanding of change versus changelessness
No one would deny you're so lucky to be totally immersed in the
　　　　beauty of the senses

because beauty always carries an air of the childish. On the wedding night
the groom pretends to be an old man, so he really becomes old
unless the bride separates out from the sway of the narcissus
queen from canary,
both bring the unreal loveliness of hand-made things
but more real than real, not subject to the rule of alchemy.

[BH, LMK, WNH]

One Minute, Oh, Heaven and Men Have Grown Old

One minute later, bicycles have grown old.
Do you really think clouds in trousers are faster cycling than walking?
Do you really think rain in a skirt is a high school teacher?
One minute, enough to have finished primary school.
One minute of Peking U, two minutes' reading in primary school.
One minute of English class, two minutes' teaching spoken Chinese.
One minute of Contemporary History, two minutes back in ancient history.
A semi-feudal minute. A semi-colonial minute. A Confucian
Or Socialist minute.
One minute, enough for you to complete a doctorate?
One hour, one semester, one year or one hundred years
Are all within this one minute.
Even a gold Rolex cannot stop this one minute in an instant.
A minute of spring will be autumn just winding the clock.
If the Chinese Studies professor on heat doesn't wear a Swiss watch
Will he wander in a fugue wearing a Chinese one?
One minute later, taxis have grown old.
One minute of buses, jammed a thousand years in half a minute.
One minute of Beijing City, half a minute in Changping district.
One minute of the American dream, half a minute of Made in China.
One minute of Global Calling, hung up in half a minute.
This one minute of *hello*, a minute of *Wei! Wei!* [31]
Space
Has become smaller and sweeter in a trade-marked apple.
An apple, one mouthful bitten out, tallies with
Local people's views on globalisation. Just this tiny bit of sweetness,
with apples and tomatoes inside, Indian curry, and Italian cheese all inside.
David Beckham is inside, too.
One minute of hot chicks, sweetened for half a minute.
One minute of speed, slowed down for half a minute.
One minute of OKE, KARA-ed for half a minute.
One minute, songs have grown old, why bother to sing?

But how come unsung songs have grown old too?
What should I do with incomers who have been OKE-ed
When they did not manage to KARA?

31. Interjection, *Hey!* Also used to answer the phone: Chinese equivalent of
Italian *Pronto!*

After a minute, trains have grown old.
After another minute, scheduled flights have grown old too.
Do you really think one minute of BBQ chicken wings
Can make the nibbled stuff fly away?
One minute, not enough to love a woman,
But enough to love two or more.
One minute of sunset, it gives another minute of early dawn.
One minute of this present life, it owes one minute of your next life.
One minute, oh, heaven and men have grown old.

[BH, LMK]

So, How About Venice?

1

Consider such a change: life is bitterly short –
do not leave Venice in such haste,
a place where you're heading to. On the train,
you overslept, though it seemed you were sleepless all night.
Sleep, made up mostly of compressed air,
shrivelled like a balloon. You woke up, like the collar of a light-
        coloured shirt
turned outward, even dirtier than the cuffs. All along the road,
locksmiths' stalls everywhere, Chengdu, locked,
will be Venice opened: emptiness was opened, too.
The whole of Venice was emptied somewhere, a vocabulary chart,
        emptied.

2

'Sir, yours is a ticket for the local.' The train
runs on blunt knives. Can they be changed into razors
So the journey can be faster: is the next stop Venice?
'There's no next stop, Sir.' Blade-like scenery,
flashing at the throat. Solomon's judgement was right,
after a meaning gives up its tail, it will escape like a gecko.
Unless time has turned its blade, seconds fall behind minutes,
and you do not ask *what e'en is this e'en?* The sense of reality
is borrowed from the good old times, you might
borrow good ears from Orpheus, or a swollen heel from Achilles.

3

A footsore journey to Venice. A blistered feeling
pushes right from the bronchia to the syringe, and right to the vein,
on that bone-freezing needle's tip. 'Painful?'
the nurse asks from a thousand miles away. The syringes are disposable,
disposed after use, but what can you do with the surplus mercurochrome?
It takes days to wash off if you happen to get it on your hands
Near the clinic the barefoot doctors' shoes are laid out at random,
but nobody is actually barefoot: even scarecrows are wearing shoes
to walk around Human Resources. Drought, pushed open by an umbrella;
the rain, in Chengdu, has just started to fall, as we arrive at Venice.[32]

[BH, LMK]

Who Leaves, Who Stays

Dusk, the little boy hid inside a plant,
Eavesdropping on insects' internal organs. What he heard, in fact,
was the world beyond the insects, such as the internal organs of machines.
The setting sun tumbled under the boy's feet like van wheels:
the Boy's father was a van driver,
the van was unloaded,
parked in the wilderness.
The father left the van, dumbfounded by the beauty of sunset's absolute silence
He hung up on the mobile phone that kept ringing,
said to the Boy: every single thing that tumbles along the skyline has lips,
but they only talk to things themselves,
only build ears and words upon these talks.
In order to deny those ears the Boy eavesdropped on other ears.
He was not in fact hearing,
but he accidentally heard a totally different way of listening –
the Boy invented his own deafness
And became a soaring, visionary deaf boy.
Will there be, behind the mortal sunset,
Another clamorous world of miracles?
Will there be another person listening, another setting sun sinking?

32. Author's Note: 'Unfinished'.

126

Oh stumbling sky –
the world is unusually quiet because of an unanswered phone.
Machines and insects do not hear each other's heartbeat,
plants are also pulled up by the roots.
The deafness of the Boy became scenery, order, nostalgia.
The van wouldn't start,
so Father buried his head fixing it,
while Mother embraced the sunset and slept for a while, just a while,
not knowing the sky was darkening, not knowing that old age was coming.

12 April 1997, Stuttgart   [BH, LMK]

ZHANG SHUGANG   (*b.* 1956)

Snow

Outside snow is falling. Yes, snow is fallen outside. Snow is
falling, outside. Snowfall is outside. Snow is fallen outside.
Maybe no snow. Of course, this is another way of saying it.
But the sky is very dark, yes, very dark, maybe a snow flurry
will be falling, or just fallen. But the sky is very dark.
Maybe. It's falling snow or no snow, is falling, not falling,
will be falling, will not be falling. Maybe the sky isn't very
dark, maybe it's just because of the drawn curtains, or that
the sun is setting, or it being covered by an iridescent cloud,
but the sky is really looking a little dark. This is another way
of saying it of course, snow, maybe, is really falling even
though the sky is very dark, even though the sky isn't really
very dark. Of course this is another way of saying it. Even
though snow is really falling, maybe, now is falling, just like
someone, sitting in shadow by the window gets up, moves
around, but is still sitting there.

8.30am, 28 December 2003   [BH, LMK]

LIAO YIWU (*b.* 1958)

Secret Anguish

incandescent lamps shade these thousand-plus days
thousand-plus steel fences
god's thousand-plus ring fingers

the earth
birdcage confined in many-fingered psychology
the swift, softly lingering song of the nightingale, calling
– delight in us!

buy us at a good price!
humanity in the birdcage
enemies inside humanity

shut the enemies in cages of eternal daylight [33]
all across the sky I hear the constellations' voices sweetly sing

my tender flesh is suffused with white
my bone marrow infested with crawling foetal hair
I am reduced to a mutant American ghost
my crime is adoring the darkness

give me a black heart and liver
give me secret anguish, a diary, mail
sex acts under cover of night
give me an Oedipus complex
and the lip-smacking sound of suckling at the breast

my home is the hell inside books

carry us away
bat!

the moon is stuffed full of salt grains
frisbee
sands under the full moon

33. Author's Note: 'In Chongqing Detention Centre the lights are kept
burning day and night. Prisoners there don't know what darkness is.'

carry us away!

take it all in with one look
like a horse dropped dead on a sand dune
soul, heart, arsehole, feelings
thrown away all over the horse's bones

blind angel
carry us away!
use your sound waves to transmit us down to the ninth level stairs
tell this shining tale from the thicket of daggers
to innocent little devils

August 1992   [BH]

New Year's Eve in Jail

New Year's Eve
the sound of firecrackers beyond the high wall
like thousands of masters in private schools
mercilessly thrashing boys' buttocks

my soul has had the shit beaten out of it

in this instant the world is a great ship
and we are locked up in the hold
glued to the wall and intently listening to the boundless waters
and the other even vaster waters of nothingness
like an arrow piercing the heart

the night-warders wade through water
their bayonets soft as fish tails
oh you dumbly shouting fish

the murderer just turned eighteen
opens his mouth wide
          oh you baby-faced
dumbly shouting fish

windpipe smashed by the garrotte
sprouting in the world of the dead

the shackled bandit
crashing to the floor
attacks the band outside the walls
the gunpowder-smoke-wreathed human stage outside the walls
the moon, that white thrashed buttock outside the walls

rise up
take that round toy of yours, so swollen it's shining
raise it to the unblocked sky
oh, give Mother a noisy kowtow for me!

New Year's Eve 1992   [BH, WNH]

ZHOU LUNYOU   (*b.* 1958)

The Difficulty of Playing Chess Against
the Hand of the State's Champion

one hand doesn't really belong to me
always unwilling to be taken away from my body
breath heavier than shadows
oppressing every part of my body
from the lips to the lungs   then to the limbs
your reckless or unconsidered steps forbidden
consciousness may even be a little more sensitive
wanting to leave   wanting to hide far far away
in a place beyond their whip's reach
beyond the scope of the hand's games
and only confined to wanting   spirit journey
just this is dangerous enough
the hand's whiskers are even more real than the point of a knife
even sharper   stabbing into the inner core of dreams
knowing everything   not having let any single bit go
details   running even faster   like falcons

observing from the sky the rabbit's motion
every single place you could possibly go
it has already been waiting, its plain-clothes collar turned up
it only takes that deadly stroke to knock you down
and alas, alack, you'll be dead and gone   leaving a six-month stink
letting you get away with it   or giving you a stay of execution
instituting a pursuit effective for your lifetime
instead of striking you dead at once   doesn't mean the hand is merciful
making you realise from your everyday terror
the patience and cruelty of cats playing with mice
the magnificent efficiency of machines   the hand even colder than iron
stir-frying raw rice behind closed doors   letting your name
be painted black on some list
and marked with a red flag too   this actually isn't paranoia
barbed wire inside and outside life and the moving walls
force you to retreat into some book
to hold firmly on to those last few isolated words
the light the hand gives out loosely referring to all things –
beyond the water, is the fish's internal network
fleeing out of the sky is the range of fire in birds' lives
flip the classics open, and there's the repressive chapter
violence and persecution pinpointing the mind
in every day's dishes   the fickle shadows of hands
even begin to interfere with intestines and stomach
making you lose your appetite
lust rapidly trapped and paralysed
hair falling out too soon and each night's impending sleep
leave the imprint of a hand   a metal component
like the beauty of tigers that's everywhere
the control of structure over crystals   theme
control over personages   concreteness of poets
can't get rid of the abstraction of cybernetic control
the hand flipping back and forth   makes you laugh bitterly
        laugh crazily   roar with laughter
tasting all that's sweet and bitter in the mortal world
not knowing at the end of the day whether to laugh or to cry   you
understand at last
it's the hand of state chess you're playing against
the imperiousness of the hand   violence in its rhetorical form
failure with no alternative   being the inevitable
ending   anyway live according to the hand's way
to show your submission   wading into the depths of time

let silence be your indirect answer
under the influence and pressure of the hand
this poem could have two kinds of ending –
initially you think of living in obscurity   learning from ancient poets
behind a chrysanthemum (hermits have hills no more:
all the hills have been nationalised)
the only way is to stay immobile on the original spot   stay out of mind
      stay out of thought
a mute becoming an idiot again
under a tree of who knows what
sit rapt in meditation   no beginning no end (*ending #1*)
or open up your tense skin   throw yourself
into the light   from the back of the armour
grab that temteratureless hand
drop your blood on it   painting its palm full
forcing it to leave on the terminal testimony of this century
the bloody imprint of a hand (*ending #2*)

in the games that follow
you must pretend nothing happened
and on a chessboard with no squares
keep on playing chess with that invisible hand

7 March 1992 by Moon Lake, Xichang [BH, LMK]

SONG LIN (*b.* 1959)

Carrying My Son Piggyback in the Mountains

Our skin was the friend of mountains and of air,
our sense of smell was a friend to the antelope –
on a little oak it left its scent behind;

we sat down to rest, the village out of sight,
the hermit's house was hushed,
there in a cleft on the snow line lay the tiny skeleton of a bird.

Square chimneys, blue windows,
a small cabbage leaf was hearth for mole crickets and bees,
on rough clay walls were human handprints.

Towards the lake district we walked, and the mountains did too,
with the rising of the sun, the mountains grew taller still,
their haloes like wheel after wheel, rolling on the leaves.

Superfine crystal poured down, and with it colours of dense cloud
colours of thundering, inspiring, cascades,
roaring like beasts we shouted at the caves.

[BH, LMK]

The Jetty That Runs to the Sea

Floating, unfixed. To sea blue's ultimate end
it's only a little stretch.

Like a gesture of goodbye,
a handkerchief, or a kiss,
to the predestined distance
it's only a little stretch.
Someone's scanning the sea,
scanning for scanning's sake,
the shape of the jetty in his memory
like bird's wing or starlight.
The boat is leaving, so before his eyes
shadows will drift down and drift down.
It's really not that the jetty can be self-sufficient on the shore:
it's only that floating has stretched meaning a little.

11 August 1998   [BH]

LÜ DE'AN (*b.* 1960)

Between the Mountains

The half-bright, half-dim glen,
the moon hanging high up, stars hanging low;
beside the little stream,
unhurried, these few households.

'I know the darkness well!'
That's just to say that I have only now
got to know a small part of the mountain path
and these few pebbles in the stream.

I gather firewood by the stream,
for burning in my winter grate,
letting you wait inside the house,
as if drowsiness already cast its spell;

the windows are faintly glowing. By
that tree and behind those canes,
right now, I'm all alone, getting on with
gathering my firewood, cold wind

attacking me, a headlight beam shining,
still the same as that day in the past;
and I can't help saying it:
'I know the darkness well...'

Now I think I actually said it to you,
but the meaning is still the same:
that small part of the mountain path, it's me
just got to know it, that day

I didn't tell you: in the distance
on the ridge the spiralling freight trains sweep by,
headlights illuminating half of each house,
all crawling toward the city as if on pilgrimage.

[BH, LMK]

XIAO KAIYU (*b.* 1960)

Two Old Ladies on a Small Train

This shower of rain is strange,
it smells a bit of periods. Old age, eh? – what can you do?
My right buttock's twisted, my right leg's twisted too,
never mind walking or standing, even sitting or lying down are sore enough.

It's hard to bear, though, isn't it?
My left leg's fine, my left buttock's all right, so the other half of me is OK –
screw it, enough! Look at you and me, both shot to hell,
never mind the seam in the knickers, or that legal thread which stitches lips shut.

Everything's already broken enough,
these rains every year, always, assaulting the nights;
this year, on top of putting up with all that, I had to bite my tongue,
a distant relative said he'd come and see me, but those were his last words.

Bone and plastic,
it's a tricky match but we still have some time left,
let's give it a shot before we get to the little stream on that big border;
let's scrub up, then you tell me, isn't fishing just waiting for the fish to fall asleep?

Every little station
we stop at, it's like there are retired girls working overtime. They quarrel,
tidy their handbags. Give irrelevant, clever-clever, answers.
Four hands lead each other on, as if such superannuated penalty boxes would
ever be breached.

It really is like the pattering of spring rain,
isn't it, sitting on the train – an endless penetration – and you can touch
itchy trees anywhere. Two people heading to the terminus, as if it were
a new point of balance, and everywhere the drip of green eggs from a wound.

March–August 2000, Röderhof-Wewelsfleth [BH, WNH]

Raining

(in memory of Kropotkin)

It's May, thunder squeezing in between drizzle,
and from the verandah I look out over Suzhou Creek:
painfully slow, the dockers are unloading coal,
and the pitch black water is fast flowing by;

an empty barge blows its whistle,
and shivering like a weakened woman in childbed
it steams into the deep shade of the locust trees;
rain is falling, thunder is booming.

Another coal barge docks at the quay,
'Catch!' a sailor throws the hawser ashore,
it's caught and the shout is 'Jump in!'
then he leaps into the hold, presumably for a smoke.

After the faintest thunder has gone,
there's a flash of pale lightning,
and this is the time I'm hoping to join them
to the shifting of the dripping coal with Bakunin's hands,

it isn't because the dark rays of the lightning have changed
the faces of the he-men in the rain:
the libation of hard liquor that's filled their bodies –
they can give me that,

but after the rain falls heavily for a while
it stops, and they don't seem to notice.
Was it for today that I once risked my life on those journeys?
Courage snatched from drizzling rain.

[BH]

Mao Zedong

All the red tape that's losing its colour and its shape
makes the VIP of correct content
partial to silver-grey – colour of the clouds – and indigo – colour of
          the sea the well-regulated exterior
of immense affairs. He is fond of this sort of country
the sun hangs on his forehead like a badge,
suspended above a sea of people.
The unlimited reality of steel new from the furnace
surrounds the square, where limited and unlimited intersect,
with barbicans not of gold, but clay.

The press acclaims the victory of the ideal
the unruly tides go on rising
the hurricane in millions of hearts fills the hollow dimensions of the banners
billowing sails command the sea's waters to rise
the sea only has ship bones and the sea bed.

He sleeps in a swimming pool full of old books
in between rebuilding work, watching the air
speaking in short hermetic lines
unanalysable meaning hidden in tough briars of language,
warrior's language from an invisible battlefield, who understands it?

[BH]

YANG ZHENG (*b.* 1960)

The Bottle's Bulletin
(for Yang Lian)

I walked too far, smelling stronger and stronger times
I want to change me into you, change autumn into September
you, the I in my heart, live in a goblet of fine jade
a starry sky reflecting the years, I have seen though your image

137

autumn comes back to autumn again, the locomotive hauling fate
setting out at every second, I need non-stop transmogrification
until the keenest of blades can't pierce my enchantment
you're living my death, see, surreptitiously I swap myself

we sink in an instant, and then there's an endless sallying forth
fire penetrates water, vanished water, ferments pain into pain
death is repeated dying, and isn't fermentation rebirth and transfiguration?
today's me drinks down yesterday, beautiful abstracted into more beautiful

I see swallows flying towards last year oh, autumn
a puzzle cycling back and forth in a kaleidoscope, I have memorised
the years like mysteries, totally gone, each and every path runs forward
if I look back again, I can only pointlessly add an annoying autumn shower

9 September 2010, Beijing [BH]

Knife Edge

what's shining is definitely not a knife: the face of the knife is beyond
        weariness
what's shining is not a dream of a knife: a dream is a dark flame devoured
        by a dream
what's shining is not shine itself, either: that's too abstract, too urgent
what's shining must come from another world: a stubborn referee
sitting up straight in the void; the more we're used to breakage, the more
        we're eager to
be split in two by it; after breakage there's a still more broken antithesis
what slices us open is never a knife, but its shining aesthetic

4 September 2010, Beijing [BH]

138

CHEN DONGDONG (*b.* 1961)

Across the Centuries

get the lantern lit inside the rock, show them
the sea's gesture, show them
the ancient fish
might as well show them bright lights, raised high on the mountain
a lantern
the lantern might as well be lit into the river water, show them
the living fish, show them
the voiceless sea
might as well show them the setting sun
a firebird soaring from the woods
lights the lantern. as I lift my hands to block the north wind
as I stand right between the gorges
I think they will close in on me
they will come to see my riddling lantern
language
watch flowers in Autumn
hear all night the wind's hoarseness outside the door. outside the door
frigid iron blades segment the rain
a sound like screaming rocks
it's been three months. I have looked for water in an arid pasture
felt the lean dusk in the mountain stream. above the matted grass
a few red birds were startled out of sleep like water lilies
I look for water, and as I turn, step back into rainy autumn
I realise the street is buried deep in fallen leaves
like a sunken ship
whose black sails no one could remember
as it dawns on me that the long night's rain was just the tap of falling
          leaves
and this poem in my hand is going to be frigid as a
withered chrysanthemum

[BH, LMK]

Windowsill

now there's no more than a windowsill
hanging suspended on the hypothetical peacock-blue horizon
gaping to swallow an unreal building is hard to
imagine – and impossible to show
the tiger of the architect's shocking style

but it could have been inferred: you pass through the windowsill
to see yourself, leaning awkwardly on
the pterodactyl's back, as if you plan an assault
have you vanished into the mirror glass that reflects the lake? maybe
it's no more than this, that you've only just sat down by the dressing table
in the nape of your neck a feline drowsiness crimping

and so once more pass through the windowsill
you can see a heap of beautiful brocade, underwear
in disorder, an idly supine lioness
if the door inside a remote backwater is starting to bang
disclosing an even remoter garden, then you can

expect this, that you can then be hypothetical: how from the
shallow reflections in a fish-shaped pond you
conjecture the remotest image – a
windowsill like an upside-down shadow, its crows set
non-existently off by the peacock-blue horizon
like imaginary memoirs, they're being imagined right now

the trial of strength between language and the world is no more than
a trial of strength with the self – the windowsill's surreality
has become your reality now. the gloaming sky
has arrived, moving afternoon tea away. a cloud of bats
return to the dressing table's gloomy lighting. and

you, seeking confirmation: the silhouette of an architect's outdoor
project, it can prolong the stare of sunset vision
whether or not you can see yourself look down at yourself
        – no more passed through, but protractedly stretched
beyond the windowsill is the savagery of words, night's
wolf pack, about to merge with daydreams.

[BH]

Toad

as if away from supervision, away from the poet's life in the well
the scabby toad, sat on mother earth's cranium that
displays the curvature of the planet, yearns even more in its vacuity

for golden freedom. and freedom is unfree
the fantasy of freedom, dragged between
the enforced rotation of the planets: centripetal force falls into

the darkness of destiny. that needn't differ from darkness in the well
in darkness the poet wrote of darkness
...in darkness the poet, he re-incarnated as

the darkness he clearly intuited in the zeitgeist: a voice
a scabby toad, a frog goddess finally golden-draped
flying up to icy altitudes

oh toad, though, the clear night has reflected again
the deep and serene well bottom. as the poet recites
as the showgirl acting the imperial concubine by the rim of the glass
        well is

a new Moon Goddess, between moon and moon
the freedom of shadows, like supervision gives
illumination to all things, just like TV drama, to dispatch

routine darkness, re-enacting the routine of darkness
it must grant you shadow fantasy
the golden one, the free/unfree

the scabby toad poet who jumps off the cranium
unexpectedly moving into the Moon Goddess's womb
in vacuity – it's not only yearning squatting there

2000 [BH, LMK]

141

Complete Renovation

After Wallace Stevens' 'The Man with The Blue Guitar'
  (for Bobo)

1

desert from a night of total lunar eclipse
that Semu Mongol whipping on Kublai Khan
a horse fast as the wind racing to conquer

his helm was apparently more imperative
it was mounted with a red crest; he had it lean over
the horse's head, his spine almost bent into a bow

asked to slant towards the waterscape at dusk
fully glazed chain mail glittering
bringing back memories: he had crossed

between shallow sleep and deep doze, the repeatedly reflecting
dream of the Fiery Mountains; the plastron he daubed
right up on his chest, it reflected the light of

the setting sun, like a bunch of arrows, from the decorative pattern
on this ceramic tile inlaid on the wall of
the bathroom, it popped out the tip of its tongue to lick

to lick through – the man in the living room
though, was using an even more exaggerated neon waistline
to head-butt his brain into a LCD monitor

2

a fantasy world inferior to the magic
of reality is his reality
a desert from the night of total lunar eclipse

in the *Age of Empires*™, his nudity
was draped with the insomniac Imperial Robes
thatched cottages becoming city-states…a silver coin

going back and forth between the paths with nothing between
the pirates and the Wenzhou real estate speculators – and it fell again into him
he dropped his pants, while hurrying to hold emptiness

in both hands, that man had already decorated
his nakedness with Kublai, a horse fast as the wind,
chain mail glittering, hung up high in the bathroom

meanwhile, the radian of the bathtub obeyed the waistline
and an arc of neon slantwise crossed the artificial lake
drowning in a sea of lights, making the colours of night become

the colours of night covering over the residential quarter
not allowing this painstaking effort
to go on the market and be called half-finished

3

this situation was equivalent to a translated poem
the man walking Kublai the doggie
dyed his short hair blonde

how could he imagine he was being imagined
his brain ejecting virtual
reality at a monthly rate, and also devoting his nakedness

to surrealism, inlaid on the bathroom wall
the remoteness this tile mural decorated
drapes himself in a bathrobe like draping on chain mail, leaning by
            the window

looking at the starry sky, conceiving just another kind of
magical memory – had he crossed between
shallow sleep and deep doze, that reflecting

dream of the Fiery Mountains? Maybe he simply
chose a path to return from
quarter, waterscape and stainless rockery. This situation was
            equivalent to a

translated poem: its night of total lunar eclipse
in a desert couldn't not say to itself
– oh god, where am I?

2003 [BH, LMK]

MENG LANG (*b.* 1961)

Even the Rosy Dawn Is Stale

1

Even the rosy dawn is stale.

So in the dark there's no need to long for so-called daybreak.

The place revealed by light
is the sky
is a crowd with blades in hand, striving.

Words, words
on the horizon, whose lips are rising?

2

Blissful pollen indulges in travel
or indulges in being sedentary – oh sweet life –
but itself has no consciousness at all.

Pollen staining the point of a knife
really can be taken to a strange place:
bliss – can never be too much,
like when you too are allotted a portion.

Carving the imaginary rootstock of the flower
the paperknife of youth is going to colonise.

3

Dark night is torturing the sun at a secret spot
bloodcurdling cries the sun lets out one by one
you will hear it only first thing tomorrow morning.

And I, the abrupt intruder
have also touched the burning brow of the sun!
At the moment of dying
I revive the world with a hundred thousand roosters –

Even the rosy dawn is stale
and even the daybreak is nothing new to foul mankind.

   4

But oh, the noble skull atop the vault of heaven!
On the horizon, whose beautiful neck is rising?

[BH, LMK]

SENZI (*b.* 1961)

Insubstantial Souls

There are still mysteries, still choices,
from sparse chinaberry to massed elms,
from one to another, flocks of birds migrate:
leaves all fallen from the branches,
and so the birds become leaves in the high places.
Rabbits retreat from the corn to the weedy slopes,
ringdoves abruptly settle on the wires,
rock-doves randomly come upon ruins;
even blinder, sparrows might blunder into chimneys,
lost in the room where nobody lives.
In my new house there's a sparrow's corpse,
specimens – a grasshopper and two butterflies – some dry leaves;
I put them on a south-facing windowsill,
and sunshine takes their insubstantial souls away.
I decided to keep them,
not disturbing the dirt on their bodies,
as they turned over in that sweet dust.

Before dawn, 11 March 2003   [BH, LMK]

HU DONG (*b.* 1962)

Your Esteemed Daughter

1

out of that obese foreign land –
the number one nightmare, the dream person that sickens you –
wake up, stand up, walk on tiptoe

beyond carnality.

like an entire House of Pleasure appearing out of nowhere, drowned
        in light,
she reassembles her openly-displayed soft jewels:

a photograph album, a necklace, a candlelit night –
just eighteen years old. the grimace of a moth before the flame
disguises

her Daddy Floodwater

she opens up, an unexpected present
possibly the tip of a breaking wave, possibly a teetering treasure ship,
possibly a scattering and re-grouping

of Spring swallows holding in their beaks our childhood's twin beds,
        whispering
a vast river of lost words...the cat's become the Kitchen God,
the Superior Man a slut:

you, Father of the *Book of Change*,
do you know where her heart has been, or what thing has caught her
        fancy, or who
she has been fondling at night's edge, under starry skies?
in the stuttering kaleidoscope – like water lilies, one by one, thoughts
        rise and fall.

divine eyes as lovely as the abacus beads.

2

your wish to uncover the ups and downs of our exploits is like
finding in this poem

a tree
(intolerable ardour)

its imaginary leaves guide us toward
the ocean that
you enseeded – multi-faceted tumbling prisms.

from the moment its falling sounds out, it urg-
es us on: differing flowers on the same tree...
or different fruit from the same flower,

drifting to heaven's heart, the Pole Star, shrinking.

3

the set rules of the puzzle: tiny stepping-stones;
the gravitational pull of its solution: star-clans in the water-butt.

you dip-and-write. the best and worst of words
depend on

the slough of your good mood, the white chalk of stars on the tip
of your nose, the snow on your baldy pate.

Come Summer Solstice, we go to the country, loaf about and wonder.

we carve roses on the pens that fence in the chickens and goats,
your smile –

the Red Boy spitting fire, the immortals somersaulting;
made a fool of on New Year's Eve, no different to country folk, we
        repeat
their country folk's tales.

[BH, WNH]

147

Frog, Cicada, Moth

The ten-million-year rotation of words, like seething swarms
of tadpoles, is because the ever-reflecting mirror of illusionary change
integrates previous lives with generations to come, and where lights
        shine in darkness,
reflecting Chengdu...Pool of a Hundred Blossoms.
A frog is calling: change! But I hope I can change,
the Goddess of Creation makes the mouth-organ reeds loudly sound,
then delivers breath and sound, ladder-like,
tuning the pitch of the sun higher, suspending multi-coloured stones
        in the air.

Famine year after famine year, blank talk blossoms on racially disturbed
tongues. The shell of scorching childhood pain splits
– a dream, an electric fan, a desolate
siesta, winding around a cyclically-repeating tree.
A cicada is singing: change! Now I really am changing,
then the Moon Goddess crosses a thousand miles, then preparing the feast,
encouraging each other, singing instead of howling –
in the wax and wane of lunar virtue, sharing clarity and perfection.

Change, isn't it just weaving sadness on the shuttle
between lips and teeth colliding? And the generations increase and multiply,
and every strand of the tapestry of the landscape of the will inherits
limits: alpha and omega –
a moth is flying: change! I can only change again,
immortal Moon Goddess never then exhausted, only then living in utter
        aloneness,
yet uncaring of who the tuning pegs of time
's chaos cast aside, or who they hold.

[BH, LMK]

34. (*See opposite page.*) *The Rainbow Skirt and Feather Dress* is a piece of
music by Emperor Tang Minghuang (712-756), to accompany a dance of the
same name reformed by his beloved concubine Yang Guifei. Their love affair
and her death in 751 at the hands of, yet again, the imperial guards, is the
subject of a famous poem by Bai Juyi, *The Song of Undying Sorrow.*

35. The Barefoot Immortal was incarnated as Emperor Song Renzong
(1022-63), in answer to the previous emperor's prayers for a son.

36. This reference to Zhuangzi's wife (via Buddha and a sheep's foot) is
so cryptic, the editors admit defeat.

The Royal We

My sun fades behind the western hills; I used to be an early riser.
Under the Imperial Canopy my unclean form used to be
passed out drunk in the front row – hundreds at my beck, thousands at my call.
The Plume-Gathering Pontifex sank into the wilderness; the football flew high
　　　　in the air.
The prince in fact changed his spots (taking the name of Mountainfoot)
What impediment was it to me if commoners came and went from their
　　　　own front doors?
But over and over I dreamed of nesting ants starting fires,
and suddenly I thought of ennobling my very own kicker of a horse.

An unbroken line of twilight on cliff carvings. Lotus blossom in the bronze vase
sent out pollen alarms: her *Rainbow Skirt*, burned by foot-soldiers, composed
a cloud's filthy array.[34] Lychees turned white-headed;
night's veins gunmetal-blue – how could these be her fault?
To pursue the royal stag still tempts, by god! (taking the name of Mountainside)
witness this yourself, and go on witnessing! Ambitious blood rises with the tide.
Sacrifice a kidney. The Barefoot Immortal, reluctant to live as a hermit,
ran the risk of turning himself into a masterstroke.[35]

The night was cool as water; my eyes, like the sodden eyes
of fish, goggled at shields: Oh, Buddha, Zhuangzi's wife, who evaded
the comb, lifted the sheep's foot.[36] To love me is
to forgive me, to leak out from places that shouldn't leak.
Poetry doesn't gush out in an uproar (taking the name of Mountaintop)
nor the missile strike the bulls-eye of the mistake of all mistakes – Dancer:
turn into the snake inside the flute player's cold jar, be a satiated
rainbow. The snake has length enough to reach back to Paradise.

I'm bursting with dawn's energy, a carbuncle without pain. In
the highest height, who has smiled, seeing without limits? This conjunction
of Sun and Moon can't prevent me continuing to scale
the nameless peaks framed by my window. Like some Emperor of every other day
fondling the globe, (taking the name of Holy Land of China)
this rebel chief sounds his shinbone flute. Ah, escape to anywhere – it's all
the same. Thick drifts of locust tree leaves in the palace, now day's shining
　　　　cobwebs
stick ten thousand nightmares on him, the King in Yellow is ready to run.

[BH, WNH]

MAI CHENG (*b.* 1962)

Granny Chronicle

when I'd done my homework up to how the wind blows away the dust
granny's Shandong accent
was lit by the fairytales in the matchbox
while the kettle's boiling
just for you I'll steep that cup of tea in the mirror

she'd kneel in front of the stove
and to my future
she'd add the village's smoke and fire
the misprints in the schoolbooks
burned with a crackle-crackle
in the flames trickling from the stove

scalding hot water
had boiled granny's reticence
she raised the teapot, pointed
to the cup that stood in the mirror
and for me she steeped my faraway years, not a metre tall yet

[BH]

Symbols

the roses in granny's hands
were planted in pots
waiting for the western metaphor to grow
when she could comb
her worries to the back of her head
she'd doff these alien landscapes
and from the village come to town

granny goes into the florist to ask
how to purchase love
the florist smiles and replies
Madam, we buy flowers in:
what we sell are symbols

[BH]

QING PING (*b.* 1962)

Evolution

These people, like me, are in the monkey dream,
A fiery disaster. Disheartenedly unrealistic.
In this life, summer seems eternal.
The spiderweb of dreams seems to be
Hung on the body by cakes of dreaming.

Scenes of solitude are always linked.
Loneliness is always denounced.
Seeker of a livelihood or contemplative, both need
A little slice of pie to settle the future of dreams.

'Life's no big deal.'
But life is actually very odd –
Cut off by the billowing broad ocean, cut off
By endless screams and silence,
Two totally different people are
Baking hatred in the same oven.

[BH, LMK]

ZHANG ZAO (1962-2010)

In the Mirror

only if she recalls every regret in her life
will plum blossom fall and fall
say, seeing her swim to the riverbank
say, climbing up a pinewood ladder
dangerous things are lovely, no doubt
but no match for seeing her mounted homecoming
blushing in shame.
bowing her head, answering the king
a mirror waits for her forever
it allows her to sit at the place she always sits in the mirror
    gazing out of the window: only if she recalls every regret in her life
will plum blossom fall and fall across Southern Mountain.

[BH, LMK]

Gently Swinging

Attic, language lab.

                                        Autumn arrives with a bang,
bright and clear, changed for the new glass of the universe on four walls,
everybody wearing headphones properly, expressions uniform as jade.

The pregnant teacher is listening too. Blurred sound's
                            feathery fragments of the classics:
Evening News, Evening News, the tape fast-forwards, whistling noisily
        round the world.
Nervous words unwilling to pass away, like streetscape and
fountains, like extraterrestrials standing on some brink,
fiddling with the sunset glow, abruptly they unload a bolt of brocade:
emptiness less than a flower!

She takes a look at the new pattern
around her, a loom in everyone's mouth,
muttering the exact same
good story.
Everyone is immersed in listening intently,
everyone baring vital organs, working –

total awareness.

[BH]

Early Spring February

the sun used to shine on me; in Chongqing one drop of
dew's early mood enveloping images one by one
I bypass stretch after stretch of air; the railway hurts
trains till they flee the light, cuckoo's light song left behind
I say, hello peaks, and parasol trees, pine and cypress too
height regardless, please let me love as if in secret
in Hunan, sun shining in the eyes of my childhood
my hands grew up, the gently fondled road was shortened
dust around the city whirls and dances round and round
horn like a brother, car wheels a kaleidoscope
teething pain changes into the scars on my backside
fruit presses me to the tree, mercilessly knocks me
down. Oh, I still can feel that I am alive today
alive in a phony place made out of paper; spring
clucks and coos, sun prods all over like a quack doctor
prods at these up-front or could it be these deferred
times, prods and prods at the utopia of this world
oh, shun the hidden sage, useless as a rotten rope

[BH]

Choir

a choir warm on latitudes and longitudes
tongues of young girls fresh from the bath
like magician's roses conjured out of thin air

who are they presented to? who are they a gift for?
head, leaven the bread of my soul
little poplars, open the roaring heat inside me [37]

raise it up, over-arching you, like straddling a
definition; oh, the numinous difficulty
of those handy disposable notes

the girls are leading me to eat ashes
at the end of the universe, ah, the pasture of the void
Wednesday passes on the baton

but some wolfish thing with the heart and lungs of a dog
is howling, reverberating
relentlessly mouthing fallen May

1992 [BH, WNH]

Motherland Miscellany

what's overflowing and running down, it's not booze
that's not yet a cherry pit, spat out with no more flesh on it than a corpse
the boy at the bottom of the well, people still salvaging stuff

till the middle of the night, till suffocation, only then an
empty bottle fallen to earth from the cloud's mouth, unbroken
will humans still tolerate me passing through the lobby

37. 'Little poplars, little pines, grow big and be the rafters of the motherland'
– a Communist Party song for pre-school children; roaring heat, lit. *internal heat*, is a term of art in traditional Chinese medicine.

154

passing through the sexy silence of typewriters
what's been spilled is still not
the moon's face installed on the water and beaten

black and blue; captain, oh your wicked women
haven't opened the window of the water yet. But I've begun to lick
I'm licking the bright clothes in the air

I'm licking the little brocade streamers pressed between the feet
of the pages; till licking is swapped for being licked
I'd rather be licked all life long, never wanting to live a life

[BH]

The Condemned and His Path

From the capital to the weedy barrens,
broad sea, blank sky boundless, and my head
locked in a pillory, my voice
hog-tied, bellflowers on a thousand field-paths
disclose death –
a meaning crowned for the walker
on a long road and a far journey;[38]

I walk and walk;
death is inevitable: this is certainly
not politics. Thirsty, I
sketch a tiny forest spirit;
her bouncing breasts, a fresh and tender unfamiliarity,
running across the never-named current,
while the razor-like fawn
restrains the clear brittle shade;

if I couldn't sleep,
I would aesthetically assume
I was making sleep sleep,
deeply and soundly;

38. This is a quotation from Qu Yuan's 'Li Sao'. See 'On Encountering
Trouble', tr. Hawkes, *Songs of the South*, p.73, lines 191-92, among other
similar lines.

if I feared, if I feared,
I would presumably think
I was already dead, I'd
made death die, and also had

taken away everything I'd been seeing:
the proletarian flavour of the discolouring scenery,
restaurants, ferries, kingfishers,
a few lands of abundance in the provinces,
a few slovenly hookers shuffling mahjong tiles,
a few fierce tigers banished from humans by humans,
thrown aside like worn-out socks,
and the distant shadows of pagodas,

even further away, there's that tiny forest fairy,
elegant, floating and lingering, a little mother you can call by
her baby name, her world flowing with fragrance

same as everybody else,
the dream of someone going to their death,
the dream of the meta-human,
it's impure, like pure poetry.

1994   [BH, LMK, WNH]

Chef

The future is a chill blast from inside a body plundered
and passed, the overturned vinegar bottle permeates tendon and bone.
The chef pushes the door open, sees twilight, like a little girl,
using the tip of its tongue to feel all around for the light switch.
Inside there's peacock-like specificity,
on the ceiling a few balloons, still living a kind of life:
the chef endures the suddenness. He cuts the tofu in two,
slices it an inch thick, puts it into the applauding pan of oil,
fries both sides golden-yellow;

                                        then changes to another pan,
stir-fries a bit of smashed ginger, mince, and bright red bean-paste,
imports the tofu; adds a little millet-wine, MSG and water,

lets it soak in to become a soft secrecy,
at this point, sprinkle on some diced spring onion and it's ready to serve!
The chef invents this reality because of some dream,
heavy snow whirling outside, looking for a name.
From the depth of his aching tooth, the sky is slowly
drawing away that little floral dress.
From myopia lenses, the past leaks out like sperm.
                                        Superlatively the chef sticks
his head out of the window, the recipe cools down into a bridge
toward the altogether unacknowledged fields. He listens, listens:
truly, someone is making this dish, and putting
this mouthwatering bait into the dark night backyard.
Two 'Nos' are on the run in the fiction of the times,
like two little tongue beasts, emitting hot air,
grappling with each other on the ice-bound river surface...

1995 [BH, LMK]

Edge

Like the tomato hiding on the edge of a steelyard, he's always
lying down. Whatever flashes over, a warning or a swallow, he
is rock steady, on guard beside the little thing. The second hand moves to
ten o'clock sharp, and the alarm clock quietly leaves, a cigarette
has also left, carrying pairs of blue handcuffs
his eyes, clouds, German locks. Anyhow, what's not here
has all gone.

Emptiness, getting bigger. He is distant, but there's always
some edge; on the edge of the cog, the edge of the water, edge of
himself. Every so often he looks at the sky, forefinger up, practising fine,
thin, but frantic calligraphy: 'Come back!'
It's true, those who lost their shape have reverted to that original shape:
New Zone windows are full of wind, the moon dipped in a lager barrel,
the steelyard, abruptly tilting, there, infinite
as a pacified lion
flat out beside the tomato.

[BH, LMK, WNH]

In the Forest

1

A few default matters of yours,
like thunderclouds, they call you to the hilltop.
Gliders of falling leaves,
a few small distant parachuting question marks wriggle and gently fall into
the bottleneck of scenery. It seems somebody in the weather is performing
a mathematical calculation.
You burn with anxiety.
Rings of the bell, rings of the bell throw headless golden armour
into the depths of the forest. There, mist
is operating in the corner of the Autumn wind, starting up
a discarded picture,
a warm generator room shaped like the insides of an alarm clock.
There, you walk about.

2

You walk about, as if the forest isn't in the forest.
Like an urgent long-distance call, squirrels split open the forest paths.
Listen: Something's wrong.
The sky is filled up with floating malfunctions,
a plaza has been reversed.

You replace the handset, maple leaves all over you.

Mushrooms, they twist the bronze screws even tighter –
making a china shop inlay itself in the fresh green of Freiheitstrasse,
making the shadows that are detectives for death
tag along in.
They shoot a glance at the zeros on the invoice;
their bodies segment and hop one-legged through the revolving door.
They turn right, and point vaguely at
the forest on the other shore.

A misty butterfly effect.
At noon, flowing water plays the flute.
The bright and clean expression of porcelain, a ballet of many delicate poses.
They say: smash it. We say nothing.

3

You're on the rampage.
That receipt is clasped right in your hand,
you want to redeem your pawned shadow.
The forest turns dark, raindrops strike the keyboard of dense leaves,
and you're lost. Yet
hope is always on the left. Leftward,
there, the abstract man mute and silent on the road sign,
he gives you a little nod;
green, staying on and waiting in the tree trunk like a mother,
flimsily tweaking the precise cogs.
Woodpeckers, working while they're talking,
circles and circles of sound waves rippling in time and tide.

Woodpeckers, permeating the whole forest, and
Monday.

4

A circle of open ground.
There, the long distance runner is repairing his breath machine.
His thirst opens up a treeful of red apples,
their scent lifts and floats into the Golden Bell Tower, returning reality
            or letting it slip away.
He feels deeply alone because of his thirst. He bends his head to polish
his warm palm: it seems to be a train station,
a hubbub of voices. A bunch of kids off to a picnic splash skeins of
crazily dappled spouting water.
Light, it sends a pointsman-like shadow to stand at the crossroads.
He feels he's got from the universe, for the first time, a pair of hands, and
            violence.

1 January 1996, Tübingen   [BH]

Hair Salon: Restricted Access or Long Shot

1

Small town in the south. Sultry as Utopia.
Electric fans blowing everybody's bones all fluttery,
but no one can fall apart. On a little stone bridge,
two or three tourists point at the landscape, one
a northern taxman on the run from his criminal past.

2

I'm someone with plenty of aliases too,
I'm stifling a fit of laughter, my chopsticks reach for the Drunken Prawns.
The emptiness of the empty air is so churned up it's utterly broken.

The boss's sixty-fourth mask has opened its mouth,
and what it says is the usual enigma: 'Cleanliness,
I'm its slave – because it's in plain view,
because it knows no limits –
you have to constantly clear up behind it'.

A woman interrupts: 'Our boss
is a good man. One time I was looking out from upstairs
and I saw he was kneeling in the middle of the road, drunk,
rolling up his sleeves to fold the zebra crossing and take it home'.

3

I go to sleep on a rush mat but wake up beside the rockery.
Butterflies usher in the future, but duplicate some Ming dynasty
morning. On a day like this, you only need to feel out of sorts
from head to foot to know the future is on its way;

you only need to feel alone, and then you know
everything's gone completely wrong, and there's no way to change it.
At a moment of dead calm, only when the wind suddenly blows upstream,
does it stand you up, and like someone in a rage, you leap forward,
tear the paper, as your true name –
an ambulance singing like cicadas – hurtles toward you.

[BH, WNH]

A Key for C.R.

Million-ton darkness. We're going home, clothes swollen with the west wind.
A glass of water is isolated on the bookcase.
$\qquad$ Hidden in the great vastness, swallows
aim their migration at a single tiny cent a thousand miles away,
while we're locked into the memory of the mountain shadow outside the room.
Your nakedness fills the verandah,
and all around us, the black magnet's night like a meditator attracts

emptiness. A key is sucking in the world.
An airmail letter delivered in error passes back and forth between you and me.
'Big', it whispers, 'big'.

The flames leap up: ah, the letter, endlessly growing,
it presses us to live inside.
You're drunk and you throw up, I'm thinking long and hard about writing
$\qquad$ a reply,
and my shadow is holding two sheets of paper, as if
$\qquad$ I'm stretching my indebted and lopsided wings.

1996 [BH]

Song Sung Drunk

Last night, as the party lurched and wobbled and drifted leftward, the booze
was so sweet it began to bow down low. Live prawns of notes
spurt-strolled from the cello, and then, pitter-patter,
stood to attention in Booze Wonderland, asking if anyone was starting a
$\qquad$ revolution.
There was a fat guy weeping and taking a string of firecrackers from his
$\qquad$ inside pocket,
but nobody was paying any attention. Hey! Don't close in so far away,
the seven or eight of you, don't swing your hair back and forward,
don't let the teapot's liberated zone shatter and flood out.
Don't bow down low to me (under the table the deer goes 'doh!')

161

There was a Party official type on tiptoe, raising a glass, with
pocket-money snout, telling foreign guests to 'Eat cock!' [39]
The booze laughed before it happened. I kept on drifting leftward, so was
I the fat guy? No way could the string of bangers catch fire.
My mind was a thousand miles away, declaiming in an empty phone box.
Could a hit man have come as contracted? The world
showed its blue tail, with only a sodden towel
passed over here, an empty boat turning back through the cold waves.
Oh, falling down left and right, let us from the body of it
refine another Manchuria, a motorway
leading to variations on svelte and slender, leading to the seven or eight of yo
Your name was Emerald, but you disappeared for a while, or maybe
as you dialled your mobile you were feeding the stone lions
to call the empty phone box a thousand miles away.
(Her boyfriend promised to wait there for her call,
but he didn't come, so she was imagining her own illusory 'there'.)
She came back here, collapsed all over us, as if
it was all hyacinths at the other end. An old chancer swayed over
to toast somebody. Character was dripping from everyone's
finger-ends, the fat guy's firecrackers stayed unlit, so
someone chucked his lighter away. 'My mind',
the fat guy spat, 'is very very clear – no – Our'
the fat guy slapped himself, 'Our Imperial Mind knows what's what'.
The hit man grew softer. Outside, ice sealed in the news.
'Left, left,' the fat guy helped the hit man into the toilet.
The hit man kissed his absence like he was kissing the chin of the King of Chi
Oh, King of China! Absent, like the hit man. But me, like the
fat guy, again and again I bowed down low before The Will of Heaven; or mayb
was that drunk, a thousand miles away, by chance beside the phone box,
hearing it ring, ambling over, but falling behind the silence.
The drunk waited by the empty phone box, singing, oh singing, oh:
'Oh far away, oh, far away, you've got an abstract of this place'.

[BH, WNH]

39. There is a pun here: the harmless '*chi ji ba*' (Let's eat chicken)
is a homophone for the vulgar '*chi jiba*' (suck dick).

Father

In 1962 he didn't know what he could do. He
was still young, very idealistic, pretty leftish, but
carrying the name of a rightist. He'd escaped home to
Changsha from Xinjiang, puffy with hunger. His granny made him
a pot of tripe and turnip soup, with red dates floating in it.
Incense was burning in the room – a snare rising upward with its smell.

That day he really was at his wits' end.
He wanted to go out for a stroll, but not very much.
He stared at things he couldn't see, laughed out loud.
His granny gave him a cigarette and he smoked it, his first.
He said that in the dispersing rings of smoke were the words 'Monstrous,
        Absurd'.

At midday he thought he might go and sit a while on Tangerine Island,
to practise the flute.

He walked and walked, then didn't want to go there any more,
but following the road back he suddenly felt:

there are always two selves,
one going forward in obedience,
one going forward in disobedience,
one sitting on a bolt of brocade, whistling a song,
and this other one walking on May Day Avenue, walking in an unperishable

truth.

He thought: it's good now, everything's just fine!

He stopped. He turned around. He walked towards Tangerine Island again.
With that turn, he alerted an alarm clock at the edge of the sky.
With that turn, he messed up every rhythm on earth.
With that turn, the road was filled with miracles, and
he became my father.

[BH]

163

HUANG CANRAN (*b.* 1963)

Flowers Circulating

Every day we see them circulate,
these pretty flowers in the city, on the streets,
in shopping malls and on the metro escalators,
on buses and in McDonald's windows,
in vegetable markets near residential areas,
their ages roughly fifteen to twenty-three,
growing up in average or poor families,
spending months saving for a few good outfits,
doing all they can to dress up their saturated youth,
they circulate, but almost all alone in the world,
breaking away from their annoying, boring parents, teachers or colleagues,
exposing sexy arms, shoulders,
calves, thighs and even belly buttons, pleasing to everybody's eyes –
if you suddenly feel a freshness in the suffocating air,
that is probably because of their presence,
and about her who endows this city with energy,
airheads, they focus instead on small targets,
like, go buy a pair of shoes, go visit an old classmate,
go pay the phone bill, go deposit a few hundred in the bank,
go get a hairdo, go borrow a pop novel from the library,
you look at them a bit too long, they think you're a wolf,
you look at them a longer while, they think they have some kind of flaw,
their bodies are filled with the energies for love and a blissful life,
but they strain to suppress these, snuff them out,
until they've hit the eight-year boundary or crossed that frontier,
figure, skin and expression beginning to change,
beginning to use lipstick, eye-shadow, tweezers,
beginning to go on dates, watch movies, walk in the park,
get married, have babies, go to restaurants with the in-laws on weekends,
eventually becoming what shows up the new generation of pretty flowers,
eventually becoming a part of annoyance, boredom and suffocation,
love becomes a bubble, a shadow, bliss postponed to their kids,
wearing pyjamas in bed,
maybe right next to you.

[BH, LMK]

164

XI CHUAN (*b.* 1963)

Commandments

you shall not kill
therefore arm yourself to the teeth
and also in your imagination exhaust the insanity of bloodlust
divinities don't punish imaginings
but be careful not to squash the ants as you rave

you shall not eat meat
so there's a necessity to assume all animals on the earth are unclean
just like your body, just like your internal organs
or at least wear the mask of sympathy
only being vegetarian doesn't guarantee you won't gorge yourself into
        obesity

you shall not drink
mainly so as not to stir up trouble when stewed
please fill your wine bottles with water
please drink cool water: with a clear head, please curse the demon drink
that you may pander to divinities, better the taxman should explode in
        thunderous rage

you shall not steal
do not peep into other people's rooms, do not open drawers
if you've ever dabbled in these light-fingered arts
you'll have to spend a lifetime defending yourself
this is one way you can scorn private ownership

you shall not dress vainly
therefore style yourself after a monk
and mortify your frail flesh, insist on sober garb
for this you'll gain the panegyric:
'Listen! His clear mind speaks! See! The truth is in his hands!'

you shall not lust
you should only talk tragedy or deep learning with that gender you prefer
but don't lead the topic towards the soul's anguish

lust is a snare
best to skirt its shores

you shall not covet
so it's not a bad idea to crown yourself king in a dark room
and why not cut a skeleton key and carry it in your hand?
walk, stop, turn: in that capital city under the light of your sun
you will disdain to open each rusted lock

you shall not lie
therefore you can choose one day in every week
to run off to an unpeopled wilderness, let off some hot air
then give a long sigh
go back under your own roof to be a lord or lady of dumbness and
        discretion

January 1998 [BH, LMK, WNH]

Cat and Mouse

> 'At the start of the month, the cat bites the mice's necks and heads.'
> Song Ci (1274 AD), *The Washing Away of Wrongs*

The mice don't give a damn. Mice who go to school still go to school, those who do business still do business. The mice don't give a damn. The mice shower with the dew from blades of grass, in praise of how wide the world is, in praise of humans defeating famine, 'barns and byres pressed with harvest, cellars filled with wine'. The more the mice scratch the itchy-ouches, the more optimistic they are – just leave some food for the cat. The mice booze the oil in the lamps, and topple washbasins onto the floor, and realise there are red beans and green beans in cardboard boxes, and realise there's a woman in the toilet ready to give birth.

At the middle of the month, the cat bites the mice's backs and bellies

The mice roar with laughter. The mice summon wind and rain. The mice compete over whose claws are sharper than their teeth, never ever having wanted to realise that everybody's belly had become plumper,

166

and nobody knew when. Should be straining to bear baby after baby. Seeing the next mouse generation, though small in scale and small in shape, they're crazy with ambition. The mice have faith in absolute victory now. The mice learn to bite through iron and steel, and to bite through gold and silver. The ultimate goal is to bite through a building and bring it down. Do the mice still give a damn about the cat biting their backs and bellies? Anyway, the mice have put on their thickest armour.

At the end of the month, the cat bites the mice's hind legs

The mice need their hind legs, between climbing up and climbing down, the mice need to stand steady on their feet too. But the mice can deny absolutely to the cat that it's the end of the month, deny absolutely they have hind legs. It's necessary to solve the problem of recreation first: moving house or marrying off a daughter shouldn't be done at the end of the month. Whenever it comes to the end of the month, the mice treasure their own hind legs even more. The mice have heard that it's the same law for tigers biting humans, so they decide to form an alliance with humans to wipe out tigers and cats. Sharing sovereignty over the world: you, on the ground, me under the ground, and the sky to be shared by everybody.

May 1997 [BH, LMK]

Khitan Mask

The nomads and craftsmen of Khitan abut upon a sea of non-Khitan people. The sun of Khitan, its speed of rising and setting: we can only make an estimate, pretending to be one hundred per cent sure.

I chose a mouse and named it 'Khitan Mouse', it's hiding right in my room. While Khitan raindrops, adapted to the vast grasslands, never ever fall on my head.

A big pair of scissors has cut off the chaotic lifeblood of the Kingdom of Khitan (This kingdom of eagles, kingdom of purebred horses and bighorn sheep); no one will ever again be responsible for the swordplay that made the illustrious name of Khitan resound everlastingly through the world.

167

Some remember the Khitan, only because 16th-century Europeans were once not sure whether 'Khitan' and 'China' denoted two separate things or whether they were two names for one country.

The 'Khitan chamber pot' on sale at the Beijing Antique Market makes the collector smile knowingly; he hears the chamber pot insistently nagging at him, 'Who are Khitans?'

A guy will sometimes have his head shaved in a Khitan hairstyle: ignoramuses think him outlandish as a British punk, and the wise think him profound as an Italian monk, but he's only unintentionally disguised as a Khitan ghost.

...but, being without the Kingdom of Khitan is like being without the Khitan princess with her amber and jade pectoral, who strummed on her crescent sword with scarlet fingernails.

Her lovely face has been dug away from her bones by time, while what time can't dig away is this gold mask in the history museum, which is a memory of that lovely face, over which earthworms once crawled.

Khitan has forged itself into a gold mask. All its dignity is only built upon gold but not upon Khitan calligraphy, which almost nobody can decipher now.

To history, this is barbaric, reckless, foolhardy: it seems the fake face can more effectively manage the darkness underground and the bluster above ground than the real face can.

Millions of rustling phantoms will kneel together around this mask. If the long-gone princess allowed, they would put on this mask in turn, take turns to stand in for the kingdom heaven never approved.

Once they had put on this mask, they couldn't see, they couldn't hear, and there'd be no way they could speak. They'd only come to the realisation of Heaven's Tao 900 years after their death.

Inside the history museum's glass case, the value of this gold mask is climbing, while its weight may be reducing from three pounds to one ounce: it might be reduced to a splendid but unreliable wrapping paper.

And maybe Khitan phantoms are rushing in to steal their princess'
mask away, totally denying as they do it that there ever was a Kingdom
of Khitan.

[BH, LMK]

YANG XIAOBIN (*b.* 1963)

Printemps in Paris

Strip off a suit skirt with the pet name Etam, it becomes lingerie.
I thought I touched flesh tone, but that was the mirror.

Hand dripping with glass, no fingers remain between fingers
and, from inside one pocket, no other pocket is salvaged.

Mirrors have emptied, sleeves worn and gone.
Turn your head, and the ripped cross-stitches are spiders' legs.

Not one springtime can be kept, except for
cotton sewn into a mood, warming up after a while and

cooling down again, so, touching it once more,
is it really the petals of Printemps?

Or a long-lost label,
grown up into the willow waists of Utopia?

Along an endless watch strap, I walk all the way to a dirty mind.
The salesgirl says, That was just the French edition of *Cosmo*.

[BH, LMK, WNH)

Daily Lament

1

shave off the beard
shave off the tobacco in the beard
shave off the fire in the tobacco
and the stars in flames

shave off the lips in passing
shave off the flowers bred in a French kiss
shave off the corals of lust

oh, shave off the strings on a nocturne, shave off
the souls infinitely stretching out on those strings
also these dancing legs
and the chanting tongues

shave off the churches
shave off the flagpoles
shave off the bones grown mad as steeples

shave off the razor
and shave off the hand holding the razor

2

take off the neckerchiefs and the leaders
at the same time, take off the tempests and the memories

take off the wounds, will the pain still be there?
take off the wings, will the butterfly's hovering remain?
take off its spots, will a leopard still starve?

take off the walls
take off the higher clouds
meaning, to take off poets' pants
take off the vital organs of rhythm and disseminate them

even more, take off the voice and speak
take off sleep and dream
and take off the whole land and get close to the ancestors

in the end, take off the skin and become a specimen

wash off the bodies, blood marks will be brighter still
wash off the bride, so the rouge will not disappear
wash off the papers, ink marks and writing will be even clearer

just the same, the hard life washed off lasts longer than faces

so, wash off the faces!
and time itself will be washed off

wash off the salt in the sea
there will be mysophobic fishes dying in the sun

wash off the nights, let daytime be naked
wash off the shadows, let everything be solitary and alone

wash off this world, leaving only the reflection in the mirror
clean and tidy, tidy and clean

[BH, LMK]

ZHENG DANYI (*b.* 1963)

Northern Diary

Those bicycles on me are in fact a herd of horses with their souls
removed, along the alameda
the throng lifts off the ground, shuttles, flies like phantoms...
fog. We place ourselves in one another's fog

the wound splits open again yet doesn't want to speak
'Speak, speak to me!'
The redundant finger of the six points at...

the shining ribs of the heating vents, so shiny like dying
while those rheumy-eyed old folk
are raising candles on my body

while those tearful old folk span this country with tape-measures
the country I enshrine in my diary... deep wells rocking
fog spreading. Fog

is like the unlike...
from the inside leading me forwards, towards

the non-existent finger of the six
writing the herd of horses
along the riverbank the non-speaking herd gallops past
the sky...the sky which stops spreading shades of blue
wild geese more like the unlike...

'Speak, speak to me!'
The girls on my body are questioning their wounds

[BH, LMK]

Oblivion Too

oblivion is also the latest memory of someone prostrate with a stomach ache
the doctor takes away the gastroscope like he was pulling out an appendix

from left arteries, syringes – that delicate vampire
sucks out a substitute again, to be sent to the lab

give us some more milk, give us some more
firm nipples, please
shouting – it's also the last hot specimen in the fridge

because, too many becauses
then the mournful cello has no way to forget
no way to, no matter how

surely only birds still use words like freedom

[BH, LMK]

HAI ZI (1964-1989)

To 1986

'like two fierce monks firing the land of wild chrysanthemums
– this is how my heart is this year'

(or the only skulls remaining when horses drowned in the lake of emeralds)
the infinite terror in a horse's brain! that infinite terror of water and fruit!

'(as I crane my neck and go wandering all around)
your lips are like rainbow clouds moving deep into an orchard
(while in my brain remains the terror in horses' heads
that terror of lips and fruit)'

'(this clear, cool well-water of mine)
washing my feet like washing two weapons of war
(skeletons of swans fly in from far and far away
graveyard horns sing for someone blustering on a swan's body)'

[BH, LMK, WNH]

Dedicated to Dark Night
(For The Daughters of Dark Night)

from the land dark night rises
dark night blocks the shining sky
the land laid waste after harvest
from inside of you dark night rises

you came from far away, where I go
on this long long journey, which passes here
the sky has nothing to its name
why does that comfort me so?

the land laid waste after harvest
they've taken away the year's yield
they've taken the crop away, ridden away the horses
people left in the ground, buried deep

pitchforks gleam, straw is piled on the fire
rice grain heaped in the dark barn
the barn is too dark, too still, too much has been gathered,
too much laid waste: I saw Death's eyes in that harvest

birds like black drops of rain
flock from dusk into dark night
dark night has nothing to its name
why does that comfort me so?

walking along the way
singing full-throatedly
the gale sweeps across the ridge
above is the edgeless sky

[BH, LMK, WNH]

PAN WEI (b. 1964)

Days
(for C.Y.)

those landscapes oozing out from every grain of amber.
oozing out from the eaves, oozing out from
the skeleton and the inner palace unmasked in faint thunder.

there is also silence, laying the dining table with silverware,
meditating on distance with the idleness of a servant.
in the distance, there may be water, newly sprouted shoots
preparing to flow.

the tiny swaying of its little wasp waist on account of one day.

that's right, the branches are correct –
making the leaves occupy the high ground, pinning the sound of the
       bell down.
there is no bronze fallen from the morning,
nor are there hovering walls rushing out from the village.

there is only distance, getting lost, getting lost, getting endlessly lost;
there is only the post office, infecting, infecting custom.

[BH]

Village Clique
(to He Jiawei)

Before you leave, already you have returned time and again to your
       old home
Now, all that you can return to is just
a wall consecrated by rain.
In your piedness, you're real as a fantasy.
The past bends its menacing knee to court you;
you're pulling back, shrinking, swallowing rusty milk.

Village clique, I'm a fill-in-the-blank question too;
streets drying out on the serrated edge of the moon.
The salt on the flagstones, it's not actually suspicious times.
The marrying rooftop, it's merely wings collecting rent.
While in the courtyard of carved doors and windows, it'll unwittingly
       reveal
the feudal mewling of our tiny thin grandmother.

But, you will get an invitation from superstition.
No need to wipe out the weaknesses flying off like fallen leaves.
Even if you could play the shape of twilight with a guitar,
not a string would be born for you.
Under the grasping skirts of our county council, there are still mouldy
officials shuff-shuffling their dominoes.

175

Four seasons a year, still in real terms a wasted effort.
However, as you return again, you're ready to bow;
village clique, I'll be like a berry in a skullcap,
offering you a yoke of water – I've been
locked up and on public show for years. And also, may amended vision
guide you to look at this: Lake Tai, my coffin.

[BH, LMK]

SONG WEI (*b.* 1964)

Chronicles of Landlordland: When SARS Was Rampant

So have I heard:[40] once upon a time in the kingdom of Landlordland,
a single female Bodhisattva in Lord Buddha's retinue
lived as a widow on the far far away
cliffs of white streams and flying snow,
her heart filled with joy!
Beside the temple gate, the mannequin egrets faced downwind;
tall and slim with back-combed feathers, they were her chilly girlfriends.
Between them they brought the rain, the feet of the rain
dashing all the way, arriving in the blink of an eye in front of my house.
What a delicate scene it was: daytime lightning,
bolts of startling thunder rolling into the yard like deep-fried crispy kebabs;
and us, banqueting above the thunder and lightning,
shot glasses transparent, meat and vegetables sooty without fire.

This is what I myself witnessed in Landlordland:
the white-gowned Bodhisattva visited the market place in person
peddling the herbs she collected and processed with her own hands –
lady's-tresses, fish mint, stemless violet, sour wood-sorrel;
I too have eaten things original and exclusive to her:
small-scaled fine-fleshed silver carp, vetch tips snatched from the pig's mouth,
as well as that chard we can weave into sandals;
I swallowed in one all the exciting screams of night-flying insects,
in order that I too could croak like a frog,

40. This is an introductory phrase used in Chinese translations of Buddhist sutras.

and so ride the enormous bubbles blown from my cheeks
jumping down from the tall tall treetops, and landing in the well.

Marvels were hidden everywhere among the fields. Stumbling at random
even the mud I would unwittingly chew was so tasty, so clean.
My mouth vast and distant, teeth hidden deeper than eels in their holes.
My arms all wound in raw silk and white cloud
as watery pigtails flowed down the mountain's waist.
I sat down to a disorderly Harvest Home, and never wanted to get up again.
I ate a lump of crispy meat, like swallowing a horse pill.
Grannies, grandpas, uncles, aunties, brothers, wives, sons
and nephews, their vows had to be witnessed, their incense fanned
by a passer-by like me. Oh Buddha of Mercy in the market place!
whose repeated incarnations meant that she had heard our chatter: in
             between these,
she swiftly came and went, already tipsy as she took her leave.

I too was panicked by those few old houses behind the twenty field balks:
their beauty as they linked together was impossible for me
to analyse or individually acquire. We walked between them,
feeling the spring and resilience of moss-mantled paths,
only to discover, built in a cobweb's centre, a planetarium
swaying up above in the wind,
its roof all covered with shiny tiles – some Star Lord
would nose about it from top to bottom in the small hours
watching huddled lovemaking, quivering ripples in water butts,
and grass and woods growing all through the night, covering the roof
in the blink of an eye: this is the mortal world even immortals cannot
             entirely see.

I was the only one – between the further away fields – who heard the toad
speak to the frog with the deep intimacy of strangers;
I saw, too, the drifting duckweed's tranquil refusal
of the long-legged mosquito. I totally got the point.
In Landlordland, I understood silkworms had nothing to do with weaving, just like
spring dreams have nothing to do with sleep: these passing dreams
were me opening wide my dragonfly eyes, to see the cuckoo
clear the way, while freshwater snails brought up the rear –
and in between a country woman planting seedlings along our way,
her rich double-petalled rump raised to face the blue sky!
Look, spring dreams are so wide awake yet so sodden with oil,
just like the crisscross field balks soaked with rain,
they were confined to an ancient bed. On the canopy with its carved bedposts,

thousands of field balks were revealed: a snail, wanting to chase the train,
had boarded its future, his whole life the same as ours –
we would all like to make long-term plans.

And the Bodhisattva, a beautiful widow living alone,
did she reject people's appeals for help
because of her fear of what others might say? – No, after our hectic desire
came an epidemic: a pestilence infecting all, like this Harvest Home
attended by all: each sprouted grain diseased, every pickled grass a simple.
Oh, the plague, given an inch, took an ell as it leaned ever closer to summer.
But nobody could see its nearly transparent geometry
within this even cleaner air, just as no words written on paper
would be recognised in Landlordland. Whether Typical or Atypical,
I thought, lung diseases were always the sickness of genius,
its toxins are aesthetic, formal,
up-to-date, advancing with the times,
and therefore widely spread and sustainable for development.

The little china horseman on the palace tiles
and the cat on the hot tin roof are both
stilt-walking high-stepping souls, their lives in the hand of fate.
In order to nip this in the bud, the Bodhisattva might have to
add disinfectant to her sweet dew, and take the egrets' temperatures,
those neighbours in intimate contact, even if
all she got was a sly sneeze, cooler even than a late spring cold snap;
she'd also whisk the dust of sunshine from the top of my head
with a willow twig, that little desert lurking in my hair.
However, now that I have taken from her slender fingertips
those rounds and whorls that hid her mysteries – no wonder she had the power
so to summon wind and rain – she could just be a
keenly attentive landlady, shouldering Heaven's scales of justice
and collecting rent on every hill and in every ditch – but if so, why would
        I still need
her thousand hands, or that scalpel flickering gracefully in those thousand hands?

That was country life, now out of reach for many years – *the emerald water
        and green hills:*
and what for?[41] – though only now are we catching up with
the reforesting of the mountains, and the fishing bans on the rivers, I still
        have to say –
in Landlordland, on the white-gowned Bodhisattva's mountains – bloody
        golf balls!

41. From Chairman Mao Zedong's poem 'Saying Goodbye to the God of Disease'.

As dawn re-assembles the sky and one by one the prostrate hills give off
aromas like freshly-baked bread, my protective clothing has grown over me
like ringworm: I am well-fed and warm, so why shouldn't I
indulge in a bit of shameless lust? Will the plague consummate my wish
       at last,
so that I could be like a statue of Guan Yin, an MDF Bodhisattva,
my heart and lungs full of sludge, living the easy life in the temple of the
       ICU?
And this is the hardest of karmas to practise, it's just not as easy
as feeding up some bitch till she's fat and white and dumb as a pig,
first letting her eat your leftover pigswill, then eating her.

4 May 2003. Late night, Nanping; copied out over 10 days and nights
[BH, LMK, WNH]

ZANG DI (*b.* 1964)

Guessing About Joseph Conrad

Sailing towards an inshore islet,
this fishing boat uses its unsophisticated organs
to plough a shallow blossoming ditch
on the sea's surface: as delicate as that
which we see in the fields in Spring.
There's a wind, like an invisible swarm,
sniffing all along its transparent
depth. Standing on the deck
every one of us is like someone hunted
by a sound that he can't see.
But in fact, spending the weekend
on a shipping route like this, 'It's very safe' –
the temporary tour guide also said that
to the woman we think is the prettiest
among us. 'A shipping route like this
is as precise as a zip'.
In this case, the ocean's surface
could be a bed sheet. Under a cover of
sky-blue, sleeping each and every sleep;

all of which seem to culminate in
a great fearless god.
Death, by comparison, appears less important.
And on another, parallel shipping route,
a flock of dazzling seagulls is practising
the correct pronunciation. A ring-pull can
somebody threw out attracts them.
The volume of the great ocean's symphony
has grown a Utopian larynx: measure it
in fathoms and apothegms.
As a way of waking up, the hooting
steam whistle just doesn't work. But,
at the moment the whistle stops,
the seagulls sound like words
acclaiming victory: they fly out
of a Conrad novel, free from
the fetters of printing or history...

September 1995   [BH, LMK, WNH]

Cosmo-Sceneriology

I lean out to look down:
a dark knowledge seems
to have filled all space up.
Meteors are like subpoenas
shooting along their seemingly ungoverned
trajectories. I can't see
our city, it's now,
much more than at any other time,
like a hollow association.
Why is that there's still nobody to establish
the anatomy of that type? What it is saying is that
the universe is made up of two membranes.
While right up to now, the way
they touch or uncover it –
is as if there is only one.
I notice that you're also leaning
gingerly out. We seem

to have come to a new place.
And it appears that something like this
is being verified:
we have left the moon down there.
At this moment, it's just like
a smart landing module
leaning on the corral it crashed into.

Further below, a spherical blue self
has been left down there, too.

[BH, LMK]

Spinach

Beautiful spinach hasn't hidden
you inside its green shirt.
You have never even worn
any kind of green shirt,
you have avoided that sort of look;
but I remember more clearly still
your silent flesh was like
an extreme seed.
Why is spinach beautiful
to look at? Why do I
know you can think
but never ask this sort of question?
When I rinse spinach I feel
as I touch its dark green mass
as if it was a child of mine and a plant's.
This is how the spinach answered
how in this life of ours we can
see the question of angels which, for them, don't exist.
The beauty of spinach is fragile
as we face a standard area
of only fifty square metres, spinach's distinctive brightness
is the most fragile of politics. On the surface,
it's a bit messy, not easy to keep tidy;
its beauty, you might say too,

is kept by the power of trivial details;
and its nutrition has corrected
its price, neither left nor right.

[BH]

A Charm About Things

On a windowsill, three pine cones.
The size of each
is almost the same.
But they vary from dark to light.

Each cone is larger than my closed fist,
in fact, not less than twice as big.
But I do not feel embarrassed. Already I see
my fist is a pagoda shaped like a cone.

The darkest is the one
which fell from the tree this year –
I hesitate in deciding when the two lighter ones fell,
but I know the colour of these two is not lighter than ash-gray time.

And I know that squirrels
have been inspired by such lightness
to make their own small fur coats.
The secret recipe of lightness remains unrevealed.

Each pine cone possesses its own source,
yet a small part of each origin
holds its mystery. Same thing with poetry.
Yet poetry won't be suffocated by this problem.

I am writing poetry, secretly in love
with the clear structure of the cones.
It asks me to take it to where I picked them up.
It asks to be placed on top of the Red Pine.

[Murray Edmond & Zang Di]

100 Years of Solitude for New Poetry

About your poetry –
I guess it's better suited to the natural
environment here than you are.
It has dodged this crux of heredity.

When it absorbs nourishment it's like a stem of waving corn,
when it sleeps it's like a pregnant wild bitch.
When it walks, it's like a small stream flowing past
a railway bridge like a horizontal plaque.

It has dismissed language, the reason being
that language works too seriously.
It slapped the subject of its service, it slipped off
the condom of metre. It has laid bare the impossible.

It's like a wooden spoon stuck to a pot commanding
the undeclared war of the peas.
Though these are round and glossy peas, plump and plenty,
they are still not words.

About the relationship between you and me,
your poetry is a room as yet unrented,
so empty is the scene,
it's as if the ring had been collected somewhere else.

It has even borne a lovely gourd,
as fresh and delicate, as suited to porno tales,
as the ones I buy from the morning market.
it's the life in the life.

It's astounded how many times you come back,
and me, I'm doing my best not to ask where you went.
This is your poetry.
And yes, for an instant, it was almost not written by you.

[BH]

True Love Society

In our life, this word
has no doubt met with more suspicion
than many other words. My friends even believe
it was precisely this word that wore down
a much-exercised age.

Stroke it sideways and this word
is a drug – stroked upwards it's a sickness,
downwards a thunderbolt inevitable
in this life. This word spent my 38th birthday
at the Natural History Museum with me.

This word's left side is a scalding morsel,
its right a moment of bliss. This word has probably
endured more internal torment than my own body.
Yet it seems there's a need for its kind of innocence –
I had one such moment, and quietly hid the morsel away

like pocketing the joker in a card game.
This word is like the brass button of summer
that I pick up from the lawn.
It's scorching hot all over, instantly accessing that life
which is always near at hand.

I thought that like the others I could keep this word at a distance.
But for me, being seduced by language
is like the way my demon flesh dominates our ego.
At twilight once, I carefully folded
two paper gliders to land on this word.

Perhaps I know why this word
can be lonelier than me.
Like the flowers of our beloved mother tongue, it knows no synonym.
When used as a verb it seems so maladroit –
like the red sun at Kunming Airport, slopping into love's frying pan.

August 2002 [BH]

YI SHA (*b*. 1966)

Wishful Thinking or the Feelings You Get from a Film Played Backwards

A shell is fired back into the barrel of a gun
Writing is sucked back into the tip of a pen
Snow floats from the ground
Daytime rushes towards the sun
Rivers run to their sources
Trains creep inside tunnels
Ruins pick themselves off the ground and stand tall as buildings
Machines break down into their component bits
A child crawls into its mother's womb
Pedestrians vanish off the streets
Dead leaves spring onto branches
The girl who committed suicide does a backward leap onto the
            second floor
The lost man jumps down from the poster seeking his whereabouts
The hand that stretches out to others is tucked back into its pocket
The bride runs away from the marriage bed
and turns into a young girl in love for the very first time
Youth grows innocent
till it sucks on rubber nipples thicker than cigarettes
She too comes back
walking in reverse
to my cramped room
I will walk away from that chilly
unfamiliar railway station
and go back to the classroom
my red Pioneer's scarf knotted round my neck
standing to greet my teachers   working at my lessons
getting ahead   studying hard

[Simon Patton & Tao Naikan]

Factory for Artificial Limbs

I was friends with Chen Xiangdong when we were kids
These days he works in a factory
that makes artificial limbs
One day, he called me out of the blue
and we arranged to meet
I recognised him   waiting at the factory gates
his smiling face was exactly the same as before
only magnified a couple of times
I noticed something odd about the way he walked
so I pulled up one leg of his trousers
It's real, he laughed
We only remembered to shake hands
as the two of us began to move off
He squeezed my hand with his fingers
Still intact, just like the good old days
Everything was intact, same as it ever was
We both roared with laughter

[Simon Patton & Tao Naikan]

I Am a Wrongly-written Chinese Character

I am a wrongly-written Chinese character
on a blackboard in some village primary school
I can't remember   whose hand it was that wrote me
or exactly what year it was
I anxiously look out at those children
They stare up at me with perfect trust
A wrongly-written Chinese character
leading generations of young kids astray
One year   I don't remember when
a teacher from some place else came along
and rubbed me out with her delicate hand
and I turned into a swirl of chalk dust
inside her sun-filled lungs

[Simon Patton & Tao Naikan]

At the Zoo

I haven't been to this zoo for 18 years
On this visit here today
I've brought my young son along to see
that there are other creatures on this planet besides us humans
In the tiger enclosure   The animal here now
is not the one I knew 18 years ago
That was this one's mother
It died one summer ten years ago
That's not important
All my son needs to know
is that it's a tiger
Later, when it growls
my son starts bawling
so I take him away
to look at the spotted deer
Because I coax it
with a handful of grass
it pushes its muzzle
up against the railing
As it does this
my fearless son grabs at its head
with his tiny fingers
and pokes it viciously in the eyes

[Simon Patton & Tao Naikan]

The Grateful Drunk

A drunk
was vomiting   in the city
vomiting in the rich glow of the setting sun
on a bridge on the city moat
There was no end to it   He looked like
he was singing at the top of his lungs
He threw up what he'd eaten
bile, even

On my way home from work
I stopped   and took in this sight
I suddenly felt deeply moved
It occurred to me that everyone has their own unique way
of showing gratitude to life

[Simon Patton & Tao Naikan]

The Only Face I Remembered That Year

To describe him as 'repulsively ugly and sly'
would be appropriate
as well as convenient and simple
but how irresponsible
It would amount to saying nothing
because you still wouldn't know
what he actually looked like
Over the past year
his is the only face I remember
out of all the strangers I've seen
emaciated   the face of an ordinary worker
by a crematorium furnace
That day   I was pushing
the corpse of my mother along on a trolley
when he blocked my path and said
'Leave it to me. There's nothing more for you to do here.'
I gave him the box
of 555 cigarettes I had brought with me
This he took without the slightest reaction
and turned away, pushing the trolley
the man who was to give my mother her send off

[Simon Patton & Tao Naikan]

My Father's Not a Well Man But He's Still a Man

Dad, even if you weighed more than you do
I'd still find a way to lift you
This is what a son is capable of
when it comes to the crunch
When you got back to the ward
from the operating theatre
it was me who lifted you onto your bed
I did this
while you were naked
There were large yellow bandages
covering your belly
A thick-tubed catheter was attached
to your shrunken penis
The young female nurse
was the only woman present
and so there was nothing to be embarrassed about
After I'd exerted myself to the utmost
in the execution of this action
all that remained to do
was to cover you up with a white cotton sheet
As I did so, you laughed
This was a result of the anaesthetic
You hadn't yet lost that feeling of euphoria
and felt no sense of loss
for the left-kidney they had removed
but feeling aggrieved you grumbled:
'Those women shaved off my pubic hair!'

[Simon Patton & Tao Naikan]

Born in the Time of Mao

I had no choice
in the shape of my belly-button
and no say
in how unsightly it's turned out

but I have no wish
to be always scraping muck
from it
to show to other people

[Simon Patton & Tao Naikan]

YU NU (*b*. 1966)

Racket

midnight racket gathers in a certain spot on a giant porcelain vase
at the mouth of the vase, the nature of the taste first visible
lingers on the tip of the tongue, in the valance, building a
garrulous rap house. lingering on the LP, rotating with it
a geometry of muscle silently moving back and forth. Those
scrapings endowed with voice
are exposed in air and so they have stand-ins
after a whole night, the suspected blackness isn't abating
but nobody really suspects, instead they notice
the one exploded shock, that is inside the taste of gloomy pomegranates

forgone fortuity testifies for foraging insects
stomachs squirm with gastric complaints
vestiges are experiences, a heap of shattered glass a day
moaning stretching into the syphon, as if spreading the ear drum
in the water, letting out a flutter-like
skirling. this is forgone fortuity, a model
the swan hibernating in the depth of blackness
hears the squalling of a baby with no bad breath
in the intactness of the glass's standing aside

in racket, categorise different kinds of shouting. loudspeakers in the thorns
inside there, wire mesh crumpled into a mass
dreaming about its variability
virtuality, or a kind of creed, passing through unrelated things
found it, passing through the lips to see the teeth

the rotation of the lungs' fan blades. the first
vocalisation caught, in the rocks
vocalising 'ah', vocalising 'oo', 'ai'
and the sound of runaway livestock. it's shouting
still in the rock, in the definition
its master makes for it

become a black charcoal-like thing. a definition of
a triangle intersecting a woman
making sense of her under this definition
fondling will then have its framework. a minor malaria
and the shivering of ignorant organs
and a green leaf, are altogether this postponed midnight moment
racket comes from physiology, and from the fallacies of physiology
from now on nine months of vegetable tranquillity
is just noise. claws. the little animal in the box
it's not her who makes the noise, it's her symbolism

her liquid appearance, it needs a box like that
needs to install wheels, starting up like a car
lost in a trance of unease, chugging all the way on
waiting for the beads of sweat oozing from the jail
a crowd wants to topple the prison with humidity
seeing the lights in the vase, the inhuman torment is
personified
people coming out from there, their entire bodies have taken
the smell and form of a jail, like a carving
the sensibility that carving expresses
makes change appear in locations, concave and convex symmetrical

an exclusive soaking-wet spindle, the narrowness of both sides
swarms toward the centre, forming an inexplicable stack
the sense of fluidity of a stack of steel balls
no ears nobody listens and attends, though noises are heard
saying that substance is female, the noises heard objective
women outdoors, clarity and brightness water dripping
midnight, the changes of location, make someone
carry two genders. turning over
the clothes they had worn, to let someone else wear them
turning over the house to the outside, to get to know the original occupier

the curiosity of midnight keeps him, on his midriff
fireflies flashing, flashing a single chance

this fright, it makes him complete his forked dwelling-place
turning around to become a guide on two roads. a thread
extends from the bypassed alleyway, from the needle's tip
to the street corner, one road is the sum of the sense of hearing,
sight, and taste. blind alleyways
plus dim light. in the blackness, he's
stupefied for a second, in the blueness he hums
black is advancing other colours, it's the promoter
of other colours, a beetle on the turntable
the rotation has suffocated its own rotation, in the blur it can't see the
axis, a dice's disgraceful behaviour
repeating and repeating. if there was shock, shock would also be
the eyes of the blind man, he's looking, pretending
he's looking, on the dropping ladder
grapes extend into the window, one grape after another
for plants this speaks to vast hunger
to a space enlarged by time
to the windows abruptly contracting

just like senility looking at youth, lethargy looking at startled waking
the mechanism beyond detached objects
just like written language looking at oral expression
midnight, an old man's spirit level
upside-down, has confused a glass of water
and ice cubes, the tedium and thrift of a certain Spring
now his tears are falling, as by the well he draws gurgling water
you can walk close to him, call him, but you can't
pull him back, away from that deep well

racket is a person, endlessly jumping
jumping over, back, and jumping again
but on the original spot all along. like lead weights tied to a kite
in the tiger's suppositions, there are
cat components
as it stretches its back
zero point self-negation, objects to be completed
as disposables, different components glittering
all packed up inside blackness, its petals open
to expose a porcelain vase. the things on the table
fall down from the table, not from any other place
a soft tender thing – and a CLANG

[BH, LMK]

192

CHEN XIANFA (*b*. 1967)

Previous Incarnation [42]

If you want to get away, all you have to do is escape into the innards
       of a butterfly
no need to grind your teeth ever again, nor evade your parents' ploys
       and potions
no need to wait till the blood is all spat out.
To be an enemy, all you have to do is be the foe of the entire human race.
Pop! He's moulted his ink-stained indigo shroud
moulted a layer of skin
moulted every stage in the journey of his inner heart
from the embarcation at dawn to the weariness at dusk
moulted the pilgrimage of clouds and water –
this is a scene to give you goosebumps: he has so lightly and effortlessly
moulted his bones!
I'm forever singing the praises of the final act when they draw themselves
       up to leap
and a butterfly that has waited billions of years on the twig trembles all
       over
and cries in the darkness, They're here!
Tonight, the clear moon is lower than the eaves
The tide rises on both banks of the little green river

There's only one line she has not forgotten yet
choking back the tears her feelings bring up
she pushes her left wing out, stretches forward
and says: well met, my Butterfly Lover,
well met –

[BH, LMK, WNH]

42. This poem relies on allusions to '*Liang Zhu*' (The Butterfly Lovers),
a play telling the story of two doomed lovers who are reunited after death
as a pair of butterflies.

GE MAI (1967-1991)

I Know I Would...

I know I would... go
to the limits of a warped
breakfast... I know you wouldn't
seize the advantage, before night shuts all eye-

lids, and take me away; I know

where two twisting stars within a stone
still face the Sicilian wind, but is there still
a ravishing, sorry person? Are the ice-cold
fishing floats still bobbing gently there

in the wind? still there, inside the black skin of the jacket

I know, after I leave, you will begin to
scatter into each and every identical petal –
I'll cry, which one is it? The petals will vanish one
by one; the bloody clay will also vanish

24 November 1989   [BH, WNH]

Joyful Sonnet

Cigars. Jodhpurs. Sea's teeth.
Women riding trees. Flowers poisoned by wild bees.
Everything in the lobby open wide. Nerves stretched tight.
Pigeons' chests. Wild beasts' breasts.
One chance lost forever. One person's solitary disease.
Genius. Defect. Flame on the surface of silks.
A busy night for the Prince of Monaco.
Nine-headed birds. Gob stain. Artists' pain.
Jazz musicians. Keyholes. Lorca.
Rumba in the air. Lolita repenting.

Squeeze. Tap. Upward arm strength.
Savings. Drying up. Under waterweed, echoing.
Bastards. Applause. Sounds of sorrow and joy in dreams.
Leather whips. Nails. Stiletto processes.

[BH, LMK]

ZHU ZHU (*b.* 1969)

Leather Case
(for my father)

1

We went fishing.
our arms trailing above the water,

past my birthplace.
He was sunk in sleep, past

another township, the dirt road sharply reflecting light
like filthy snow; on the rooftop of the village hall

hung
dust stirred up by cars:

forty miles per hour, equals the caretaker's
half-smile,

us not knowing why she
stood there, sending her smiling salutations to a car.

On one gable
a fading slogan,

softly flickered across its lips; after almost
half a century, its volume turned right down at last.

195

2

Passing fields, villages, fields,
the car stopped beside a ditch, every puddle on the road

like a pleading, glowing fish,
waiting for a rising river.

He began to talk to me about the names of crops,
his tone had never been this gentle –

spoke of the cat,
how the last time the whole family moved, it suddenly jumped out of
        the car.

Then he stopped talking, like here,
silent, vast, in the noisy pecking of feeding birds;

a layer of silvery-grey plastic
covered the horizon; and I felt

that he had begun to touch on some things at last,
and had put my fingers, with them, on one side.

3

He fell asleep again, resting his head on my chest.
The fishing tackle back in the latched black leather case,

before the leather case was put in the back of the truck,
it had been on top of the big wardrobe at home,

for many years.
My young eyes were always attracted to it,

a case never opened before
in my sight, its solid shell

as steady as a gravestone, welded in layers of ice.
Opaque. When sunlight shone through the window

like turning a key,
it lit up every object in the house.

4

He fell asleep again, resting his head on my chest.
Muddy roads, the open hood trembling like chattering teeth.

The radio brought news of
the meeting of the Estonian President and

Boris Yeltsin.
The rear-view mirror like a flash camera captured:

my chest
rested on by an elderly Russian head;

grown up, my pride like the tide through the canyon
dribbled toward the plain:

oppressed, and oppressed, by a weight constantly
jolted into decreasing, this oppression

even put me at ease in my
warm blood. The linked floats

would soon be trailing across the water,
and while casting our rods

the nosegays of fierce light
made the river's wavelength riotous and dense –

holding the fishing rod for that long long time,
it was the first time ever –

at the silently expanding end,
a serenity long years awaited.

5

And now he is placing my fingers
on this fishing rod

taken from the leather case;
correcting my hand position,

as well as squeezing the little cut worm
onto the hook,

lightly pressing my hands down
until the line drills into the depth of the rippling water.

And now the case is lying at my feet,
the leather on its base damply dissolving, as if –

contrarily, from inside it, countless fish are
swimming over in a shoal,

along the curving fishing rod in my hands
swimming into the heart of the river.

I touch the latches,
and opening the case is like opening a vacuum,

I sob in this vacuum of love:
except for this, no love that isn't a fearsome illusion.

September 1999 – July 2001   [BH, LMK]

JIANG TAO (*b.* 1970)

Tribe of Palaeopithecus

the forest was filled with fallen fruit, a scarlet carpet
whose origin lay in geological change
the waters had receded, the tiger's sabre tooth was rotten
around the empty ground we discussed the future
the old ones had just crawled out from evolution, waving their old fists
the young ones could no longer hold their tongues, they'd got to be the first
to eat the sika deer: ambition to move a mountain lacking
though they could ford the river, north and south

the fields were just a dining table
the so-called republic too rumbustious
nevertheless autumn's despotism drove off mosquitoes and flies
fortunately we were all standing upright
able to watch the stars, fight empty-handed to free ourselves from the
        food chain
but the October work force
still inclined towards surplus: no need to paint our skin, or to cook
with flesh for firewood, only the males kept on
up-ending the females, chanting the beauty of it
until to say 'I love you' out loud
at least with spring flowers and autumn moons, it still took two million years

[BH, LMK]

JIANG HAO (*b.* 1971)

Song of the Wandering Immortal

Vol. I
Scrawl on the finite window's screen, outline the desert's mammaries.
Lamp, cast this onto the lower lip, then blur. Say static is discharged
        across the pass
between the breasts' bunches. An LP dies in silence, the Magpie Bridge[43]
        returns
to between the thighs; pull her legs' steel cords apart, dangle the remains
of our nation: adorn your temples with her ice-cream summits.

Me? The moon folded in my pocket, the crown of a tree
screwed on tight; how many shadow-puppets have wilted in performance!
The whole station in a frenzy, wave-tips dazzling *en pointe*;
you trudge at an angle into the wind, the ocean steps lightly towards its
        decline.
But the lower throat's deep winding path leads to the bosom, and

43. The Milky Way.

199

the grippers that twist the stamen's black hairs, in the gentle heat
of a papery sac, step out of character and are tempered. I endure the
      imagination,
which, really, involves transgressing reality; innocence
drives the procreative spasms: Dame Nature both conquers and creates.

Vol. II

And what's natural? Intimate and close as shoulderblades, sprung up
      like a row of trees:
joy and unspeakable loneliness, necessity's smooth tongue
and sharp tooth; three and a half years, while I gnawed on the horizon,
the drifted snow asked my heart, is it as cold here, as brittle?
The books you've read, do they keep playing the word-games? But then
      reality

burnt my fingers: 3000 per reading, changed into dollars for a good time.
Love and lust seduced me from civilising, poetry combing students' heads
with iambs; in those days, education was led astray by romance,
is binding together better than forever-knowing? Who'd aspire to a
      selfish heart –
that white horse which is not a horse? Bearing booze and fags, you abruptly
      sprayed the stairs;

why was night thus – a burning horoscope, a love drama?
I say: will we go to Mount Tai, watch the sun rise and set,
console the needy sky? Bring the landscape back for a tattoo,
please get used to my unusual beauty: do not smile knowingly or play at
      praise.

10 April 2006, Urumqi [BH, WNH]

44. (*See opposite page.*) The third of the 24 Solar Terms, a traditional
fortnightly weather calendar.

MA HUA (1972-2004)

from Snowy Mountain Canzonets

1 *Asleep in Spring*

At night this year's new snow turns to a mountain spring knocking
        on the wooden door.
Its creaking and crackling will drive you dafter than
the lowing of the cows and neighing of the horses in the day time.
        I was dreaming
the worn-out wooden door was me,
knocked on again and again by transparent snowfall and the new moon.

2 *The Village Schoolmaster*

The fish-scale cloud that was here last month came back from behind Snowy
Mountain, bringing much-needed pink for peach trees, much-needed
        green for barley, but
for me, no much-needed love – only noisy pupils followed it in.
Twelve dark red faces, familiar as all my days hereafter,
a bit brightly-coloured, a bit dirty.

3 *The Peach Blossom*

Sometimes the fall of peach blossom brings with it a huge rumbling
like thunder in the weeks of Waking Insects.[44]
Shut your eyes, and the slender fallen blooms will return to the branches,
a flock of jade-green butterflies will suck on stamens, and a jet-black eagle
will start picking at my heart.

5 *The Mountain Stream*

The rise and fall of the rocks is uneven, the rise and fall of snowmelt
        follows the moon.
As newly-peeled timber follows the torrent down,
its crashing is mixed into the water I loaded in the barrel.
After all the boiling, they wrap a couple of shiny green tea leaves,
to go on floating inside me.

8 *The Glacier*

The glacier's muffled avalanche dazzling as if nothing has changed, only
        pale blue sunlight
oozes out from cracks in the ice.
Burning juniper's smoke and fragrance give it a life,
make dumb earth and stone disappear, make my body, and with it its skin
tone, pale to the point of invisibility,
suddenly shivering between the mountains, hesitant.

9 *The Wild Orchids*

The little purple sparks all over the hillside
can't burn the grass dragon's pale green tongue,
but they have burned the feet of cows and horses going messily home,
and the sloppily gluttonous butterflies'
tender lips.

14 *The Primary School Pupils*

The sloppy choir is all awry, meandering along the Lancang's western bank.
In the old bus bright-coloured Primary Fours long for summer and two
        years later.
twenty faces glide in the wind, sparks rubbed out by grains of fine sand.
The setting sun is dim, a pale yellow halo
covers clouded-over Snowy Mountain and the temporary teacher choking
        back his sobs.

20 *The Autumn Moon*

The humid day disperses in the valley, and the sky pales along with it.
Four boys sit idle on the face of Snowy Mountain, waiting for the ice-
        cold moon of
autumn behind the snow. There's a full moon with water flowing through it,
like a hole in the sky, pierced by the back of an anonymous hand;
like a lotus blossom, that thunder in the firmament.

28 *The Evening*

Recklessly trotting rats mock the lone human in the log cabin, mocking his
idleness and his tolerance. As if it had been
foretold in another age, he counts the alien footsteps,
contrasting them with his heartbeat and his excitation –
a match surprisingly good, and unbelievable.

31 *The Spring Snow*

Newly-green pine boughs are too weak to bear more white, more cold.
This is the last time: excessive white
has lost its shape inside pale light and fine mist.
Ice is pouring down the glacier,
snow is melting under Snowy Mountain

33 *The Peach Blossom Feathers*

The light yellow bird has gone, the pale pink one,
head pillowed on peach blossom, is staring blankly and snoring.
As she turns over, the whirlwind she's long awaited sweeps her pillow away.
The pillow has flown, as if her own soft shiny feathers
are falling all around from the sky.

37 *The Mist*

The hill a hundred paces away – here then not here – in the end vanishes
        with the darkening green.
Four miles away, the river has thrown off the ringing of its waves.
The world is three hundred metres high and thirty metres wide,
squeezed in by rain.
Two shiny brown mules are muddling back from beyond this world.

[BH]

SHUI YIN (*b.* 1972)

The Dictionary's Song

At every input of a frequently used sentence: 'Tomorrow,
sunny', 'Make a short sentence with *innocent*',
'Spring, now – what more do you want to know?'
'Keeping fit takes time, too'
– All you need do is input these sentences
as you wash your little finger. If this is for
remembering your letter, you will begin.

Harbour Coffee House. Harbour. Coffee House.
What is its proper address? The awkwardness of released mistakes
should be pointed out by others. As for your *beforehand*
idea, it's easy to mistakenly think it's only
one word too early – 'solve', solving is
so good, you have already solved the problem once!
These have no doubt added to my confidence.

Have I sometimes thought about using a foreign language?
Yet when it comes to *nitrate*, I haven't even got
the confidence to spell it. I recall there was one day
you diligently helped me to learn 'bad taste'
– kitsch – and also to retain the
following suggestion – 'Sir, you may also use
taxonomy. And Japanese-style *Gemütlichkeit*.'

[BH]

HAN BO (*b.* 1973)

People's Park

Our people. Why do you
hang the sunset into
the birdcage of the park?

I can't figure it out. Maybe
rays of light have their own little

melancholy. Didn't you once go carrying
sorrow home, too? The whole evening

has ended in a blink, primary school's
bluntness, though, has only been half-sharpened.

I cannot let go of it. The days
are so good to look at, though they can't be

lived through. With patience
you grow up, as you
recede to drown in the lake.

2 February 2003, Mudanjiang – 28 April 2003, Shanghai
[BH, LMK]

HU XUDONG (*b.* 1974)

Armadillo

It makes me think, suddenly seeing the date on the computer,
of this day last year, in South America, on the beach of Paraty.
It's a little town panned from grains of seventeenth century gold,
located somewhere with sky-engulfing sea views and Portuguese
　　　　　poverty.
At nightfall, in our hands we carried back to the shore a body of
　　　　　foolish, fierce
clouds and islands, roaming every street we saw, sighing over every
　　　　　antiquity.
In the flickering of red lights, a furtive place, the people coming and
　　　　　going:
it was all highly-strung guys and a fleshy landscape of slapper and
　　　　　floozy.
All at once we were delighted, thinking that we'd come to
the local red-light district, but realised as soon as we got down,
this was the art quarter, where intellectuals from a hundred miles
　　　　　around
brought along their intellecules,[45] to solemnly re-collect here
from the coastal Indians of Brazil, a résumé of blood and tears.
Mounted on the walls as art, there were Indians;
lectured into academic tongue twisters, on stage there were Indians
and in the lobby the unfamiliar dry female tinder and blazing male fire
took Indian names to instantaneously cohere.
We didn't see a single living Indian in the place, until
outside, on the corner a few dozen yards away
we encountered Indians selling handicrafts in the dark alleyway.
They slept on the streets, hawking clumsy carvings, macramé
and feather ornaments. They didn't bawl out their wares,
growing stiff as calluses in the throat of the dark night,
even the few price-related Portuguese numbers they couldn't slight,
like chapped calluses, were rough and sore.

45. The wordplay in Chinese here makes a neologism out of 'intellectual'
and 'molecule'.

The caution in their eyes linked to defences of five centuries ago:
on the other side of the line, we warily bought
an armadillo carving. Umm, right, armadillo…
the docile one of the *xenarthra* family, armoured from head to toe,
living in the jungle like their ancestors, a quiet life all they sought.
Umm, right, Paraty… I was painfully popular with the elite just now:
the Indians in this place used to be stately and orderly, they spoke bright
Tupi-Guarani, and then were hunted to invisibility.
The elite was loath to mention those stuck in the throat of night,
mute as a tiny callus, the invisible posterity.

[BH, LMK]

Into the High Mountains

They chopped off the foot of the mountain, and stretched out a
          mountainfoot village
to frighten us, but we're not afraid.
We take the whole village walking,
persimmons all the way, dogs all the way. Even autumn
has followed us into the little outhouse,
breathless in the shit-stink of farming, as it steps on a basket of
          veggies
chasing after the ceaseless freshness on our tongues.

Plucking from the mountain's waist, they cast a mountainside of
          velvet
onto the slope we walk on, so soft that even stones
melt in the wind, so the eeriness of stones that rage in the ancient
          temple
flows in the spring water. The ancient temple
decays in the wind too, not inhaling incense, only vomiting a string
of cars out from its gate. Each class sits idle as crabs in their cars and
          buses,
tourist crabs waving claws, clipping a wisp of autumn wind from our
          eyes.

207

Filleting the mountain's tenderloin, they took a bare mountainspine
to feed the autumnal vultures perched on our backbones.
That pair of gluttons have no scenery to devour, circling wing to wing,
seizing only the agony of mountainbones trussed with electricity
        cables
and a little medium, shot from a launch pad, who can't talk to the
        dead.
Lucky that there's still two or three sentimental little trees, their little
        faces
blushing all over, giving us a touch of that fickle autumn feeling.

What about the mountain peaks, then? They couldn't risk provoking
        those.
The peaks would rather pull out all their hair than turn into
the reddest of their red-tapeworms. We sit on our arses
upon the male-pattern baldness of the water meadows, going nowhere.
Everything downhill from here, according to the old rules of poetry
        and painting,
is everything North China should be. But we, fighting that cold war
beyond the horizon, have handed the whole mountain over to the
        other side.

1 November 2005 [BH, LMK, WNH]

Sex Shop

She was his silicone hole, he was her
blue vibrator. Removal sale! half price!
trumpets in daytime besieged them, the salesgirl
vividly explaining away the shades in customers' minds.

They were locked in the shop window, facing
the dirty glass, male and female customers choosing
the soft and hard of their separate vision. And they quietly
gazed at the calm in each other's raw materials

208

all the dark night long. Occasionally, there would be one or two
resolute shades left behind, in the darkness
provoking their unplugged shyness. Even
so, it did not hamper them from using their thirst

to connect with the power, passing through the fragile glass,
vigorously vibrating together. She was his
heartrending tightness, he was her reckless
speed. They were the parts, the parts of love.

Summer gave them warmth and eternity;
before the shop closed down, they fierily
transcended. The salesgirl hastily jotted this down:
'Two samples, female A, male B, missing.'

[BH, LMK]

QIN XIAOYU (*b*. 1974)

Fare Thee Well

Plants are failing, willow twigs long and leggy,
in the Wind-Stilling Pavilion on the old border path,
a horizon of toasts, cups of tears.
Wild-goose cries are faint thunder in the heart's chambers,
an electrifying final year for a terrified aristocrat.
I give you the hot ice in this poem.

The so-called cosmos is only
you being south and me being north,
you being iamb and me being trochee.

[BH]

Lyric Toast

Roast squirrel canapé. Ragout & black bread zakuski, pesky fly tapas,
       taboo bar-snacks.
Canopy canapé.
Zakuski of raven-digested roe deer. Bar-snacks of cuss-words.
Tapas of autumn's first draught under the door. Canapé of cawing.
Starry sky zakuski.
Blueberry & red bean tapas. Bar-snacks of barking & wind soughing
       in the pines.
Zakuski of a nip in the air & a well-stoked wood-burning stove.
Tapas of life's triumphs & tragedies.

So many of these guys – anacreontic reindeer canapé or the Earl of
       Hell on toast.

[BH, WNH]

Livestock and the Great Wall

Plough-ox Du Fu, cowherd Tao Yuanming.

Confucians keep pigs,
the grasslands are like Islam.

Sheep are Taoists, easy-going wanderers.
If distant water is sweet, autumn and winter will be late in coming.
Slaughter is poetry, the figure in the wind-blown grass is poetry.
Poetry of sculpted snow at an open window, poetry of clouds gathered
       and sheared.

The Heavenly Horse's homeless nostalgia,
isn't a broken battle-line in space, but a dream vision in time.
How much more so is a white horse, galloping onto the cairns?
Who to ask? My horse's plaited tail, but your horse-head fiddle?

[BH]

Rock Painter

I carve game on stone, my quarry,
so they become beasts in fur coats, mastered by me.

Lines of dry branches, sharp here and there as if broken,
terror having a pretty grain to it.

I paint antlers like dense thickets
so the fawn on the crag will linger at the mountain's foot.

This is how I paint *SLOW*: the sun sets between the round hills
and I let the evening light tint it.

And *FAST* seems like it can shrink the road's riders
and the slenderness of their horses' backs.

I carve things that amaze me, in my ox-eyed amazement.
I love to carve what I love to do: we look like a gecko.

The masks I carve can make plants grow faster.
I hope the universe is a bit simpler than that.

[BH]

WANG AO (*b.* 1976)

The Complete Collection of Myths

an ancient ginkgo tree, growing in a middle school
its fallen leaves are golden, combustible, as if it had been drinking
as the moon rose, it transpires peach fragrance; under the tree
     appears a ring

of coloured pebbles, conversing in the language of the night sky – at times
there'll be debates; as though it were walking the path home, and had
        stopped
midway through its life, watching children sleep soundly in the surrounding
blocks, it feels itself infinitely remote, and not because
it's the oldest species here, or because it has mused on the unfathomable
        atmosphere;
it has taken off its long gown, and the sea breezes blowing from far,
        wafting the fallen
leaves, and the clarity of the moonlight
all make it raise its face, paddle the pirogue of itself, transform lines of
        longitude and
latitude into its concentric rings
it used to envy the burning logs, who know in just this far away manner
        that, like birds in flight,
their formation will alter to Sci-Fi before and epic behind, while drifters
        with faith in
religion still wander toward the Pole; its primitive cries are no different
        from
the night wind; at this time, the dispute over so many rings of pebbles
        may dazzle – but
finally it's up to myth and the *commedia* to persuade each other.

[BH, LMK, WNH]

212

PART TWO

1. NARRATIVE POEMS

QIN XIAOYU

Building the Labyrinth of Time: On Narrative Poetry

In classical Chinese, Narrative was known as 'the ordering of things', meaning putting the elements of a story in chronological order. The ancient book of rites, *Zhou Li*, spoke of 'keeping the order to rule the music'. In the Tang dynasty, Jia Gongyan (*fl.* 655 AD) said, 'one who narrates should follow an order, as we do when we are listing the musical instruments.' Classical *yuefu*, or poems in the style of folk songs, often used musical forms, as indicated by their titles: *ge* (song), *xing* (march), *qu* (tune), *yin* (recitative), and *yao* (ballad), such as the well-known 'Orphan's March', 'Xizhou Tune' or 'White-hair's Recitative'. The common element here was the use of straightforward linear narrative.

Another feature of classical narrative poetry was respect for brevity. This was not only a poetic virtue, it was also linked with historical narrative from its inception. For Chinese historians, brevity in a text was a chief indicator of narrative beauty. The Tang dynasty historian Liu Zhiji (661–721), in his *Generality of Historiography*, wrote 'the beauty of national history must consist of good narrative, and to be good, narrative must maintain brevity and simplicity: the meaning is greatest when the text is brief…rich meaning within simple text is the particular beauty of narrative'. The cultural centrality of Chinese historical studies deeply influenced all other types of narrative, including narrative poetry.

Since the May Fourth Movement, one group of poets trying to write a new narrative poetry in the language of daily speech were intellectuals influenced by Modernist thought and literary concepts from the west. Driven by ideals of a proletarian or realist literature, they turned to the lives of ordinary people, and, through focusing on lower class subjects, communicated their ideas of humaneness and liberation. Most of these works could only be called quotidian accounts written in rough language. But there was one exceptional case: Feng Zhi (1905-93), called 'the best lyric poet in China' by his famous contemporary, Lu Xun (1881-1936), was also admired for his narrative poetry. One piece in particular was highly thought of: 'In Front of

215

the Temple Gate', in eight-line stanzas, with one rhyme per stanza, and the rhythm just monotonous enough to suggest the tone of the old monk who narrates: the quiet, even contained surface, together with a shocking and magical story, created an intense narrative.

In the late 1920s, the Crescent Moon School tried to paint portraits of Chinese national character, such as 'The Death of Li Bai' by Wen Yiduo (1899-1946). Their focus on portraying the 'National Soul' through epic narrative made their work different from more realist narrative poems being written at that time. Over the next 20 years, there was the leftwing 'Shouting Narrative', and nationalist epics written during the Japanese invasion, as well as folk song narratives, but most of the work was still problematic, in that, though it was able to recount an incident, it failed as poetry. Exceptions include 'Liu Yi and the Dragon-girl of Lake Dongting', by Wu Xinghua (1921-66) which blended modern dramatic speech with modified classical poetic forms, creating a unique narrative style.

Narrative is not only about a succession of events, of course, for there must also be a chain of cause and effect, and we cannot find the borderline between narrative and lyric poetry simply by assuming the former tells a story within a poetic form. One feature of narrative is the significance it attaches to identifying the speaker: a lyric may have a narrator, but it is not as important to the reader to identify who this is. There is an 'I' speaking in both Zhang Zao's 'Death Sentence on the German Soldier Shermanski', and Zhu Zhu's 'Robinson Crusoe'. But the readers must establish who this 'I' is: is it the poet or is it someone else? From the titles, subtitles, and the opening lines, we can easily say that Zhang Zao's narrator is Shermanski, while the narrator in Robinson Crusoe is neither the poet Zhu Zhu nor the character in Daniel Defoe's novel, but a Chinese man whose boyhood friends gave him this nickname.

The traditional respect for brevity is preserved in narrative poems like 'Shermanski' and 'Robinson Crusoe', rather than in the contemporary Chinese novel. As in classical narrative poetry, 'Shermanski' talks about the whole life of the soldier in just 81 lines, telling about his birth, how he grew up, the war, his falling in love, the trial, and his death. This would seem suitable subject matter for a novel, but we don't feel this treatment is at all slight – witness how at the end the narrative is counting out his last minutes and even seconds.

This is the way of writing invisible text – as Liu Zhiji said, 'There is visible text and invisible text. Here 'visible' means using a complex method to fully explain the piece; while 'invisible' means saving words and limiting the text to create the story beyond the sentences... If someone can keep the important elements and leave out the minor ones, writing a sentence which touches both the general and the details, using a few words to stand for so much, this is the Tao of writing the invisible text'.

Zhang Zao knows all about this: for example, Shermanski's Russian lover cleverly pries the information from him that gets the German pillbox destroyed:

> Tell me, how do you say that in German?
> I answer, *Ich liebe dich, Katya!*
> > After that our bunker was blown away,
> guerillas, eh, lovely Katya?

Another feature of this poem which makes it distinct is its use of narrative imagery. As we mentioned before, the narrative rhythm focuses on the minutes just before Shermanski is executed:

> darling Katya, I still have ten minutes,
> daybreak still has ten minutes,
> autumn still has five minutes,
> we still have two minutes

Compressing dawn and Autumn together demonstrates his proximity to death. We are shown the beauty of the world and of the individual life, as well as our love for them. The images here serve a narrative function, but also carry a lyric charge, adding to the appeal of the story, as well as creating aesthetic meaning beyond it.

'Clearwater County' is a playful imitation of the anonymous early 17th-century novel *Jin Ping Mei* (Plum in a Golden Vase).[46] In it, we understand Zhu Zhu's complex attitude towards his source text, which was itself a continuation of an episode from the Water Margin: he is fascinated by, but satirises, critiques and corrects his original. In his re-writing, the villain Ximen Qing becomes a philandering bad guy; Wu Song, the hero who kills a tiger, becomes a pitiable man who suffers deeply with lust; and Wang Po, here Granny Wang, the woman who designs a murder, becomes one of the Chinese prototypes of a force of nature.

---

46. Jin Ping Mei takes up from an incident in the earlier novel *Shuihu Zhuan* (Water Margin), and follows the life and career of a minor villain. See Clement Egerton tr., *The Golden Lotus*, 4 vols (Routledge & Kegan Paul, 1938), with the erotic passages in clinical Latin; or see the revised edition of 1966, which translates these passages. David Tod Roy tr., *The Plum in the Golden Vase* (Princeton University Press, 1993-2011), 4 vols, is useful as a crib.

'Clearwater County' is a narrative poem composed of a group of character studies and monologues. Each monologue is at once the expression of the character and also a reflection of the poet's version of the original, and these two voices create a type of dialogue within the monologues. For example, in the section about Ximen Qing, he says,

I'm the kind that's so gorged, I can't taste my meat,
I'm the blind man in the story, groping at the elephant

while in the section about Wu Song, he says,

people love lies,
and all I did was fight and kill the flickering shadow of a tiger

The poet's interpretation is clearly expressed in these lines. Within this dialogue, the characters are no longer puppets manipulated by the original authors of the stories, but have gained further dimensions of their own. This rethinking of the characters means the story has been totally rewritten.

But how can a novel of more than a million words be rewritten as just six poems? Zhu Zhu's method is to select or invent particular incidents and sub-plots and make these the stages on which the characters can explore their new possibilities, turning the original novel into raw material, as though its hugely complex stories were just waiting to be out in order by this poem. This way of shifting some elements around and thus changing the whole world of *Jin Ping Mei* corresponds to Bloom's concept of 'clinamen', or the swerve.[47] At the same time, this group of poems uses its brevity to encourage readers to join in, to replenish and create a rich brew of new meanings.

One way it does this is through the figure of Pan Jinlian, Mr Wu the Elder's wife and Ximen Qing's lover, the most important figure in the original novel. In the poem, however, she is not named and does not speak. She is the reason why Brother Yun is exhorted to 'run'; she is the 'gallows tree' of which Ximen Qing says, 'let me step up and kick the stool away'; she is the 'illusory knot' in Mr Wu the Elder's eyes, she is an 'enormous lure' to Wu Song. So, who is she exactly? Zhu Zhu's narrative introduces a note of mystery and doubt.

Time is the key point in narrative. 'Shermanski' follows a clear linear narrative; but there is a significant complication in 'Clearwater

47. Harold Bloom, *The Anxiety of Influence: A Theory of Poetry* (OUP, 1973), pp. 19-45.

County': if it followed the time-line of the original novel, 'Cleaning Windows' should be the first piece, with 'Treasure Chest' second, then 'Troop Commandant Wu Song', 'The Bad Guy', 'Run, Brother Yun!' and finally, 'Dignity'. But the poem smashes this order, substituting a non-linear one, and these isolated incidents somehow float independently from the story. In another words, it cancels time out, thus creating its own space: Clearwater County becomes a form of abyss.

'Hugely open yet closed, suddenly broken yet linked, complex and then again different, one can never guess what will follow' – this paradoxical statement describing classical Chinese narrative poetry was written by the scholar Qiao Yi (*fl.* 1730 AD), in his *Speaking of Poetry in Sword Canyon*. Poems like 'Clearwater County' return to this tradition, even as they point toward the future.

SUN WENBO (*b.* 1956)

A Soldier's Life in Xi'an

1

Daybreak, damp mists coil around the treetops; birds,
pictogram-like, beat their wings out of lethargy.
A jogger hoping for immortality opens his mouth, spits out balls of bad
        breath,
he's aiming for Xuan Zang's statue at the Big Wild Goose Pagoda.[48] In
        the army base
the duty officer has blown reveille,
half-asleep soldiers spill out of the doors, fall in.
Back in the Tang Dynasty, this was the place where the emperor
and his ministers would drink, dine, debate. The walls are unchanged,
though in some places they've collapsed, but
the Bell Tower in the central square has been restored time and again,
its colonnades brand new: a good place to imagine the ringing of long-ago
        bells.

2

The Mao suit has replaced the mandarin jacket. Telegrams and the
        telephone
have replaced soldiers lighting beacons one after the other.
Standing beside a new aluminium revolving door, you can see
high up in the air and written in English,
the shop sign. One letter has peeled off already,
and it's covered in a thick layer of dust. Bikes one by one,
like ants linked head to tail, ring their ear-piercing bells,
very like voices. Walk into the restaurant, and inside,
that mutton soup with flatbread, and those big bowls you so rarely see –
exactly as the ballads describe them. Once you've seen it for yourself,
either your appetite massively increases, or you turn on your heel and
        leave at once.

48. Xuan Zang (*c.* 602-664 AD), the Tang Dynasty monk who brought
Buddhist scriptures from India, for which the pagoda was built.

3

The girls you knew, not one was a looker, but still
they made the guys around you jealous: only a soldier
would see a woman as forbidden fruit. No options –
you lost no time in cutting those connections. Sunday,
that endlessly boring day, you wandered aimlessly about the town;
your pocket money was pitifully small, what could you do? You
just sat on the steps in front of the cinema door,
looking at the posters; or borrowed a paper from a stranger's
hand, and maybe it carried news from thousands of miles
from your home – a train derailed,
pork off the ration, eggs still in stock.

4

Your parents and your sister, what are they up to? They're fine, of course.
'Write letters to me.' 'What will I write about?'
'Big things have been happening in our country recently: the leadership
has been changing regularly.' 'What's that to you?'
'Life is really boring, like the endlessly droning engines
on the cars I fix.' 'We went to this beauty spot,
temples, monkeys, and then your sister tripped and fell,
but luckily she was caught by a branch.' 'Now my
shooting has improved, but I kind of don't like it:
as soon as I see the muzzle flash, I'm afraid.'
'That's enough! You shouldn't think of your gun as some embodiment
        of death.'

5

The country is country-shaped: from clan and tribe
to democratic system, war is a symbol of progress. We little people
shouldn't try to get these things right – reverent awe is all that's needed
        from us.
Look at the Terracotta Army. So many foreign tourists come
to its arch-framed steel and concrete museum – what for?
To give us the thumbs-up. How can we not be proud?
It's an incomparable symbol of our strength and prosperity. And glory.
You know? And there's still a lot of brilliant things we haven't dug up yet
that will attract the slack-jawed admiration of others. Anything else
we could complain about? Happiness ought to be
commonplace here, so straighten up, stand to attention.

6

Under Baqiao Bridge the Wei River is a stream of baby urine,
but it will join the Yellow River, and reach the ocean, so beside it
your so-called 'golden years' lack allure.
It was Wang Wei and Li Bai whose tears flowed from Baqiao Bridge,
so how was it? Did they chant quietly or sing like loons?
That calendar you flipped though – sheet upon sheet of wasted paper,
piled high. As you think about that, past and future become
the army camp at night, the 9.30 order for lights out,
the sound of your sergeant's shoes inspecting the corridor, like
the Devil coming closer and closer, step by step. Do you sigh?
Do you hate? No point. It's a part of your life you can't erase.

[BH, WNH]

ZHANG ZAO (1962-2010)

Death Sentence on the German Soldier Shermanski

            Russian was my destiny.
I grew up, this orphan on the border,
on the edge of bread and windmills.
And oh, the picture book villages!
Apart from mother tongue German, my Russian
grew at lightning speed,
so fast it overtook secret trains my teeth my age
and trees.
Kakaya choroshoya pogoda!
Hey, what lovely weather!
            After that the war broke out.
First I went to Greece, full of daytime and
stones; eucalyptus trees and the murmuring music of
streams silenced me.
Three months, I didn't say a word,
never even said *Jawohl* to the officers.

After that they transferred me to Russia:
the Neva ablaze,
Stalingrad trashed –
this seemed to be all my fault.
Really – words are the world, and the world
doesn't actually forgive in words.
Eh, years of hate, down-at-heel words, how long do I have to suffer you?
                    After that we were billeted in
some village, and though I'd never seen the place before,
it seemed like I'd been there many times. What, *davay*?
'Funny that what we know best is strange
places, eh, Captain?'
And the Captain says, 'Shermanski,
we've got to fix up a bunker,
like a dagger to the enemy's heart!'
Because of my Russian,
I was sent to scrounge up some eggs, milk and other grub.
So every day I was in and out of the lanes, with their walls of wattle and
          daub,
October sunshine tracing my shadow liquid as running water,
me happy as Schubert's Trout.
My quick tongue flipped open door curtains,
playing cuckoo to tease my crimson Katya
          – All set, Katya?
          Give me ten red apples today.
Katya's armpits are a bit rank, like mine
but it's no problem; through the night
the moon plays warm across our bodies.
The first time, weren't our bodies
like vocabulary, colliding, turning into idioms?
Katya, *Ya tebya lyublyu!*
          – Tell me, how do you say that in German?
I answer, *Ich liebe dich*, Katya!
          After that our bunker was blown away,
guerillas, eh, lovely Katya?

          The court martial convicted me of treason,
gave me forty-eight hours.
I used twenty-four for an escape,
but they dragged me back; I used another fourteen to plead for mercy,
writing *Bitte, bitte, Gnade!*
but it was rejected. Then they gave me another ten hours,

eight hours, six hours, five hours;
after that the chaplain came,
and he was so well-meaning it was like an eternity:
eternity's no substitute for me.
Just like a bullet's no substitute for me,
me, Shermanski, what a guy!
The chaplain cried, held me, kissed me:
      – My son, my son, *Du bist nicht verloren!*
      There's still time, do you want to write a letter?
      You dictate and I'll write/But do you speak Russian?
      God knows all languages, my son.
So I'm in a hurry to say, Katya, my darling
darling Katya, I still have ten minutes,
daybreak still has ten minutes,
autumn still has five minutes,
we still have two minutes,
one minute, half a minute,
        ten seconds, eight seconds, five seconds,
        two seconds: *Lebewohl!* Katya darling!

        Hey, shoot me in a vital organ.
Don't shoot me in the heart.
Katya, my darling…
I have died a death – really, what is death?
Death is just like how the others died.

[BH]

ZHU ZHU (*b.* 1969)

Robinson Crusoe

My name is Crusoe – you know the one –
I've been called that since I was a little boy:
my pals compared me to the comic strip
and said: 'It's you!' So that's who I became.

I was happy with that, because he's a hero
who stayed for years on a desert island, all alone,
with no headmaster telling him what to do, no homework even.
Right now, I'm sitting in this chair
in a big house,
and you can see the Arc de Triomphe.
I'm waiting for the nurse to do my drip, and feed me,
say how well I look and praise the weather in Paris – we're both on
         the mend.
Thank you, my angel: I say that every time I use up
the two hours in which she belongs to this house;
then I watch her fixing her make-up in front of the bathroom mirror,
carefully pursing her lips like every woman fixing her make-up;
taking her bag from the sofa,
never forgetting to turn and smile at me as she leaves.
I bow my head to listen to her footsteps stop at the lift,
I listen to it droning its way down from upstairs
like a drip-feed, then she goes in
like a drop of crystal-clear fluid, dripping,
dripping all the way down and I say it again, thank you, my angel.

I say it again, then fall
into a deep sleep, and don't know how long I've slept,
maybe a few minutes, maybe a day or two, or maybe
until the next time she comes: she comes every week,
twice.
Usually, I'm woken by others:
friends might come to visit;
or sales reps, like hotel staff doing morning-calls,
might wait solicitously and stubbornly by the door.
Or the insurance people, twice a year –
sometimes I think that's more than enough.
It doesn't bother me at all...
I want to keep a tapir – I read about it in a story –
it eats nightmares. I also want to keep –
this appeared in the jottings of a South American –
Nothingness: apparently it always stands behind you,
no matter how often you turn around.

I always used to paint, and then
I left China.
On the plane to San Francisco, I resolved

225

I would be a better painter from now on,
with the Pacific Ocean as my witness. Unfortunately
I haven't painted a single picture since.

A hand. White tape holds the needle in place.
When I can feel the sting
that means blood is flowing from the vein to the drip,
I treasure this stinging, this feeling of still being alive –
right now I only have an upper body.
I'm curious to see what my blood is going to do:
first it reddens the little plastic bag
that adjusts the speed of the drip;
then, like a red arrow rising on a battle plan,
it shoots into the big upside-down
drip bottle, and blossoms
in the water like a little flower,
or like the ink an octopus emits,
the spread of a mushroom cloud.
I'm dazzled by what I'm capable of,
glad I can still move, still lie to myself
at last I'm painting a picture, just in another medium.
And so I spend half the day
raising my arm, and finally manage to cheer.

Paris is better than America, there's more to it
than cars. Here
regular travellers will touch down
to admire this city and me; for this purpose
I've hung a blackboard beside the door
and invited them to sign it,
these young people,
très agréable,
these Man Fridays –
and so they sign,
as if entering a historic period they don't understand,
a prehistoric period, a hidden
but (since I'm not dead)
still extant historic period –
they look at me with respect, meaning
we've signed, what's next?
so I smile at them, act simple
so they see what they want to see:

the great master of ages past,
the silence of his manner.

In fact, I'm nothing of the kind –
I've even gone beyond my own piss and shit;
I'm no longer in either pan of the scales,
too many massive, newly-cast weights
came flocking in on me:
already inside the hourglass that measures time past,
I am the sands of my remaining years,
already the shadow of Nothingness,
its slave. It's that shadow
which lives in this big extravagant house,
funded by the compensation from a car crash.
Thank you, America:
footing the bill was big of you.
No point being difficult about this. Of course, I prefer living in
Paris –
oh yes, and another thing – I remember now,
yes, I remember everything now.
I'm not Robinson Crusoe, I have a name of my own.
And I have never lived on an archipelago
in the Pacific, I have never been a European,
nor an American, nor am I a rescued aboriginal,
no, I'd really prefer my pals
to call me Pilgrim –
like the pilgrims in *Monkey* or Wu Song in *Water Margin* –
even though I'll never walk again,
even though I've done all the walking I'll ever do.
I'm going to die in this Corbusier chair,
die with my head bowed, even though
they've sent me word:
I can go home.

2001   [BH, LMK, WNH]

Clearwater Country [49]

Run, Brother Yun!

He is this morning's most anxious individual:
he's just missed knocking over the fortune teller's stall
and the whistlers busking in the market,
and his pears spill from the basket
in his hand as he runs.

He's running toward the little wee fella's patch
to bring the news. Anybody that slows his pace
will come to a bad end in his mind's eye.
He's running so fast he's as light as an arrow.

We follow his headlong run intently,
as if we're watching a flashback pinning scenes together.
We are the teahouse, tight-lipped as a bottle, we are
the audience, too late to tell him the ending:
his flat out run is fervent as a severed head.

July 2000

The Bad Guy
(The hoodlum Ximen Qing speaks)

1

On the way to the herbalist the rain comes on,
the light like dragon scales,

---

49. This poem refers to an episode in chapters 23-32 of the novel *Shuihu Zhuan* (Water Margin), which tells the story of the hero Wu Song, who with his bare hands fought and killed a tiger; his brother the pancake stall owner Wu the Elder; and his lovely young wife Pan Jinlian, who is seduced by the local hoodlum Ximen Qing. He is aided in this by the disreputable Grannie Wang; and Brother Yun is the street kid who alerts Wu Song to the situation.

This incident is also the starting point for the anonymous 17th-century novel *Jin Ping Mei*, which follows the later lives of Ximen Qing and the other characters.

Shuihu Zhuan has been translated into English several times, under different titles, and has been made into several films and TV series, of which the best known in the west was the 1977 Nippon TV series *Water Margin*.

steam becoming demoniacal
as it rises from the cobbles and evaporates away.

Leaves flow out from gutters:
though I'm hiding under the eaves,
I can feel the raindrops melt, like liquorice spread on skin,
leaving behind a cool, fresh scent.

As I get my horse settled,
up above, across the street,
a lattice window suddenly opens wide –
and a woman is standing there.

A woman,
wearing a camisole, red with green flowers,
looking off beyond the horizon.
She stretches out her bare arms

to feel the spray blossom on the clothes pole.
When she stands on tiptoe I can only guess how lovely her feet are –
that would need a lamp behind her knees.
I've had this happen a good many times: every time

a vision like this has appeared,
I've inveigled her to my mansion.
I'm the kind that's so gorged, I can't taste my meat,
I'm the blind man in the story, groping at the elephant.

I have exuberant energies,
I'm a rich man, with the physique of a trooper.
I have time on my side too –

now her gaze
begins to drift across and nibbles at the back of my neck,
and my plump Adam's apple bobs
as if I'm swallowing a jewel.

2

The rain is falling between us,
between two eager voyeurs
the door bolt is loosening, and,
raised on this, the grass is even greener.

The rain tastes far-travelled,
the rain will soon be double rainbows arcing over the towns,
on the plains in between, carts that were snaking forward,
in an instant are stock still.

The rain bouncing and dripping from the roof tiles
is heroically generous, like a hermit teaching me
to recite the spell for wasting a whole life.

Now the rain is something too heavy to measure
which just suits you and me –
oh girl, my gallows-tree,
let me step up and kick the stool away.

August 2000

Cleaning Windows

Mr Wu the Elder speaks
A chair supports her here,
a force, a force is running through her body,
transmitted from her tiptoes upwards:
it ought to be a straight line, but it kinks at the hollows
of the knees and the groin. Says the body to the force,
You're the illusory knot the magician loves to show the audience;
says the force, But that's all you are. As she picks up her duster
a gust of wind sends her skirt flying, her belly shows a fin's transparency.
Now force and body stop fighting and start to work together.
It's an old rickety chair, tied together with rusty wire,
but now her body bears down upon the chair's hollowness,
pressed down on, this rapidly gathers together,
as if all the townsfolk were pushing upwards.
She's smiling as she finds, when cleaning the window, clarity's not
            possible
and part-clarity is a trap; her hand keeps cleaning the wrong side of the
            stain:
this is when the stain is like a trick unfolding from her hand.
What gets clearer bit by bit is a sure test of a person:
tired, she stops. She's running with sweat, it drips onto her dusty,
            coarse nipples,
soaks both her thighs, and even

her most secret seam is unmentionably aroused by the stirring of the
        breeze.
She carries on cleaning, and we make ourselves dizzy looking her up
        and down.
It's one net in motion, all knotting and meshing.
Ah, it seems we've left Clearwater County now, we're far away,
ensnared by a great emptiness outside ourselves;
my hand, gripping the chair back, begins to tip it,
and you, in the distance, just stand there.

August 2000

Troop Commandant Wu Song
(Mr Wu's brother speaks)

   1

My quarter-staff is idle now,
my felt rug covered in dust;
in my dream she drowns and I don't reach out a hand –
in fact, she's just downstairs.

Chignon undone, the vortex of her hair hangs to her waist
with the exhaustion of her dying day,
face like a sleepy lotus, a rounded blossom
of static discharge loosed across a clear sky.

She's so light when she walks,
like steam from a pot wiping itself out;
but the staircase is swaying,
a dam about to burst.

She makes you think of
a lightly shimmering bolt of cotton still slightly shivering,
made to jump by the tailor's yardstick,
waiting for the judgement.

I'm netted by my own gaze,
every other sense deadened:
an enormous lure
is rising right now.

231

2

On these streets,
on these ancient city streets that make me foresee a bloodbath,
I feel bewildered, enmeshed, not clean.
See those roof ridges so crowded
that even the swallows can't turn round.

I think of my elder brother as bigger and stronger,
from the broad leagues of his breast
where I lay my head,
to his shoulders that tower like an encircling city wall
and keep wild beasts at bay:

the stockade of kinship.
For me it's warmth, straw-like, wordless, sun-flecked.
When he's out selling his pancakes
the whole block seethes like a midday pot,
each ingredient suddenly

floating to the surface:
her body is a potful of sweet juices
wriggling like gold filigree,
about to swallow me up.

3

I'm under house arrest,
imprisoned by the legend of my yesterdays:
in order to slip out of its handcuffs I've lost weight,
right now I'm wide-eyed and staring into an empty bottle,

on guard against the rumours blowing beyond the curtain.
I dream all the neighbours are here, laughing
as they check through my filth-spattered pants;
I dream of her, too, kneeling before Big Brother's coffin.

I have to get away and not be caught up in this,
let all the stupid folk come and sort this out.
Please let my quarterstaff and halberd remain a hero's props...
and that sedan-chair hasn't been paraded around for a while.

With trembling hand I grip the goat's-hair brush,
I'm training myself to write my name;
people love lies,
and all I did was fight and kill the flickering shadow of a tiger.

September 2000

Treasure Chest
(The bawd Grannie Wang speaks)

1

Oh whirlwind,
my dear,
your blackened body
like a water-warped diamond-tipped drill,
spins as it rises:

its drill bit, sharp, hard and biting,
has pierced the glass sky,
every white cloud is sucked into you one after the other,
spasming like piss and shit through the guts of beasts.
Autumn is too serene, its blue too deep

and we hate that.
Ah, dear little sister, so easily angered,
when you blew through my teashop till it rocked and sank –
only then did I feel alive,
only then did I feel good.

I push back the hair blown from my brow,
my gaze recoils involuntarily
from the light outside the shop,
black spots big as bins dance before my eyes:

perhaps I shouldn't be staring
at the sun like this.
Piercing pain like a dagger
climbs from my burning retinas
to my temples.

2

Today no one
came into my shop
with lowered voice and reddening eyes:
one sidelong look
would have turned me to cinders,

a few coppers flung down would be like
a filthy mouthful of tea dashed in my face.
But that's their mistake:
this worn-out old body of mine
is still simmering away, each bubble

bigger and rounder than the last;
they swell and burst like cervical mucus,
generating a web,
and on every strand of these tightropes

my tottering steps
criss-cross the whole county.
See, your old granny bent over the counter
as if I'm asleep –
but I've never let go of a single passing human fly.

3

In the afternoon, an earthshaking roar,
people flood on to the streets
to stare at the hero who beat a tiger to death;
when he passes my door, from far away,
I see that crimson muscle

like high-class stone,
the big beard flecked with booze,
chest deep as the carved lions before the courthouse –
rather, he's like a festive dragon-boat
eating up the waves,

stirring up our fouled channels.
Shaken by so much heat and wet
my dry, shrivelled breasts
begin to distend
judder in time with the drumbeats;

I almost want to follow
in the footsteps of that wild, joyful crowd,
past all the blocks afloat like water lilies,
go even further to view
the city wall through its arches, suddenly magnificent.

But people look down their noses at
me when I'm out greedily taking in the sights:
they want me to shrink away into the depths of my shop,
bundle myself in this sack of a body, and furthermore,
guard against the tiniest of gleams leaking out of my eyes.

4

Eyes twitching, I come to the bedroom,
and open a big wooden chest:
it's packed with gold ingots and grave clothes, and also
a trousseau I've been treasuring –
silk and satin finger-smoothed and faded,
spilling out like a water-spattered flame,

as I look it
uncoils in all directions.
Such extravagance! To keep them alive I choose the chill
and the grippiness of the poor,
I choose unending dry seasons and a gloomy teashop. I want me to
          become
the oldest of living things,
squatting hidden,
not like a whirlwind, but like the draught beneath a door;
I escape each and every doom of easy destruction.

Now they've gone away,
so now I can rake through the discarded hair grips,
the jade pendants and kids' shoes.
I will gather them all up one by one,
and put them in this treasure chest.

September 2000

Dignity
(The hoodlum's son-in law Chen Jingji speaks)

When we set out from the Eastern Capital
he was already with us; all he cared about was
the gold in our heavy bags. Only that
could make his smiling face as round as a wheel,
and throw off every speck of dirt; he'd lash himself to the barrow
       boy's back
and show off his balancing act. His flute playing would put you at
       your ease,
he'd keep turning his head to wink at us;
but I knew we were the lightest things in our luggage,
the ropes that bound the bags together,
and in the end, just the device he used to untie them.

Wife, I hate it that, of your blood,
half is his,
you're like a pitiful spoon reflecting his face:
even at the moment we make love
your body, with a final miserliness, holds back,
harbouring him. That's why I always
hurry to the finish.
Does your period carry a touch of purgatory?
Dumbly you chew on your handkerchief,
you weep, and I'm fed up.

There is only him left of your bloodline, and
still you wouldn't hand him over, let me go one on one with him, let
       me thrash him,
kick him: he had no crowd of friends and servants in the Eastern Capital.

The Eastern Capital was like a sheer cliff,
but Clearwater County is scarier than an abyss, all-devouring,
in its every block, loaded coffins
heaped up everywhere, its denizens
live like they had all fallen at once, dead from the sky,
howls barely begun before they're hurled out.
Do I know what I will be like there? A stone-cold stove
standing by a wall –
the lightest of touches would shatter it to cinders.
I've seen its shape through the haze of our wedding party,

a huge coiled serpent
forever drooling black spittle strawberries
and felling the bewildered reeds.

My fear of this refuge is like
my fear of passing through the wise woman's hands again,
being pressed back into the placenta;
she'll peel back my face for the switch that shuts down my ears and eyes,
thump my internal organs with all her strength
making them spasm and contract.
And he'll be looking on, arms folded,
until the time my voice turns childlike, and in the end
it'll be as if I've fallen asleep, and there will be no stain on the floor;
you, little sorceress dodging out of the moonlight,
with a bowl of hot chicken soup in your hands
to position upon his chessboard.

September 2000

[BH, WNH]

SUN LEI (*b.* 1971)

Travel

> 'I never told anyone what I knew. Which was that it wasn't for
> anyone else what it was for me'
> – Ted Berrigan

1

I left all of a sudden,
taking only a book, good for
boredom and disgust. On the train
a woman was sitting opposite me,
sweating constantly, so even her shoes were wet:
I passed her a tissue, and when
she raised her eyes abruptly, I saw
they were full of rain.

2

Every time it stopped, I watched
the people getting on board, and tried hard to guess
their age. Sometimes
we would sit shoulder to shoulder,
exchange pleasantries, or
keep silent. All the way, I held
my suitcase tight. And the train was so worn out,
it aged some more at every station.

3

I stepped down from the platform, sat
on the steps outside.
The weather was cold. This was a little station
in a mountain pass, with rubber trees everywhere:
I couldn't follow the dialect, so, as I
shouted in Mandarin, at the same time I
gestured, pointing
at myself from head to toe.

4

All night, I slept by myself
in the waiting room, I slept
really cautiously, and for ages didn't dare to move.
Otherwise, the train might have suddenly pulled out
of my sleep, losing all
the momentum in my life.
But this station wasn't on the map,
express trains never stop here.

5

Come morning, I left the station
and followed the crowd,
found a bank, broke
a big note, then ate breakfast
at the market. Typical local food,
but so spicy I couldn't open my eyes. I turned my head
and saw a man waiting to make a phone call,
weeping, flipping a cigarette into his mouth,
fiercely inhaling a mouthful of smoke.

6

I strolled along the street
and stopped at random. On the telegraph poles
were lots of ads for VD clinics and private schools,
and one, printed on yellow paper,
was a death notice. I tore it off
and ripped it to shreds,
but there was no way this could hold back
the actual news of someone's death.

7

Once at the crossroads, I hesitated.
I wanted to leave the market.
I wandered around for a long time, but still
couldn't see the end of it.
When I asked a man selling pears
for directions, he handed me
a black pear, saying, 'Buy this.'
So I bought it.

8

Come afternoon, I went to see the sights:
a huge temple, not too well-restored,
and tickets were only forty yuan. I went in,
fascinated by the giant bell. The attendant
said with a smile, 'Bang it,
ten bucks a bang.' But I knew
whatever I knocked on now
there would be no sound here.

9

At that moment, as though it were the train,
the ground shook: the petrol station on the next street
had exploded. I was very close to it,
and was knocked flat. Fire whooshed over my scalp and away.
I was deafened, someone
carried me away. When I woke up,
I was lying in a village hospital,
the drip bottle was high up, almost a tiny moon.

10

At dusk I left the hospital,
the smell of burning all over me.
I recalled my childhood, burning wheat straw
on the ridges of the fields, so choked
I couldn't stand up straight. I was seven then,
poor but clean. That was a time
when the patches were on my coat
and not yet inside my body.

11

For more than half that evening, I was humming
a nursery rhyme; then, at the end of
one street, I was singing with all my heart,
and couldn't stop the tears falling.
A policeman came by, glanced at my
ID card, and said, 'Phoney.'
At the cop shop, he gave me
a form, so I wrote: *windy*.

12

The moment dawn broke, I got older,
I didn't want to speak any more. I lay upon
a bench at the station, covering my chest with a newspaper.
Everything around me was
travelling at full speed. An express train
suddenly stopped, and I made no move to get up,
preferring to wait. I knew
if I didn't get on board it couldn't leave.

2 October 2000   [BH, LMK, WNH]

2. NEO-CLASSICAL POEMS

QIN XIAOYU

River Spring Enters an Old Year:
On Neo-classical Poetry

Following classical models is a Chinese literary tradition. Such statements from pre-modern writers as 'Music must rely on tones, Poetry must follow the classics' (Wang Kaiyun [1832-1916], *Xiangyi Lou Shuo Shi*, 'Talking About Poetry in the Xiangqi Lodge') or 'Poetry that doesn't learn the classics should described as savage' (Shen Deqian [1673-1769], *Shuo Shi Cuiyu*, 'A Poetry Primer') were almost self-evident laws that, for centuries, no one thought to argue with. Even though, post-1919, the New Poetry's aesthetic revolution rejected the laws of Classical poetry, its very resistance was in one sense an acknowledgement of that tradition: within its continuous attempt to reimagine poetry, there was always an inherent desire to transform the classical.

For instance, among the post-1919 poets, Fei Ming's 'New Zen Poetry' tried to inherit the philosophical thought of classical poetry, while Bian Zhilin's poems tried to copy the style of Tang Dynasty poets like Li Shangyin, or the aesthetic feel of the Song Dynasty collection *Huajian Ci* ('Among the Flowers'). Wen Yiduo imitated the forms with visually square, fixed-metre poems whose regular rhythms and regimented prosody were intended to copy the classical tradition, but Xu Zhimo, Wen Yiduo's friend in the Crescent Moon School, commented, 'everyone knows how to cut a piece of tofu, and everyone can plan some nearly-similar rhythms, but where is the poetry?'

Despite Bian Zhilin's argument that national spirit and style are more important than national form, in this book, the neo-classical selection is focused specifically on form, and how a transformation of classical Chinese poetics takes place within modern language. This is addressed in three ways: conscious usage of the rules of poetic and musical form; using classical language and grammar to bring the soul of classical poetry into contemporary writing; and following the influence of classical poetry in developing modes of thought and rhetoric rooted in Chinese characters.

In classical Chinese poetry, there were strict rules concerning both tone patterns and rhymes. A fixed tone system separated the four tones of the Chinese language into two sections, known as 平 ('*ping*' level) and 仄 ('*ze*' oblique).[50] *Ping* contained the first and the second tones and *ze* the third and fourth.[51] '*Ping*' was considered to be more open and louder; *ze* narrower and darker. The beauty was held to lie in the way that *ping* and *ze* contrasted with each other in various patterns. This included the principle of antithesis whereby characters in the same position in a pair of lines must mirror each other. These perfectly designed forms were rooted deeply in the nature of classical Chinese, in which each character was a word, and each sentence a chain of linked monosyllabic characters, allowing poets considerable flexibility in creating the poem's sound structure: how characters were linked or separated in parallel structures was always meaningful. The single character syllabic system was the foundation of classical form, but since most modern Chinese words are made up of more than one syllable, many classical forms have lost their linguistic basis.

Rhyme is another central principle of classical poetics. If we were to take the relationship between rhyme and poetry as a way of looking at the difference between classical and modern poems, then we could say classical verse had very strict rules regarding rhymes, meaning the rhyme-patterns often created the poem, while modern poetry has no fixed rules for rhyme, therefore, the poems often create the rhyme-patterns.

Chinese critics have debated for a long time over the relationship between rhyme and meaning, arguing for instance that, in the classical form of *ci* form, some of the prescribed metrical patterns were more suitable for emotional and heroic themes, so that if a poet used a heroic pattern to write something languishing or introspective, even though they followed the pattern perfectly, there would still be a lack of harmony between sound and sense.[52] The five-syllable line was often used by classical poets to write bold, striking poems, which the poet Liang Zongdai (1903-83) called 'universal poetry'.

The pattern of influence between rhyme and meaning goes both ways. The *ci* scholar, Long Yusheng (1902-55), thought the organisation of

50. In Modern Standard Chinese – Mandarin – every syllable has a fixed pitch contour: level, rising, dipping, or falling.

51. This is a simplification of which scholars of the subject would perhaps not entirely approve.

52. *Ci* is a lyric form in which poems follow the metric pattern of an existing song.

lines, in terms of their length and the tones at the line-ends, 'could show different moods and feelings'. Following this theory, Yang Lian's 'Imperial Palace at Jehol' is almost in *ci* form, its lines, though their lengths vary, often end with descending tones (the oblique *ze* sounds). This form is traditionally thought 'good for expressing loneliness of spirit', and this poem is about the beauty and the loss in an emperor's mad sexual life.

The linguist Wang Li argued that, 'the ancient modal particles in Chinese have been almost completely lost in contemporary speech: they have been replaced by new modal particles that came from other sources'.[53] However, these ancient modal particles haven't totally vanished: they appear from time to time in the poems of Xiao Kaiyu and Jiang Hao. In fact, these words don't only express the modal: rendered highly rhetorical by their use in classical literature, they became keys to help readers read and experience the writing. Even though they themselves don't provide meaning, just like the blankness in Chinese landscape painting, they can mark where spiritual energy comes and goes, and, when used expertly, contribute to musicality and rhythm.

Many writers have noted that the subject and object pronouns are often left out in classical Chinese poetry. The Song dynasty poet Su Dongpo (1037-1101 AD) wrote: 'the halls are silent / scattered stars sometimes cross the Milky Way/ try asking the night how it is'.[54] Here, who is it who listens, who sees and who answers? Even asking such questions is already to diminish the image-world created by the poet. This kind of omission is neither because of the rigid forms of classical poetry, nor because the poet deliberately tries to create an unbroken beauty by mixing the subjective and objective. This use of a subject-less, tense-less language gives universality to the poet's experiences: the absence of a fixed subject becomes an invitation, drawing the reader subconsciously into the world of the poem. Compared to this, modern language, controlled by logical meaning, has lost a lot of grammatical freedom, and it is now rare for the subject to be left out.

One exception is Yang Lian, who doesn't only leave the subject out, but goes further, linking this omission with the Buddhist concept of breaking through the limits of the self, developing what he terms a

---

53. Translators' note: modal particles show completed or continuous aspect, and imperative or interrogative mood, etc; they are also known as 'empty words'.

54. Burton Watson, *Selected Poems of Su Tung-p'o* (Copper Canyon Press, 1994); Lin Yutang, *The Gay Genius: The Life and Times of Su Tungpo* (J. Day Co., 1947).

kind of 'non-personal' thinking. As he says, 'the word itself is an absent condition of existence, yet it announces the absent world again…"non-person" is not an omission, but a deletion: the individual has been deleted, so that their absence can become everyone'. We can see this at the end of 'Holy Lilac Sea', the final poem of 'Sailors Home':

This instant   the shine of shattered sex organs is a long look of goodbye
Spring's perfume like smoke's smell   silken parasols opening one by one
Final day lowered into our mouth   all your cries learning from a bird's
    cry

Only the body's image isn't enough   at last a tear drop has fallen
Leaving for the garden   stars tenderly drifting
Each breath of wind blowing away the ocean

We don't need to ask who opened the 'silken parasols' or who is leaving for the garden: the 'final day' belongs to everyone.

Classical Chinese poetry's aesthetics often focus on the liveliness and energy within images. This is no doubt linked to the way that the Chinese character is built up from visual, aural and conceptual elements. We can even argue that the nature of the character holds the key to the fundamental poetic of classical Chinese poetry. In the contemporary scholar Guo Saoyu's essay, 'Developments between Literary and Vernacular Versions of Chinese Literature', he points out that while classical texts were densely textured intellectually and rhetorically, those examples of folk literature, which often only survived orally, were similarly complex linguistic structures. The first has often been termed 雅 'ya', meaning elegant, and the second 俗 'su', vulgar or inelegant. The main lines of development in Chinese literature are influenced by the interactions of the two, particularly when the inelegant is brought into the elegant.

The May Fourth Movement saw the triumph of the idea that spoken and written language must be brought together, and, since then, classical poetry rooted in the nature of the Chinese character was replaced by a New Poetry based on daily speech and imported theories. Only very recently have a few poets emerged who, inspired by the classical tradition, have started to reconsider the links between characters and contemporary poetry. These writers have begun to conceive of a poetic derived from the character, demanding of themselves that they not only write poetry in Chinese, but poetry in Chinese characters.

It is not so long ago that classical Chinese poetry gathered its rhetorical energy from the character, and it is not so difficult to separate each syllabic sound into consonant, vowel, rhyme and tone. The poetic significance of rhyme and tone is clear enough, but pronunciation is a rich and complex field. There is for instance the rhetorical effect of homophones, such as 丝 ('*si*', silk) and 思 ('*si*', think, yearn), where two different characters remind the listener of each other because they share a similar sound. There is also the effect gained by multiple sounds, where certain characters have several different ways of being said. Then there are assonance and alliteration: there was an expression, 'alliteration is loud and clear like two pieces of jade knocking together; assonance is smooth and dexterous like a chain of pearls'.

There are also the aesthetic effects derived from the character's visual appearance, which include three elements: the pictogram; the radical elements; and the effect of combining or separating characters.

The effect of focussing on the pictogram can be seen in this couplet:

江南可采莲
莲叶何田田
picking lotuses in the South
lotus leaves in field after field

Here, 田 ('*tian*') clearly depicts a farmed field.

To focus on the radical parts involves select one part of the characters to develop the poem, as in the following:

寄寓客家，
牢守寒窗空寂寞；
远避迷途，
退还莲迳返逍遥。

Living like a guest in a stranger's home,
looking through the empty loneliness of winter's window;
if you wander too far on lost roads,
return to the Lotus Path to win a mind that's free.

Every character in the first couplet shares the top part (宀), meaning 'house/home', and every character in the second shares the bottom part (辶) meaning 'walk away'. The content of the poem exactly reflects this: a dialogue between the lonely wife and the departing husband: thus the silent radical components also express the poem's meaning.

The effect of combining or separating characters is playful: normally, poets separate the characters and readers combine them to understand the poem. In a line from 'General Sima's Song' by Li Bai (701-762):

狂风吹古月
crazy wind blows old moon

Here 古 ('*gu*', old) and 月 ('*yue*', moon) can be combined into the character 胡 ('*hu*', foreign), creating an image of the ancient moon – readers would grasp that the moon hangs in a cold foreign sky.

The rhetorical effect of homophones is frequently encountered in modern poetry. To take one example, Jiang Hao wrote in 'Spring and Autumn Explained':

深能照影，亦能造影；
浅能流云，亦能留云。
Depth can light up shadows and make shadows;
shallowness can make clouds flow and hold clouds back.

Here the homophones in the first line are 照影 ('*zhao ying*', light up the shadows) and 造影 ('*zao yin*', make shadows), while in the second 流云 ('*liu yun*', flowing clouds) echoes 留云 ('*liu yu*', hold clouds back).

To turn to Yang Lian's 'Imperial Palace at Jehol':

Jade bowl shattered   We command you to serve another cup of tea
Made with melted snow   water gurgling like an omen of dying early
Son of Heaven suspended from the sky   drinking   focuses us fairly

This life We could throw away if We wanted to

With the exception of poems written by the emperors themselves, this is one of the first poems to use the imperial pronoun 朕 ('*zhèn*', We) since the first emperor of the Qin Dynasty (221-206 BC). When this word become the imperial first person pronoun, it also became a symbol of absolute power, and indeed terror. To hear it in Chinese, *zhèn* (with a descending tone) sounds both powerful and cruel, like an imperative. If we remember the plotting and politics of the Imperial Palace, then the sound is also linked with 震 ('*zhen*', shock) and 鸩 ('*zhen*', poison). All emperors die eventually, but this character never did, because it embodies a way of thinking that continues today in centres of power.

In 'Imperial Palace at Jehol', the imagination of this 'We' moves from a cup of tea to the melted snow, and to the sound of flowing water. The reason why this sound symbols 'an omen of early death' is because the word 潺潺 ('*chan chan*', the sound of flowing water) can be linked with 孱 ('*chan*', weakness).

What follows this is shocking: 'Son of Heaven suspended from the sky'. Here, the image of an emperor hanging upside down is evoked by the character • ('*diao*', colloquially, penis), which combines two characters: 尸 ('*shi*', corpse) and 吊 ('*diao*', hang) – visually, this represents the male sexual organ hanging from the body. It's also worth comparing 天子 ('*tian zi*', the imperial title) with 天空 ('*tiankong*', the sky) where the character *kong* actually means 'empty'.

This is a typical example of the multiple level of meaning we can derive from the character. There is a homophonic effect whereby 饮 ('*yin*', drink) echoes 瘾 ('*yin*', 'addiction'). This opens up the question of who drinks what? It's perfectly possible that the emperor is being drunk by something else, that 'non–person singular' which haunts Yang Lian's poetry, its emptiness swallowing the decadent life of the 'We'. The poem, finally, is not about sex but about the nature of being.

BEI DAO (b. 1949)

Mother [55]
(for Di Yunxia, on her 80th birthday)

as you were young and easy
the cry of gulls accompanied your journey
plum blossom brought blood, eastward wind bitter tears
obstacles – how thou hast scattered them
the slow, slow echo of dawn songs and gloaming drums

your hair has become very white
an eagle's wing on nightfall darkened
up on a high fail dyke, the sunlit mirror sings its evensong
your guide and comforter, needle and thread in hand
the colours of spring again in your own, your native land

sleepless before the morning watch
your past rows its boat ashore
drunken lights and a running tide,
curfewed curtains and the tolling knell
old friends gone into the ends of the world
gloomy as the willow catkins' last farewell
having once turned round, the sky is old
the waning moon witness to one land, one throne
attentive words, forever sad and weary
earth's the right place for love
signs of rain and chimney smoke on the long road home

[BH, LMK]

55. The original presents itself as pastiche, seemingly constructed out of partly remembered scraps of familiar quotations and half-recalled lines of poetry. By tying together a rag-bag of similar scraps from texts in English, the translators have tried a restatement of both the denotational and connotational sense of the poem. By showing how Bei Dao's poem works, we hope we can better suggest what it might mean.
56. Dōgen Zenji (1220-53 AD), founder of the Japanese Sōtō school of Zen Buddhism.

YANG LIAN (*b.* 1955)

Imperial Palance at Jehol

bashfully the palace girls put on Our invented trousers
their privates exposed   till brocade loses its colours
in Our eyes no more lakes and hills   painted junks   curving corridors
empire   less than the triangle's scented crease
a point of pink among the hair   oh Our masterpiece

anywhere at all   only for stag's blood in Our heart springing
only for Us to be hard again   and a cry of surprise fiercely penetrating
jade bowl shattered   We command you to serve another cup of tea
made with melted snow   water gurgling like an omen dying early
Son of Heaven suspended from the sky   drinking   focuses us fairly

this life We could throw away if We wanted to
how entrancing!   The way they fall as if brushing themselves aside
and strip Us bare too   their meat tightens in the golden seraglio
so We can't pull out   a hot spurt of come   in action
spreading wind and water   on the loveliest shortcut to destruction

[BH]

XIAO KAIYU (*b.* 1960)

Sunday Farce
For fans of Dōgen [56]

1

Wow! A 400m tower is taller than a plane at 20,000m –
a counterfeit flashlight poking about in the permitted void.
In that case, to shift the bedroom's autumn breeze out into the lounge
is harder work than the North commandeering the fate of the South.
And moreover, by relying on rented welfare-statist sperm,
a marriage will then become about as urgent as a drawbridge.
Go or not go – but will not going to the suburbs cause anger?
If you delete the day then you have only deleted next week.

2

'World's road adds dawn to dawn; men's hearts grow weird and weirder.'[57]
You come out wailing, the final farewell not heeded,
as if body and mind rebel against the reasons why:
breaking ground and topping-out, neither of them exist now.
Where can those tasty Kyoto nights be re-heated – Kyoto?
Where are those hometown trees, and their peach pickers – your home town?
As countless worlds are there before your eyes and yet not there,
so you are those Kyoto nights, those peach trees, those peach pickers.

3

I once read *A Song of White Hair*: with white hair comes compassion –
the camisole across the street answers with a promise.
The road takes on a female air, and complicates the day,
delaying father, who's raising cash, from signing the will.
So don't leave yet – ancient grudges are knocking on the door,
and I'm no narcissus conjoined with its own reflection.
Night's pitter-patters wash out sky's limitless transmitter,
as though it won't defend that fiddle which broadcasts regret.

4

Better than eyes meeting or break-ups are withered, waning thighs –
wash your hands in the golden bowl, touch the warm surrounding shores:
hands return to hands. Left, India's matrilocality;
right, China, a hallucination of the kaleidoscope.
Machines ascetic by nature are best for the tumbrelling;
when it's stripping-time, the cosmos will turn mystery's blind eye.
Either, how do we build our road toward modernity, or,
fragments of original mind, how do we begin again?

5

A shape-shifted wastrel reverting to an instant basement –
hell is cosy now, so I have the gall to dabble in politics.
Looking idly on as country and people push into the wasteland,
it's enough to make me weep, and idleness must of course be critiqued.
The first big item is moving the capital: find the Promised Land,
build ourselves a portable city, and clean up the ballot a bit.
Law-enforcing bureaucrats – dealers in symbols with nothing in stock:
Master Du Fu took beauty with him, declined Chang'an's invitations.

57. The quotation is from the court poet Yu Xin (513-581 AD).

6

It's certain you'll be ensnared by Katzler Strasse's dives,
for none of these shuffled places spring from inspiration.
You're still pursuing strange heaven-sent fish in Eastern Europe,
I'm looking to see the wide steppe in a Muslim's expression.
Every cloth for bandaging politics used up long ago,
the new soldiers of the trading floor swap punches one by one.
No need to talk of time's victory over woody fell and fane:
look at the *pencai* trees, where each flower is a *gongan*.[58]

7

Your 2nd Person is a burst seam, the air has the taste of glass,
the squabs have vomited up an entire week's black smoke and steel nails.
After the great right, the key here is every second's great wrong:
if you're no hypocrite, the chance of sacrifice remains unreached.
The edges are full of the room! Every step is fired off at random,
blackout a hindrance more than a help, the profound still more profound.
Unity is easy, dreamlessness the same as a dreamless dream,
all the contractor's express deliveries returned to sender.

8

Because time takes its time, the levée calls for six or seven wise old
        hooligans,[59]
the other me ten thousand miles away settles for the sweet spot.
Coming out fighting, the empty vessel's just following orders.
What is Zen? What is Tao? What is this unending disputation?
I just want the screws, dropped in the drum of my washing machine,
        fixed;
play-dead Christianity in the end needs odd-job man Hui Neng.[60]
Your deliverance system actually a nuclear alert,
yoked by commission, you orbit earlier lives and deaths to come.

[BH, WNH]

58. These are terms relating to Chan Buddhist matters (*Chan* is cognate
with the Japanese *Zen*): *pencai* is the term for dwarf trees or bonsai; *gongan*
the insoluble problem or *koan*.
59. The poem specifically names Wang Rong (234-305 AD), once a famous
general, later one of the drinkers, pranksters and eccentrics known as the Seven
Sages of the Bamboo Grove.
60. Hui Neng (638-713 AD), the Sixth and Last Patriarch of Chan (Zen)
Buddhism.

YANG XIAOBIN (*b.* 1963)

Three Ballads

Ballad of Recruitment

Shouldering rifles, they marched from flower to soil,
fired into the depths: moles
in their mole souls fled to their tails
so abrupt are the world's terminals.

Who had tasted the grain in the tunnels:
First Emperor or Ming Dynasty Founder? [61]
Folk shuddering in burial urns were
maybe sulky, maybe cold or even frostier.

Boy soldiers the vanguard in autumn's new battles
in a blink blood was gushing, mist and clouds clearing
mares ridden above tree-lines, gone and not returning,
the remainder retreating to barracks still burning.

The general's genitals concealed murder,
cocked for action, awaiting the aesthetic of the gun
he strips his uniform off, then, bollock-naked as before,
he charges at a new city state, bellowing *King's Regulations.*

Ballad of the Beauties

These floating tongues, drifting down the Whampoa;
as gentle and tender, these fish and shrimp.

As the women taste the seafood
in the Swan Star Restaurant, midnight passes.

Breasts that the light of a lamp couldn't dim were
the only sunshine seen that Spring.

61. The 1st Emperor is Qin Shi Huang; and the founder of the Ming dynasty is Zhu Yuanzhang.

Breathy elegance of those voices – steps on a dance floor
flowing from the end of the month to Friday.

What's in those hands? Watermarks on banknotes,
the full moon on dominoes.

What do you see when you look back? Passed out in the bath,
a beautiful body soaked and swollen.

Another, hem in the booze, her form lovely under flowers:
swept-up dust, thrown into another tomorrow.

Short Ballad

One cup of ginseng soup and a nursery rhyme,
a winter day, lived through, is longer than a life.

The tonic was boiled in the river
fortified with tortoises from the future.

The walnuts were diced like a brain,
a paring from the god of long-life's forehead, an aping

of the compasses' geometry, living from antiquity
till tomorrow, an abstraction in an empty shell:

when crows fly away from the five senses
the people vomit up even more wings.

Only a young person full of sorrow
can see sunlight in the dew.

And the master of eternity sits on the sea,
a heap of bones under the moon, blowing a bamboo flute.

[BH, LMK, WNH]

ZHANG DIAN (*b.* 1968)

The Night-soil Truck

At dawn, the good weather that readers bring on
Makes the green land excrete viscous poetic juice.
All at once, the night-soil truck's giant syphon
Gathers the heritage our authors struggle to lose.

Dear listener, my maggots bow before you,
This big tub of soul can be managed as you choose.
Look here reader, turning your head to spew black clouds,
The innocent green land is holding its nose.

[BH, LMK,WNH]

JIANG HAO (*b.* 1971)

from Spring & Autumn Explained

1

Eyebrows lift an inch of spring, the sound of eyebrow-trimming
no bigger than a palace, no finer than a feather.
Spring heads up the four seasons, a blockhead
bird comes out from the middle, moves here to Mount Tai to practise,
joints itch halfway up the mountain.

Ant's eggs were upset on a spring jaunt, can a good mood
be renewed by the spring grasses? To lend your mobile to a white cloud
is to send a polite note. Mountains high enough to pierce clouds,
mountains high enough not to block clouds.
Human clouds are clouds too, they all say.

3

A photo is a tile, rain rinses and fixes flying rafters.
An empty room whitens, what's seen just a break in seeing.
Oh cold lonely city, the animal shape of drinking yourself sober;
oh island beneath the city, like a wine-soaked grain of pepper.
Wind-undressing gaol, skirt-front of undischarged water.

Water is clothes too, counted as flower-painted shoots,
noble discourses like they're pattern-cut, for five forwards
five backs, fine as the watery enigma of according-to,
depth can light up shadows and make shadows;
shallowness make clouds flow and hold clouds back.

7

Bits of news fill the estuary, and ships are the result.
Middle-age masts, old-age anchors, childhood waves,
undulating questions overleaping youth's rain.
Into the sea to kill a dragon and get a lizard, the learned Way
is a monkey clutching at shadows, grabbing fur.

Mark of the full sea, organ of virtue,
eloquence mixed into vast waters. Bait adorns the hook,
fish escape the net, each asking itself, is it all desire-contaminated?
The fun of wickedness, hoisting the sail to fan the cheeks,
sea horizon not wrinkling brows, but wrinkling faces.

10

Deep in stamens, deep in oceans,
bees gather waves of ultrasound & infrasound,
needle mouths spitting bright fire, hollows palely hosting bright water,
cooking a slice of broken cloud. Lovely, dusk,
a single flower teases a single lamp.

Deep in fallen leaves, deep in fruit,
hug a bag of caltrop to break the shell and come forth.
Little thorax-mounted bells, nests of sound,
empty stars in the horseplay, crazily barking.
Tongue broken as a snapped stem, broken again like wisdom's root.

12

You're sentimental. Hollow-eyed in your hollow robes.
You leak. Sea horizon a thousand miles a day.
You shut the door. You enter a calm in tune with trivial times.
You are mistaken. Wait only for winter winds to equalise.
You abandon yourself. A phone rings under the sea.

You're talking. You you you you you.
Stars circles the sky, sun traverses the zodiac, moon again conjunct sun,
marsh firms its belly up, ice tweaks water's sideburns.
Your bitter & sweet is harmonised, black & white gathered in.
Your single scale, it's half claw.[62]

10 February 2004, Haidian Island, Hainan
[BH, WNH]

62. Author's Note: 'This verse relies on *The Book of Rites, Monthly Tasks No.6*.'

3. SEQUENCES

QIN XIAOYU

Coiling: On the Sequence

In Chinese every character must be regarded as a kind of 'independent kingdom', an apprehensible unit constructed from visual and aural elements as well as meaning. It is both free-standing and linked with nearby characters to make up words and texts. This aesthetic principle, based on the separation of character and text, can be seen in the structure of classical Chinese novels, in highlights from operas, in the multiple perspectives of landscape painting, and in calligraphy, seal-cutting, garden design, and so on. It demonstrates a non-hierarchical, anti-autocratic relationship between the part and the whole: even though the part belongs to the whole, it does not follow the strict logic of the whole. Before anything else, the part is independent, complete in itself. In this respect, the sequence could be seen as a particularly Chinese form.

A sequence can be thought of as a specially structured group of poems in which each part must be both independent and part of the whole at the same time. The basic unit of the sequence must be written as a single poem, perhaps even with its own title, and it should not sacrifice its independence for the whole. But these poems must also form a unified piece, recognisable by a strong linking theme, style or form, rather than simply a gathering of separate pieces.

For instance, Zhang Zao's 'Conversation with Tsvetaeva' relates to her drama, *An Adventure*, and the poems display elements of dramatic plot. In Act One (poem 1): the poetic 'I' and 'you' (Tsvetaeva) meet up even though separated by death. In Act Two (poems 2-7), their relationship develops: the 'I' even discusses the Russian poet's death with the 'you'. In Act Three (poem 8) comes the climax. Pointing out that both the half-human half-ghostly 'I' and 'you' are talents who best understood each other, an end is announced. 'Every day, I dream of *Immemorial Tristesse*' in the second poem hints that this fortuitous meeting actually happened in a dream.

When Zhang Zao first arrived in Germany, he didn't speak to anyone for three months, but he carried on this conversation with Tsvetaeva in his dreams and in this poem. In Act Four (poems 9-12), having woken up, the poet's solitary voice continues to talk to himself, and the whole sequence ends with a question: 'How should we say "No!"?'

On the one hand 'No' points to a Keatsian negative capability – exactly the level 'Conversation with Tsvetaeva' is seeking. On the other, 'No' is a key word for Tsvetaeva's nature and her life. From birth onward (her mother had wished for a boy), the proud Tsvetaeva had been saying 'No' her whole life: from her mother's demand she become a musician, to the groups of poets she refused to join, to the White Russian exile circles, to Soviet Communism, up until the final 'No' of her suicide.

The reason Zhang Zao wrote 'Conversation with Tsvetaeva' was because both Zhang Zao and Tsevetaeva's exile began in Germany. Zhang Zao treats Tsvetaeva as a model: they were different (one left, one right), yet they shared the same pain of exile; he agreed with her idea of poetry as a craft, a technology, and thought that she would have understood him.

In Gu Cheng's sequence 'Ghosts Enter the City', 城 ('*cheng*', city) refers both to his own name, and to Beijing. Gu Cheng described his isolation in New Zealand after the Tiananmen massacre in these terms: 'Once I opened my eyes, there were layers of simple things around me: hills, seas, trees, grasses and stones – I could talk of the world around me with perhaps fifteen words. But when I closed my eyes, I stood on the streets of Beijing. At that moment, my real life was like a dream, but my dream-life became a reality carved into my heart and bones.'

Because of this, Gu Cheng wrote two kinds of poetry. One was a kind of song of innocence. These poems were light and Zen-like, achieving a uniquely Chinese spirituality in exile. The other kind was typified by 'Ghosts Enter the City', in which he dreamed himself back to China. In this sequence, he returns as a ghost, and the effect is both gloomy and terrifying. He called this 'Ghostly Reality.'

The sequence is made up of seven poems named after the days of the week, plus another piece called 'Qing Ming Festival' (also known as Tomb-sweeping Day, the traditional Chinese Festival of the Dead).

'Monday' explains some features of the sequence's ghosts. These are the 'fine folk'; they can swim underground like the dwarf Tu Xingsun, a character from Beijing Opera; they call themselves 'old rose', a pun on 'unlucky ghost', and walk home under shadowy street-lights. 'A gust of wind rolls the mist away' hints at both the Misty Poets and the 'Storm' (the Chinese government's word for the student movement of 1989).

'Tuesday' presents two disturbing images suggestive of deeper meanings: the laughing kites and the sick red fish. Then from

'Wednesday' to 'Saturday', Gu Cheng portrays the Tiananmen massacre.

'Wednesday' uses the Beijing street snack of popcorn to describe how, on June 4th, protesting erupted everywhere. (In 'Saturday', this becomes the 'Popcorn Revolution'.) When corn pops, it floats out from a hole in the machine, and here the political popcorn machine is seen as having two holes: one representing the huge wound in people's minds, and the other the dead. 'Wednesday' ends with bottles being thrown everywhere, which was how people expressed their anger with Deng Xiaoping ('Xiaoping' punning with '*xiao ping*', little bottle).

'Thursday' begins with the banal calligraphy of Chinese political documents, followed by the cruelty of:

> The ballpoint pen twirls around some adults
> spinning them   into a round ball
> then eating them

Then reality is rewritten: 'she changed her name so there was no trace'.

In 'Friday', the character 枰 ('*ping*', chess-board) is a transformation of 砰 ('*pang*', gunfire) from 'Wednesday' – both associated with Deng Xiaoping. As the player in this political game becomes intensely aggressive, he dare not ask if he has or has not collapsed, and is hopeless wherever he moves – even if he doesn't lose power, he will still go down in history as the villain.

In 'Saturday' a large group of soldiers hand out gifts, alluding to the proverb 'politeness before force'. The ghost asks 'why is the flower so   red?' alluding to bloodshed. Then

> students lift their benches   into the sky
>   thrown   but not thrown like this
>   we need three to stand on benches and throw ropes into the   sky
>   thrown well they can be kites

Again, 凳 ('*deng*', bench) puns on Deng Xiaoping, while the reference to three alludes to the character 众 ('*zhong*', crowd), which consists of three iterations of the character 人 ('*ren*', person).

In 'Sunday' the ghost who has been walking home since 'Monday' seems finally to arrive, although it seems the ghost has no home to return to: he still sees Monday's 'shadows cast by the light'. This completes the week – however, the sequence doesn't end there, continuing with 'Qingming Festival'. This changes the whole process. In 'Monday', the ghosts are depicted as

> Standing high above the water
> Swimming out of a stream of gold from the earth

'Qingming Festival' ends with the line, 'only on the diving board does the ghost fall from grace', linking it back to the ghostly journey to Tiananmen. We realise the ghost will return to Monday at this point: like Sisyphus, he is eternally on the way home, but can never arrive.

T.S. Eliot's *Four Quartets* imitated the form of Beethoven's late quartets, and in turn Yang Lian's sequence 'Where the Sea Stands Still' not only parallels this poem formally, but echoes it verbally: the stillness in the title relates to Eliot's 'Still point of the turning world', and also refers to the Buddhist idea of *samatha* (rendered in Chinese as 'calm abiding'), the meditation state where all thought ceases. As with *Four Quartets*, 'Where the Sea Stands Still' is inspired by music: its four sections, each with the same title, resemble four movements.

The beginning, as in a slow overture, summarises the basic images and themes of the whole sequence:

> blue is always higher   just as your weariness has chosen
> the sea   just as a man's gaze compels the sea
> to be twice as desolate

The ending resolves these themes:

> stand still   this shore
> is where we see ourselves set sail

Each of the four sections is made up of three parts as in the sonata form with exposition plus development, then fantasia and finally a recapitulation. Each third section repeatedly uses passive verb forms, stressing the agent marker 被 (*'bei'*), which indicates the passive voice. After the Cultural Revolution, Tiananmen Massacre, and years of exile, for Yang Lian, this condition of passivity indicates the particular pain of the Chinese experience, while allowing him to relate this to the concept of the 'Non-Person Singular', which for him crosses history and cultures. He took this to mean the less choice in a given situation, the more the situation can be re-thought as complete spiritual freedom.

Another structural element within the sequence is the four seasons. In the first movement: 'hate   has united the ashes of early spring'; in the second: 'the little church steeple squeezes into this night each August / a storm   required reading in death's lesson' (August being the anniversary of Yang Lian's departure from China); in the third movement, 'the one harvested stone' uses autumnal imagery; and in the fourth, 'briars   drag out winter's questioning'. In this movement,

Yang Lian sums up this aspect of the poem:

> kids   almonds roasted by the seasons
> become every
>   imagination denied by being seen
>   inspired by destruction
> the pomegranate   is wrapped in blue calcified pips

These pips become the image of the present moment, which like a black hole sucks in all light from the past, so that 'Where the Sea Stands Still' becomes a paradoxical locus point: now is furthest away, in the now there is no time.

The setting of the poem is literally the road Yang Lian would come home along from Sydney University, presented so exactly that it can be used as a map, but it also symbolises the fact there is no home to return to, and the floating life that comes to comprehend rootlessness is its only root.

ZOU JINGZHI (b. 1952)

from Pictures at an Exhibition

1

unfolding the oilpaper
he didn't know that the inside of an apple
was a chemical factory
he didn't know that in the statue's
eyes, the dents were black
he didn't know that in the clean, bright hall
the pictures were attentively losing their focus

she had been seen
had been wrapped up in the sweater she knitted
it was winter outside when they looked at her
she was moving about in here
while nobody was looking someone changed the world [63]

the pictures that hadn't come were still hurrying over
on the way a flock of sheep ate up the sunlight
the dark night, pulled out, spun and rolled

2

drinking water during the visit
the glug recalled
days of growing vegetables

your hands had been replaced with
another pair, so you couldn't blame
these palenesses for being familiar enough

raising your eyes looking right at her
beautiful knees
the sound of gulping water brought the world to a silent accord

63. Literally 'stole the rafters and changed the pillars', a military strategy
whereby you steal away the enemy's support before he realises it's gone.

3

no shouting allowed here,
but don't you see the heart as
a golden fleece either, and when she's delighted
you should put on a stethoscope

there are things only collected by silence
but exchange requires the iron of argument
the distance between those people and the statues
makes movement meaningless

here, you should lift up the hammer and,
stroke by stroke, nail the wooden poles
to where the horses' hitching post is

then comes mowing the hay
then blending it with corn, black beans, yellow beans
then the rooster notices the out-dated dawn
but it still crows as loud as ever

4

I had just come from a meeting
on my way, exhausted, there was a fat man
using his belly for
the material of a street collage
this almost made me go into the exhibition early

not one familiar face
those pictures were exhausted too
I was looking at a hand on a canvas
really wanting to grab the apple behind the table

summer, and since it was hot the colours,
racing onto canvas, preferred to go to war
why do these people also know about shooting

there are things must be returned to canvas
such as that visionless woman
they really have to be taken away, which will sadden us all

5

I had come to think that nobody would be here tonight
it only took a chisel to change that
so I didn't sign the register

some people exhibited tanks in a world of ice and snow
others had seized the seals' bathing pool
when I was starving I saw kitchen smoke –
some people couldn't pull through a day like this

this man was getting ready to modify that piece of grey
he wanted to creep quietly in tonight
to preserve his right to modify other people

6

cleaning out the most retiring of
paint boxes, you whistled,
your lips like candied fruit –
they can't smile now

this moment's song ascended
flying from tree to tree
it was endlessly drying honey in the sun
trying as much as it could to make itself different

it was really dangerous, autumn leaves had faded and fallen
almost as if everyone had come to think about death

7

there was this one man who had a moustache
he ate more green maize than he should have
his eye was like an apricot

he walked past everything; from a faraway place
he came to the corner, eating a slice of
bread that was even further away

in front of his feast hung lots and lots of pictures
if he was in a Shanghai restaurant, he would
order the Hibiscus Chicken

there were colours on his hands
angels had seized him by his shoulders, even though
before he came, he'd changed into clean underwear

8

light leaking from the skylight
shines on the pictures; people have to stand in the shade

I don't intend to walk over, open my
eyes wide for a single brush stroke – it's nothing
before this, painters
turned their backs on the pictures, and looked at the visitors

(some texts get washed away down the toilet and are lost
what I'm referring to isn't just newspapers and books, it's
genuine piss: out of all the urine passed in one life, only
a tiny drop can be solemnly placed under the microscope
to reach any kind of conclusion)

I flung myself here
borrowing the right arm of a heavenly deity
and the action of David slinging a stone
fated, and I mean ineluctably
to wound something

9

Spring within Spring
you promised once not to describe life
so why have you sent the kitchen smoke up?

knowing within knowing
actually there was no rice in that pot
I had no idea that you were boiling paint

all the white
washed dirty by flocks of sheep
you can use a nickel
to block the loophole or the bullet hole

you would be able to find something
on the coloured patches. the snorts

horses let out on the snowy ground were joyous
and nervous too

10

among all these people coming to see the pictures
you were able to recognise one
a street vendor on Yongan Alley

11

in the world outside of this world
there too a picture was stored
it was so extraordinarily far away
it almost couldn't be delivered
it was subtle, and it was turbid too

it could have been placed in the lobby
but not against these colours
some people were wringing their hands
they'd crawled up to the gullet that was leaking secrets –
at this moment everything became fragile

12

people weren't hugging themselves because of the cold
but because of the need for weight
once you too held yourself this tight,
it being easier than holding a rock

cough. no. oh. don't. really.
such sounds were like thundering over the hills in a cart
you've never driven a fully-assembled horse-drawn cart
among its parts there's always one mule using more muscle

no big deal, but only with it
can we dash downward from some higher place
and such velocity
is ecstasy

13

'got to dig transparency out from blackness'
when you said this
I thought of the process of sieving cornstarch

and also the human game of digging for treasure
when you, startled awake,
pointed to the cockerel, I thought briefly
that it had been a long time since the city had
gone to war for a woman

most comforts have already ascended
out of mercy into splendour
suddenly I was moved by the food at lunchtime
you saw all this with your own eyes

when snow became an insurmountable whiteness
Andersen wrapped himself tightly in his coat
the world he set out in the dark
was the result of mirrors and emaciation
I wanted so much to find a drawing-pin
to pin back the corner of that picture properly
when it's not perfect, I feel
there's someone else like me dying in this world

because of how they were painted I just couldn't move
away from those almost tangible silks
nor could I throw away the word scarlet, because
of its association with brothels

we've destroyed the props in our dreams
all soliloquies have become
private performances, you face a
big fat man, and you earn his money
by being as self-confident as General Lü Bu
riding in on his red roan [64]

[BH, LMK, WNH]

---

64. A military hero of the Three Kingdoms period (*d.* 198 AD), a kind of
Chinese Achilles.

YANG LIAN (b. 1955)

Where the Sea Stands Still

1

blue is always higher   just as your weariness has chosen
the sea   just as a man's gaze compels the sea
to be twice as desolate

going back as ever
to that carved stone ear where drumbeats are destroyed
where tiny coral corpses   fall in a snowstorm

gaudy speckles on dead fish
like the sky that holds all your lust

go back to the limit   like limitlessness
going back to the cliffs   stormheads all around
your pipes doomed to go on playing
after your death   tunes of corruption deep in the flesh

as blue is recognised at last   the wounded
sea   a million candles   stands dazzlingly still

2

reality   belittles the madness of poets again
a child has the right to reveal a brief death
flame brings crowds of bodies back down to zero
hate   has united the ashes of early spring
thick smoke spat from stamens   grows prouder still in tranquillity

the pure terror of your wish
this one day   has used up each day's bitter grief
when fire   chokes the lung's lobes
seawater   watches mother's limbs swirl and evaporate
last year's garden is squeezed out on the sea

rising to the zenith through the blank cries of seagulls
the non-licit deaths of young children
make death   understudy for spring
a chance enmity   the enmity of all your future in the darkness
because of a refusal to live in this moment

3

what's drab and what's drably copied   is criminal
someone living alone on a cliff is closer to the edge than the cliffs are
you   are battered by a thousand tons of blue rock
eyes   can't dodge the ocean's battering
what watches the day and what's stripped bare by the day
time   the hardcore pornography of the dead

a fishbone polished still sharper can never be wrong

a drop of blood   has diluted waters that embrace sunken ships
ivory archaic and ruthless as a balcony
trees   net green shoals in their branches again

in this snow-white sickroom   that white is breeding
breasts bared on rooftops   gales
change each hand too gentle
the sky's legs pinned down by the bedrail

for the sea   the ocean slides more dumbly in dreams
a cockroach twitches terribly like a human

what's past and what's spat out by the past   is only flesh
in this reality   you called to memory   there's only faraway flesh
rejecting blue cliffs
the sea that rejected wings is smashed to pieces
on your face   the lying biography each wave writes with light
and an eye staring at the edge is a fresh oyster
where the necrosis of last night goes endlessly back

Where the Sea Stands Still

1

on the tarmac sea a ghost-white bird

smells its way to the shore   the lighthouse sticks
at the left   the place where we met our untimely end

on the tarmac sea an anchor is a broken plough

with the leaning of tombstones   a century
rewrites our names
seen beside the table of red rock as we dine
on seawater   the green bonfire of pine needles warming the skeleton
baring a rust-blackened mouthful of teeth   dancing

the little church steeple squeezes into this night each August
a storm   required reading in death's lesson

light stops   where more dead congregate
the anchor chain has snapped   the anchor sunk deep where infants wail
lovers clasped tight beneath the tar

after a century we grasped the blackness of the clock

2

the flower's defences have the ocean in their sights
a beerglass waits for sunset   to paint gold and yellow
like a steadily sinking disease on the lips
that talker   still talking through the glass

that singer   electrocuted into song
at ten-fold volume to seal up the deaf
smile   is recorded
food   breaks fingers off

drowned silhouette of a sailor   presses in
multiplies between chair and chair
between in-breath and out wind on wind is a rank salt beach of bloodstains
that one called a man   makes words split and crack

stone's snow-white heels stamp on the primal earth
paralyse the stairway of heartbeats
the days   since they neither ascend nor descend   have reached
the final   drunken   cud-chewed   sea

3

paralysed years and years forced in by paralysis
years in sunken ships
this flesh which has forgotten how to banish pain opens wide its skin
insides finally touched by the ocean

liver washed clean, a single white jellyfish
face pickled   pinning down a thousand stars
bed captured by a turtle   still playing a shining instrument

as moonlight is clearly our phosphorescence
tides   endlessly scrape younger wombs clean
cries for help cease in   all the ears not there

in   a quietly suspended moment before the shark's feeding frenzy

we don't shift   rust piles up over the sky
we're shifted   the ocean's purple shadow tightly clasps
a century   a pair of hands spit ink
touch   powerless and powerlessly attained sleep
shame   riding on a lighthouse
touches   the masturbating flesh that the dead bequeath the beach
wheeling birds are tiny bows that shoot into five fingers
our coffins compelled to pursue this night

dig it out   that bottomless wounded seabed   stands still
where a storm can never stand

Where the Sea Stands Still

1

who comes with you close to each of your deaths
who says   the one harvested stone
makes the sea sink to the level of your water
as you look   you can only hear birdsong as funeral music
you listen   but dream of the ocean's carmine dustjacket
placed on the windowsill
picky nightmares read you more closely still
corpses stuffed with recalled-again chalk
who shares this doleful distance with you

now is furthest away

your standstill is as full as the ocean's madness
the fullness of solitude   makes an ear think long
in every dry shell predators have been drained of fresh blood
snow-white poison milk   one drop enough
to suckle your sunlight

eyes open and fall into reality
shut tight   is kin to the dark

2

this death-like instant   this instant of passion
this instant simultaneously blank on the black bedsheet
and suspended on the sea   flesh
escapes itself through the mirror of flesh
the blazing organ is a corridor
paralysis   the bright blue goal that makes the ocean dazzle
girls urgently cry for rest   when being stands still
the tenderest windows are damp, pushed open by the sea

fling yourself in one direction   this direction that never was
far from the strumming fingers   the instrument itself is music
far from the wind   salt settles into the wound of all the past
only the now is like being forgotten
lust's blank water on noon's black bed sheet

the further from blood ties the brighter it is   this instant that lights up sin
in the now there is no time   no one slowly waking
to say   illusion apart, no sea can come alive

3

alive powerless with no way to go back

in the ocean's collective panting
names   vulnerable planed-down nuts
fingernails resist the seasons   the attempt at murder is utterly immortal
bird wings have chilled the images

you are   someone's and what someone makes of a dream
what stands still and what's painlessly changed by standstill
you are   always your mirror's more vicious imagination

when more are missing   it's even more the world
each drop of water denying the blue that fills the vision
death's compacted sands   spread on night's city
the festering journalistic fish
a foul shade able again to find the woman in labour

only   when someone hears another's tinnitus
will reality open   like a syllabus of the darkest learning

this language which has no past   forces you to learn
what's fearsome when you look back is your own
face   a ghostlike fake reflected by the grave
history   the silver white of tree trunks seen by autumn
its leaves identical to the worst news of all
neither is true   yet a thousand times dying in the sky
the sea   so sharp it snuffs you out   makes you the you of this instant

where the mirror's fictive ending stretches endlessly away

273

Where the Sea Stands Still

1

King Street   straight on
Enmore Road   turn right
Cambridge Street   No.14
the sea's tongue licks into the grate
            the old house discloses
countless places to watch us in the dark

we are so worn down   looted and left still more dilapidated
that shadows will show themselves at this address

           unfamiliar words are only curses
inbred neighbours all jumbled together
dead pigeons spew out city scenes age on age
      glass   inlaid in eyeballs
sky   beyond the railway proudly preserves colour blindness
a map elegantly printed with everyone's ruins
          can't help owning the sea
everything not there   vanishes more
is a poem   leading us back down to the house of nowhere
and everywhere   an utterly demolished life

2

the thousand-part encyclopaedia of the waves hammers the sentences in
    stones have deleted the choir
    no poetry that isn't cruel

    to finish its interview with the poet
cold   flows in clots from snow-white skin
briars   drag out winter's questioning

    always picked clean by the very last line
the carcass   is always the nest where chicks cannot hatch
reflection of the sea on a morning wall

let word and word in full view bury a man below ground
nothing's left but the poem's black cloud
who   is eaten up piecemeal by his writing

like an invalid   leaks out in the brooding of his illness
the autobiography of death   embraces the dead in the sky
no beauty that isn't cruel

no poet's finger not sawn away
calmly burning   setting sun between white pages
speaking out   unspeakable fear

3

at some address   kids slice open a pomegranate
some address   imagines kids as
eyes   white nuts in flesh
blood   chirping bird congealed into glass
half a body twisting invisibly in the hands
and chewed-up pink jelly smeared on the teeth
death   kids have seen

what forgets us and what is pitilessly restored by forgetting
lamplight abstracted from a city at dusk
is again   but never for the last time

what strips us of direction and what is stripped by too many directions
blue   always unfurled in the heights of the head
blackening in a stare
must always have somewhere for vain hope to sortie out
to let the words that make addresses   get used to the pustulence of the crowd

blank   in the eye-socket
only in symmetry with
the sea   shapeless beneath blind men's hands
some address is assigned to plant silvery perfumed bones
to strip away our depths
kids   almonds roasted by the seasons
become every
imagination   denied by being seen
inspired by destruction
the pomegranate   is wrapped in blue calcified pips
the sea never yet slapped beyond solitude
never yet had another   shatter below the cliff
we hear ourselves   fall elsewhere and shatter

no sea that doesn't slip into the void of the poem
kids sliced by long-dead light   stand still   this shore
is where we see ourselves set sail

[BH]

ZHAI YONGMING (*b.* 1955)

Jing An Village, June

Moonless night – the wind is high and boys practise killing.
Desire stirs in the wild wheatfield –
I can smell the drunkenness of the village.

For half a year I stare at the moon
until this twisted body of mine melts
and the spinning moon is a rusted hinge.
Everybody is drinking, having fun – no one
notices me. At the garbage heap
I can feel an echo from the very heart of the earth.

A dusty farmer touches a fissure
in the old ebony table.
I think of legends from the great dynasties.
Tonight there'll be a lunar eclipse
and the farmer's wife will take a bath,
her eyes full of blind fear.

The veiled sky shivers and shapeshifts.
In the graveyard where ancestors lie
the baked mud walls crack open with dead eyes.
At dawn, tomb diggers will find
the coffins crawling with termites.
My body – all the bodies we are born with
decay in the dark and the light.

[Pascale Petit & Zhai Yongming]

GU CHENG (1956-93)

Ghosts Enter the City
Eight poems

The ghosts
of midnight
walk carefully along
afraid to fall on their heads
and change
into men

Monday

Ghosts are fine folk
they sleep   then awake
they scan bulletins   go for a swim
standing high on the water
swimming out of a stream of gold from the earth
flip fish   flip head over heels   blow on weeping bottles of wine
they like to watch things up above
and to catch, all at once, the golden

leaves

Ghosts too can sometimes read: 'Indeed, they're well informed'
then place their hands underneath the document
'This old rose beside the river'
they say in unison   exhaling a cloud of smoky mist
at dusk people say
'It's time to go home'

Along the road the streetlights cast shadows
the ghosts don't speak   the wind blows through the streets
writing at the station   grazing   faces turning grey
a gust of wind rolls the mist away

Tuesday

Ghosts see people
with closed eyes   but not
with them open

A giggling kite
sometimes seen in a dream
now along the rail of the balcony
it falls   the ghost goes carefully down
and all through the hallway nothing but laughing

                                               kites

'Half for you   half for the others'
he unfolds clothes
looking inside   no one's there   he unfolds some more
a short blue skirt
'The   hospital   sala   slips into the water'
      fifth   room   mander
                he's surprised
      to see a large red fish staring back at him

The fish is now sick   written on a sign
the fish slowly opens his sweaty palm

Wednesday

Into the city on Wednesday
the ghost thought for a long while
                      with a
'crunch', he stepped on his own shadow
discovering he had punched a gaping hole
popcorn kept tumbling down
      adults five cents   children three
      just two for the little ones

Hastily the ghost squatted down mending his clothes
and mending the road
with a 'crunch'   someone else punched a gaping hole
      the sound of singing surged upward

never to hear again the news of Jing Chunchun [65]
everywhere they erupted into parade
the prince began to bring in his winter garments
you stood on the bridge
                        beyond the moving cars, trains stop
'the metadefinition of affection is
in the very beginning I wanted to fight'
                        children
throw bottles here, there and everywhere

Thursday

The ghosts judge   the ballpoint pen
        twirling flowers
        three cents for a blossom

The ballpoint pen twirls around some adults
spinning them   into a round ball
then eating them
                    she changed her name so there was no trace
the ballpoint pen ate one word   and wrote again

        Surname   Single
        first name   Full Lips
        the volcano is cold   it comes from the North
it won't do to just babble on, blah blah blah
one person spits out another   the tall get to talk

'Just three minutes left until the flowers blossom'
who asks   the air gradually becomes transparent
Someone   in the study is piling wash-
ing   off with the collar
the brush strokes are becoming even fewer and the more
one paints   the fewer the hairs on the ghost's head

65. A childhood friend who disappeared during the 1989 Tiananmen inci-
dent.

Friday

(He gets worse and worse)
       pushing people   up the glass
       the ghost retreats
people, however, turn into pancakes
with mouths and faces   he dares not ask if he himself
has fallen   raised mouth, seeing the licence plate on the side
the ghost reads
       one horse
       five clouds   five soldiers

Sandwiched in a book a horse yelps   at the same time he noticed
the square-jawed writer and the fluffy brain above

     Five horses   five soldiers
           walking back   making
  the balance   balanced   **to balance**   five armies
    (so hopeless, wherever he goes)

That's a chess set from the north
grapes wither   soldiers are heroic   flowers flourish
the first time he broadcast the news programme was in the movies

Saturday

The ghost
is in the movies again
              Popcorn Revolution   that's the title
people beat up on him
he says   be brigade leader, be division commander, that's fine
        but not commandant of the army   that's for me to be
        don't try and deceive me
        a troop of soldiers is passing out gifts on the ground
        everybody knows   when the red plum blossoms
        changing from green to red, she is on the other side
        needing someone   needing to need negotiation
        why is the flower so   red?

First: register for marriage
    if you change your name, change your nickname   with a pen
second: students lift their benches   into the sky
    thrown   but not thrown like this
    we need three to stand on benches and throw ropes into the   sky
    thrown well they can be kites

Third: giggling
with a laugh   the director fills the air with enfolding mists

Sunday

'The dead are the beautiful people'   after saying so, the ghost
looked into the mirror   and he was actually only seven inches tall
    he was pressed down by a pile of glass   the glass
                    brushed clean
'The dead are all pretty'   like
            glass without shadows
                white projection screen   lit by lights
                passing through the slides   layer upon layer
the dead are at the emergency door
a huge pile of glass cards

He stuck his finger in one nostril
the light shone   he stuck it in the other
shadows cast by the light, the city disappears from sight
– she still cannot see –
you can hear the sound of bricks falling to the ground
the ghost is very clear
the dead make the air tremble

there are stars far away   and farther still
there are stars still   only after a long while
did he know there was a transparent poplar above the chimney?

Spring Festival Day

The ghost doesn't want to do the backstroke
                                            bulletin!
the ghost doesn't want to fall on his head
                                            bulletin!
ghosts won't become men   bulletin number seven   ghosts

                                        playing a lute   relaxing
ghost   **ghost**
          no faith   no trust   writes letters   turns on the lights
          no love no hatred   **eyes**
ghost   **all at once**
          no dad   no mom   **open**
          no son   no grandson
ghost
          not dead   not alive   not crazy
                       not stupid   just now the falling rain
                            put in a bowl, one look
                              and he knows those blinking eyes
              ghosts swim under water
                                        seeping through the deep
              the conclusion is
only on the diving board does the ghost fall from grace

[Joseph R. Allen]

66. (*See opposite page.*) It's not necessary to distinguish in Chinese whether this is a translation of the place name Unter den Linden, or just 'Under the Linden Tree' (or 'Trees'), or indeed 'Under the Bodhi Tree' (or 'Trees'). The linden shares its Chinese name with the pipal or bo tree (*Ficus religiosa*) under which the Buddha achieved enlightenment.

67. An allusion to the wicked last emperor of the Shang dynasty, Shang Zhou (*c.* 1046 BC), who is said to have had a lake filled with alcohol, in the middle of which was an island adorned with skewers of roasted meat – the famous Wine Lake and Flesh Forest, a symbol of decadent excess.

XIAO KAIYU (*b*. 1960)

Under den Linden[66]

> But how sly the breezes of spring –
> a mess of blowing, a mess of falling, a mess of wet mud
>
> Jin Nong (1687–*c*. 1763 AD)
> 'The Book of Talent, Painting and Daftness'

1

Just like in poetry, the rain starts to fall on
time, but it's not as light as in a poem,
it's instantly heavy, loaded with violence. I cross the street quickly,
draw in under the linden trees' long avenue.
Drops of water (joy!) have unpeeled the high-altitude cold,
tears start from eyes. Middle-school bombshells
are so soft and delicate in the haze. I never thought there'd be
another bruise stuck to the Brandenburg Gate,
another Chinese plaster on the Flesh Forest.[67]

2

For a long time, since the 30th of last month, I've been
content with tranquility and anticipation of this flood peak of crowds
(oh, crowds). In that time the trees in the yard have
exuded a soporific green god, a Pluto for the household,
and a convict girl with her head half-shaven. Whoever arrives,
ah, her liquid hand will wash their body all over
with a perfumed soap, while a good natured Swiss
comes to report on the floods in the Yangtze delta (now and hereafter),
she brings in sheaves of umbrellas to my empty house.

3

Whether talking or shouting, no one hears;
mouths are shut, yet strange sounds come out –
sounds of whistling, cursing, screaming. Imploring, praising,
mumbling with no significance at all, and sirens too...
how harmonious it is, joined in concord with the thunder.
From Unter den Linden to Strasse des 17. Juni
it's become a living moving wall: you can see kids'
shadows, kids flying in the air, oh, little mums and dads
giving birth all night long in front of the Adlon Hotel.

4

I sit at the windowsill, indicating that
a female Hui Neng can slap me on the head.[68] Sixteen years ago
I looked everywhere for direction. For the sake of the future,
we practised staying still, Hope and I:
he told me, I didn't tell him.
I escaped from home, and in the end stitched together a new home.
There were still sutras hidden in the fridge. Our quarreling
confirmed that everything was wrong. We were looking forward to
one rare flower, a gift to thank us for all our fear.

5

They are on the lorries, their bodies cover
the parliament building's unfinished dome.
She's the sweetest of the students: catch the moment before parting,
catch the moment, before parting, before someone else does.
It's reached the point where, between the gongs and the drums, I hear
the soft sound of her navel. I even hear
a nameless person come running over,
maybe a young lad, maybe with a knife tattoo, maybe something
        achingly sad,
maybe something easily-digested, caught up right in front.

6

I waited on the windowsill until this morning,
the storm followed in the lightning's footsteps, the thunderclaps' paces
obituarised the Yangtze's broken dikes. The little temple I want to
        live in –
a bubble in the slurry. I get to the hall,
can't find a raincoat, carry the bike
down to the basement, floodwater follows me in.
Oh, that village kid is so like me, standing
on a mountaintop in Jiujiang in the newspaper
watching the sudden vastness, so huge, so lost, and so hazy…

68. Hui Neng (638-713 AD) the Sixth and last Patriarch of the Chan school
of Buddhism; the slap on the head is still used as a teaching tool (as it is in
Japan, where *Zen* is the Japanese pronunciation of the Chinese *Chan*).

69. (*See opposite page.*) Tao Yuanming (365-427 AD), poet, first in a long
tradition of scholarly recluses, and Hui Yuan (334-416 AD), founder of the
Pure Land school of Buddhism: both lived in the area of Mount Lu.

7

...one, two, three policemen,
undressing. Kids kneeling down.
The gale cheers the storm on. Stiff penises
knock, knock against trumpets, music drip-
drips with blood – twelve, thirteen-year-olds' music;
one, two, three o'clock blood. Three or four pimples, planted on me
by the news. Put on a pair of cow's horns,
wear a little golden moustache –
my friend is here, the news from Beijing in his pocket.

8

It wasn't in Beijing, but on a south-facing slope
in Sichuan, a broken dam
in Zhejiang. I escaped from our conversation
to Jiangxi, to a yard two or three miles
from some village. Then the bloodsucking bugs of Poyang Lake
drove me to southern Anhui, far from Mount Lu,
from the clouds of Master Tao and Hui Yuan.[69] A woman threw me
          and my room
into the marinade of sea-stink from the Kowloon Hill nuclear power
          station.
Now where will I put my house?

9

Carnival on the main street, and again it lacks
Beijing-style pain: up ahead you can go to
the statue of Victory (wine bottles and bodies mercilessly
smashed, as if the Franco-Prussian War had started again), back this way
you can go to Unter den Linden, find a coffee house.
The rain still squeezes out thunder, still stuck between naked buttocks,
When all's said and done, to look back is quick, to feel quicker still.
One drink of coffee and the street goes quiet, flat and straight as a
          woman's belt:
the few people drip rain as if they're looking for love.

10

Oh, all our plans give off a delicate perfume.
You come to the kitchen, sit down, I make tea.
They come to much the same thing, those plans, though difference
          was our only intent;

285

and the grave, those rebellions of ours, are utterly without meaning.
Worrying about chopping lettuce; being shy about
swimming naked – utterly without meaning. I paint a room,
and what I promise myself is less than I'd get from a painting of a
        beggar;
the sense of guilt I get from listening to a trial
is less than the sense of comfort. But the guilt still grows and grows.

7 August 1998, Berlin   [BH, WNH]

CHEN DONGDONG (*b.* 1961)

Deprohibited Book

1 *Reflecting the Light*

... falling fast from the heights of a million storm clouds –
                        opposite new Shanghai
will the supersonic lift bring down a new snow-
                        fall? a new kind of hardship?
a new toothpick–chewing horror movie hero?
                        a new nationalist?
a new cartoon fan? or fate, that metaphysical, unfathomable
                        new decree? when nimbly it

collides with the earth, here, the old world,
                        not necessarily unperceived –
Earth gave me another little tremble, like
                        great waves, like a dream's deciding
to approach the daybreak. the western bank's great marble embankment
        is solid,
                        but the old city it shelters
still can't avoid the shock of waking...the quadrangle

                        is slapped...
the quadrangle faces the future across the river. – now that bunch there
                        can perhaps fly down, here
in the dawn light the lift girl whose charms are diluted

assiduously rises upwards, taking me to
pluck the constellations. – after climbing past Seventh Heaven, on the
roof terrace's

high-pressure pump paradise, I know

I'm placed in the middle of a contemporary mirror-image. the curtain-
glass towers

sky-scrapingly modern, from all ten
directions crowd me, engulf me. (...the quadrangle is

overlooked...)
– in ten reflections around me, in the lookout pose

I'm nearly accustomed to, once again I'm
back in my old shape, going round and round the vast asphalt spirals,
pacing –

oh, running, hoping to reach as soon as I can
the utopia of writing, a forbidden zone of early morning altitude chill

between the clear spacious tools of purgatory's
mountaintop peaks. I once had a black desk there,

there was a dictionary, and a pair of
binoculars. yet as I sat down in front of those things,

a cave screamed,

in the dark depths of the quadrangle, distortion mirrors memory's maybes

2 *Quadrangle*

It presents a simplified spiral to the sky, as it stands completed on the
city's triangular river island.

Door lintel supported by six columns, it faces out over Suzhou
Creek. The heavy stone ornaments on the lintel are ambiguous, with
the appearance of either a pair of beautiful but weary women, or a
double wave neatly bent in two. Underneath, the great bronze doors
open wide to the steamboats on the river, and Odysseus sitting calmly
in the bows would find that this building, so unassuming on the out-
side, is filled with fierce sunlight inside. Once through the abstruse
arched lobby, he will see a supercilious caryatid gleaming in the dead
centre of the atrium.

As far as the exterior is concerned, we might also mention that
these courses of crudely finished stone reach all the way up from the
ground to the seventh floor. The external windows are narrow and

fitted with black iron grilles. These give it the look of a prison, or a breathless, callused asthmatic. But it's not like that in reality. On another surface, the internal faces of the quadrangle, huge panes of clear glass from basement to seventh floor reflect the sun above in a cloudless sky, the sun at the head of its noon table. The atrium formed by the quadrangle's embrace is generously-proportioned, to the extent that it can hardly be called an atrium – because that tall caryatid pillar has been jokingly dubbed the Inner Penis Plaza. This is why the gender of the block is unclear. Standing in that Inner Caryatid Penis Plaza, looking out through the oval-steel-framed windows at the other end of the lobby, you can see the Huangpu River the building backs onto, a busy river scene. The little playgrounds that have recently begun to line the riverbank. A sign – definitely not a rumour – whose inscription warns Dogs & Chinese Not Permitted. Bicycles are Not Permitted either.

From ground level to seventh floor, like entwined railway carriages leaning on the outside of the quadrangle, there are many doors linking huge dark offices. Just push open the door of one more room and you can reach the inside of the quadrangle, and the annular corridors that thirstily drink in the sunlight. Sometimes, standing at the western end of the sixth floor corridor, a monocled German will notice that, in a corner of the fourth floor southern corridor, a dark Indian janitor is *flirting* with a British accountant and a skinny old maid.

It is one product of those foreign firms who competed to build the tallest tower on the beachhead of this city. The marble floor of the Inner Penis Plaza covers a bank vault packed full of stashed gold bars, silver dollars, pounds sterling and opium. Government boats are berthed by its doors, and there are parked carriages and vintage cars in front; drifting through its lobbies, staircases, corridors and rooms, always the mingled aromas of eau-de-cologne, cigar smoke, perspiration, copper coins, body odour, leather, onions and printing ink; going in and out through all of this are the swaddled in tweed jacket and fur coat, the zucchetti-crowned, the walking-stick supported, the silk mandarin jacket-encased, the Oxford shoe-wearing, the crocodile-briefcase-underarm, the side-parting-combed, the hunch-backed, the straight-backed, the pert-breasted girlfriend-cuddled, and the deliverers of battlefield communiqués. On each and every writing-desk, in every circle of lamplight, in the depths of drawers, inside strongboxes, under brass paperweights, beside telephones and in secretaries' armpits, are the bank cheques, ledger accounts, handwritten originals, unbound duplicates, market prices and market statistics, private correspondence, inbound company mail, petty cash and diaries. These are the sort of sounds to be normally heard: one or two dry coughs, one or two dry laughs, Handle-With-Care footsteps, hoarse whispered conversations, the click of abacus beads, and in addition, amid the sudden thunderclap of feet stamping in rage, the crack of a left hand smacking a comprador's face.

And then, or perhaps at the same time, on Suzhou Creek and the Huangpu River, in the increasing stench, the blackening and the high tides, the shore roads have sunk beneath the horizon of these two filthy streams. Exploring the embankment are alder shoots, solitary yellow streetlights and the upward-turning pigtails of the trams. As if bidding farewell to legendary times, a youngest son, newly set out from his father's generation's airline, has flown by, flapping arced wings of feathers, linen thread and beeswax. Three times he circles around the quadrangle, and afterwards whips out to the mouth of the Huangpu at Wusongkou, to vanish into the Pacific Ocean.

3 *Self-portrait*

anti-popular transformation: Icarus' defeated spirit turned into
the Jingwei bird that tries to fill the sea with pebbles...to biting
          carpentry in a dream...
Shanghai's sprawl is barbaric amongst all this – facing unlimited
          expansion,
it has shrunk the now of the world that writing can't contact.
it's exactly the now, the new whirlwind rocking the old quadrangle
          from all directions,
opening the cave that controlled sinkings. after it has whistled, a
radiant silence, it's a trap, it's the eye of the storm –

it's the suspended wake-up call from the bell of nothingness,

but you are woken in another quadrangle – the shrill klaxon
subtracting another day from every confinement, making me, so reliant
          on dream
journeys to go on living, only a prisoner of your body, as always. On
          the winding
corridor, precise as a dial, the green–clad custodian is daybreak law &
          order, is
a dizzying iron vortex that drags you from dark to the burning
          temptation of dark.
...you're dashed at the gutter at the far end of the cell
...you're bent over the freezing river of bleach...you see you...

the non-existent face-shape already frozen in the clamouring cold –
        and deep

in the face's shape, a funerary lamp is hanging lonely.
– more illusory than the abstract concreteness in
the circulation, a high window that doubles as water outlet, making
        you unable to guess
the structure of the lower world outside the high window, if it's the
        quadrangle
superimposed on another quadrangle, like the detention centre I'm in,
        like
time, like the steel barriers and barriers you sit so bored behind,
as you take the whole morning to set the chessmen in carefully
        interlocking rings –

both kinds of unreality play chess with the possible.

the unreality of desire will make you grow staring arms, gazing
hands, till you take a pale-smeared moon and from outside the high
        window
you enfold it in the needy embrace called 'me'; that destined unreality
        has a box of
tapes, and it has a cassette recorder, and it will make you listen to
me taped whole and entire, and moreover, there's no way to wipe them,
– they've been gone over. but, as a shaft of sunlight shoots through
the quadrangle's interlocked set of quadrangles, reflecting off the
        gutter –

that dark, deep, skimmed-over daydream seems in the act of parachuting,

about to take me from a suspended you and fix me in a distinct
you. – Earth gave me
                                another little tremble again
in the cavern of the spiral structure of that jail, an iron vortex
restrains the raging roars...custodian, on his epaulette of daybreak
        law & order
a new star has appeared: he lifts you above the exercise terrace,
personally opens for you the seven forbidden locks, he forces you to
        submit, like evil –

he signs each and every imagined offence with nothingness's name.

the shrill klaxon is confiscated by the new whirlwind. a fabricated me
comes out its aperture, able to suppress, like vomit, the nausea of
       gradual liberation,
to become a you of another sort. – however,
Icarus can only in fact become that mythical Jingwei bird: if you walk
       into
the old quadrangle, step into the old lift and slowly rise to the heavens...
you will be tenderly loved by the lift girl, chewing a toothpick you
       will fill her
cavern of sorrow and resentment in Shanghai's diluted charm –

experience death in the false resurrection fixed by rules & regulations,
       broad daylight

levitating voidness, the ten-faced mirror like a hermit besieged!
she'll take you up to a time of calm, you know what you want
is not really paradise – you, you want more to sit so bored
in my invisibility, leaning over the black desk...on paper,
who knows but in the ugliness of the lift girl's curvaceous waistline
you will describe it all over again in writing, and you will even outline
– the darkness that's brought by those punishment-seeking funerary
       lamps.

4 *Noon*

rays of light add to the Caryatid Penis's
perpendicularity. in an overseas phone call
the former owner brought up the quadrangle's past.
the radio under the skylight broadcasts
extra time from an on-going football match.

from inside my mirror image, I can nearly escape from my body.
between her breasts, I once had
extra activity. I once had a kind of
limited freedom: let every line of new verse
pawn noon's incandescing rhymes.

on the roof terrace the high-pressure pumps are droning.
the sun climbs to its zenith from the opposite riverbank.
the decision I hear is maybe a fair one:
never mind the red-carded players,
give the finger to the rules and say Fuck You!

in the instrument room she echoes Fuck You!
as my middle finger has slipped past her
 caesarean scar, she squirms with pleasure,
like the concurrent world sloughing off its shell,
to emerge for – the forbidden writer who

isn't necessarily staying solitary and silent. in the overseas
call, a tropical rainforest is in an uproar, an
old hand in the middle of telling all things
to rely on yourself. there's very likely a sound of
whistling at the final curtain, the radio giggling...

the sniping match's telescope shifts its direction,
another destiny in its sights: one
supersonic reaction, one free fall...
magnified hope on the other riverbank so
close you could touch it – if the language I

use is poetry, is an exposed organ, isn't wearing
a condom, it is this noon, it is noon's burning
sun, melting the quadrangle down into my hopes
like observation and meditation. there's the crime,
faith, the metaphysical & unfathomable True Way, and hovering in
        the air –
scattered through a closed dictionary.

5 *Take-off as ritual*

From the superposed quadrangles to the suburban airport is a distance
of over thirty kilometres. To be certain you won't be late, that you
will be able to board the flight you want, and that you will get on that
supersonic plane, you've overdone it just a tiny bit: you set off three
hours in advance – that's to say, you want your departure-related
activities to last for three hours. Your luggage is simple: one arch-top
suitcase with pull-out handle and three bakelite wheels, the dark blue
of its brand new material a shade lighter than your coat. When we
say colours are *dark* or *light*, is that metaphor? Or maybe it should be
classed as a simile. As you wait for the air-conditioned airport coach
(the 505) you're thinking of a pamphlet you saw that time you were a
prisoner. If we didn't say *light* or *dark*, then how could we compare or
differentiate between the two similar but distinct colours of suitcase

and prison clothing? Because you knew there was plenty of time, permitting yourself to not go because the coach hadn't arrived would have made you seem apprehensive, anxious, and if *plenty* is used of time, doesn't it mean something? But *meaning* on the other hand is time being bored. Maybe someone seeing you off is even more boring. You did once have a faint thought of that sort, but you're already seated on board the 505 now. For those who set out much too early, the one doing the seeing-off is just dispelling boredom. Your departure, though, has never included someone seeing you off, you have always turned down the seeing-off at departure. Even though seeing-off can dispel boredom, seeing-off is in and of itself more boring still. The 505 is fast and smooth. You shift your attention outside the coach window, realising that you're going all the way across this city, that you're right in the middle of your ritual of de-prohibition. And the post offices, schools, opticians, cinemas, restaurants and zoos you pass have all once been the destinations of your desires. As your desires get remoter and larger, the termini of your past are included in your departure. The 505 enters a residential area, and rapidly and crudely you size up every little roadside villa, the picture woven into the carpet of your brain an endless succession of rubbish mountains, one after another. That view is one from many years ago, for sure, of the flight you're about to begin. So maybe it's a much earlier arrangement. Into your field of view come a golf course, then a weather station, then a tractor pulling a load of bricks. Oddly, you think of your father, Daedalus. A plane appears on the horizon, conclusively proving that you've made yourself leave much too early. The 505 slows down a little to negotiate the airport concourse, and stops in a dark alley behind two quadrangles. At the moment you grab your arch-top suitcase to get off, you still haven't seen your travelling companion. She really should be standing underneath that orange bus stop sign, beside her a suitcase a shade lighter than your dark blue coat. From the suitcase she will take the plane tickets and put them in your hand. Then you two will cross the concourse's autumn sunset and walk through the portico of the Departure Hall. You both enter through the rusty iron door. You are not carrying her dark blue arch-top suitcase for her. You walk on the right. In the diagonal slash pocket of your coat of a darker blue, your left hand fingers a plane ticket. Once through the enormous glass screen of the main hall, you notice that not only has night risen, it has also gathered at an altitude of thousands of kilometres above the vaulted roof. Night is rising, not falling, as people usually say: this is a recent, important and unexpected discovery by a certain poet. But you think as you step on to the escalator, when earlier poets said night was falling, or night was coming on, weren't they also trying to convey the poetic truth of the world as they discovered it? Your travelling companion has also stepped on to the aluminium alloy escalator, and at this moment maybe, looking up to see the time of day, she notices a plane sweeping by, looking twice as huge because it's refracted in the glass screen. But the Departure Hall is looking like some crystal undersea palace out of a legend, utterly unmoving despite the howling of the planes. Because of its mysterious stability, because of the rapid revolutions within its mysterious stability, the two of you step from the escalator to the red mirror-tiles of the first floor, to see there are already people in long queues in front of all the check-in counters that process boarding passes. You feel a touch of waiting's drab insipidity. Your travelling companion, more in the mood to enjoy herself, is looking right and left at the décor and the lighting effects, as well as looking for the possibility of there being a cartoon fan, a new horror movie hero, or a new nationalist in the crowd. It ought to be said that you are her travelling companion. You pass through security, where your metal card-case has caused you a little hassle in the past. Before she sits down in the high-backed plastic seats where you wait to be summoned to the plane, she phones her family. On the big screens, all the arrivals and departures are scrolling by, but in particular, it's the voice of the PA announcer dyeing the air lake-green that gets you the tiniest bit excited, that makes you think back and compare it to the shrill klaxons at dawn that began every day in the detention centre. You're on the point of being moved by a kind of autumn evening melancholy, and what the announcer sets off in you needs no great billowing waves, then it's as if it's remotely sensing you, giving you a so-called 'physical excitement'. Well, you stand up, step forward, and embrace her. This sort of surprises you and her both. As you open a notebook in an economy class window seat, you're about to record your departure with her on this night flight, but you don't know how to describe it. Maybe you should write in an interrogative tone, but it's hard to say whether satire might not be a better strategy. You've heard that satire is a recent advance made by poets in these last few years, but is that not because their attitude to their destiny is a cold one? She's sitting beside you, leaning towards you. Her breast presses on the notebook that lies open in your lap, her face is pressed to the window. The night scene she sees is the same one you see: the main hall with its glass screen is a fair distance away now, but it's still a huge piece of finely-crafted artifice. Twenty years ago, you described the starry sky above it as being a cloisonné leopard, and right now it could be so described once again. You reach into the glory of her splendid silk shirt to fondle her back, smooth as the night sky. The plane has begun its slow taxi. As it gathers speed, you calm down. The little pain behind your eardrum becomes silent, remote. The 'I' in your heart leaps forward, expecting to fall. In one evening, you and she have taken off.

1996-1999 [BH]

ZHANG ZAO (1962-2010)

Conversations with Tsvetaeva
A Sequence of Sonnets

> 'C'est un chinois, çe sera long'
>
> Tsvetaeva

1

Black eyes disclose a smile for you, affectionate,
I try to peddle you an embroidered wallet,
kingfisher blue outside, with such exquisite phoenixes,
and in gold thread the lucky 'double happinesses' –
Two? *Nyet*, two francs fifty. See, how
the fifty difference makes a bad rhyme now;
like us both stepping off to walk on each pavement,
and yet again you can't understand my southern accent;
waiting for the lights to turn into the green anchorite,
you keep on left, and I, I go stumbling to the right.
It's not me, but suddenly towards me, someone
hair flying, rushes towards you, raising a hand,

some kind of thing, not foliage, but like foliage,
has passed into the tender hush of your theatre loge.

2

Every day, I dream of *Immemorial Tristesse*.[70] Drifting clouds of white,
Marlene, and you're brewing a pot of your private coffee,
lump sugar beyond the blue of near sight distantly guilty
like a houseboy. He longs for the big issues of wrong and right.
Doing a job, like a craft, the result of poetry
is a series of still-lives, in human symmetry,
maybe even usable? But its restraint can't surpass
the pair of brackets that shadow two lovers. The looking-glass
can do poetry too, if anyone wants it, but he must, to be frank,
guard against its habits of confuddling left side and right flank,
the two fronts face to face, bickering over some angry pretext,
while white and red duel over the word *not*. Someone, perplexed

sees themselves in the mirror, the revolution's houseboy home from
         banishment;
finely ground, suddenly devoid of people, the coffee drops in
         astonishment.

    3

…as usual, I bury my head in an empty tumbler;
you're done for; as it looks for grave-clothes, the future
gets rid of the afternoon with fragments stretched tight.
Russia's done for – a negative from the era of black and white,
a bass voice: Good morning, sir, you high-school mite:
ah – let's go – oh, come in – so cry, then – all right?
The masked ball of titles, R, trembling after the pronoun's said,
motor-like revs secret treaties, birch forests and kisses of red.
Paris is done for as well.
                    I'm sat here under an umbrell-
a, looking round and working. A new library is being constructed,
flower gardens and glass bookstands set into it.

People, they're done for too, if-words everyone's vade mecum,
not like the butterfly, terrifying the veins of the blossom.

70. By Gui Zhuang (1613-73 AD), a lament for times gone by, written at
the very beginning of the Qing Dynasty (1644-1911 AD). The Ming Dynasty
(1368-1644 AD) was the last native Chinese dynasty: the Manchu were related
to the Mongols, and so foreigners. This was a large genre, the lament for the
old ways.

4

Our eyelashes, how come they jump for joy in the alien corn?
We're nervy, routed, unable to invest in how it all looks.
The mother-tongue boat is cast away on a boundless bourn,
going ashore, I'm on foot outside myself, the letterbox
opens like a Trojan horse, empty words swarm,
cover over the bleakest of frosts for the early morn;
unfamiliarly, on the gas stove the snake kidney prances,
the waning moon in exile disperses the misery of your menses,
mum, Cassandra, professional prophet of your folk,
they forced your silhouette to inhale foreign smoke,
but sunlight, its worst penalties are still unrolling, so:
the more precise the birds, the less serious the people, though

a sheet of paper crackles in the fire, vanishes in a gale,
the actual soul escaping life young – ash, it's history's tale.

5

Sunshine can occasionally be a wolf, too, strolling farther
across the land, as shadow sucks the olive pits of remembering:
those are gods, giving your mouth the aftertaste of the lather
of sex, rendering you useless, the box of foretelling
powerless to take on a cargo of zombies,
bathing at this beach ruled by dazzled blindness.
To see means to speak it out, and say it really is the sea,
at this instant. Round. See epilepsy. See.

Life, where? 'Hector, I see you sitting
in a million pairs of eyes, in a trance, sobbing' –
you stand here, but your corpse has long since paled. Once again
you go back outside, the hero invisible early, and all that will remain

will be an inhuman thug and a cola bottle, the flesh's body-building,
spare parts of lobster-like ferocity, magnifying what's coming.

6

Cherry, bright red, as if you're waiting for the homecoming of someone.
some things, I want to go and get. Afternoon
I sat and sat, then went to sleep, my ears just dead done,
I agreed to go somewhere else to bring back a book in Russian.
You sat in your own dispersing hair, a skylark for your helmet.

Pen, it's warm because it's looked-for. Far off, visitors.
In my dream your hand is dripping broken fingers,
I want to go and get them: people, train, trumpet;

Cherry, bright red, the pure logic of waiting,
palpitatingly I calculate the time I have left for doubt,
there's no you, how the motherland's windows are emptying.
Breathe. I'll go and get them, new words to lead you home like trout;

you go and get them, the little rascals in the door lock are spewing out
          static –
it hurts, but the startled choir is soaring on high, insulated and perfect.

          7

You're back in Moscow, your requests refused so rudely,
but life's stumbles also equal poetry's stumbles exactly.
On Old Year's Night the crow's children, in all their finery,
wait for the bells, but they have to disperse: the times are awry.
The telephone operator reclines in stretcher-bearing scenery,
the real arrives late again as the Writers' Association number rings on
          emptily:
this one dead, this one gone mad, complaining, complaining,
as the long-legged mosquito of complaint buzzes its air-raid warning.
Perfect, oh, perfect, you always have to suffer
a short-term but golden-voiced line manager,
a sentence-reading (Pekinese) lapdog, sometimes saying this
has got too long, sometimes saying how naïve your thinking is,

as rooftop colleagues shout *fire!* after the fact, they haltingly race
over with congratulations, come to taste death's door slamming in your
          face.

          8

          'Wenn du mich wirklich sehen willst, so mußt du handeln!'
          Tsvetaeva to Rilke

The east turns white, a classical act coming to its conclusion:
two lovers, one to the left and one to the right, part-human and
          part-demon,
the tangerine of heart speaking to heart rips the fragrance of their prose,
it's love deep inside, a tranquil flesh-and-blood rose.

Craftsmanship is touch, however distant your separation;
the possibility of impossibility is the name of your habitation –
you softly speak of these things as I am yearning
to carry you on the dawn breeze to your home that is burning:
words, they're not things, this being the point that must be made clear,
and so it becomes necessary to live a life that has interest and allure,
like this moment – magnolias exuberantly independent, confessing
the alarm is over, like the hair of lovers drifting and falling.

The east turns white, inside your name you vanish away,
afforested flocks of birds sing in chorus: beware of the sky.

9

People can't explain the things that are all around them, can they?
Like how come the visible razor blade can snatch the soul away?
What connects the two? Rope, cobblestone, knife,
self, every little thing, these can all demand a life,
the man-made world is an unmitigated enemy,
vacant flower-shadows angrily cheer the walls of the room,
frightening you. It's not other people, I always presume,
even less you yourself, who cross out your body,
but it's those articles like coil springs, scuttling out there,
that shut down the lodgings of the eyes, forcing
you to shout: *Outside, oh, outside, always elsewhere!*
Even death is only joining up the parts of this aimless drifting.

Who's fiddling with the up and down buttons of the rootless lift?
Most of all I'm afraid that the self is the self's one and only exit.

10

I take off my glasses, wishing to be an interpreter for the deaf and dumb –
children of the universe, stony silence reigns in the auditorium;
the air is reciting this poem, and what it implies is the chance
of blossom being hustled by the butterflies of gesture's dance.
The inside story on reality is that it's another invention:
he's not in this place, this moon's homologation,
he's not in the village pub, just like here and now there is no me –
a glass anonymously sipped, and the scenery
's structure has suddenly changed. In fully loaded time and space,
the drinker crosses the bridge, and he looks back stunned at his face
marooned on the other bank, declaiming a torrent of verse. Some

pity for the world and its ways, and a plan for reform
let his steps be concocted out of all the world's weightlessness.
Oh Your Honour, Sir, look, see, everywhere, the moon shadows ...

11

...yes, Your Honour, the moon is rising before us here,
brightness all around, sir, mountain peaks sticking to your whiskers:
below us, streetlamps in the south of the city reveal the soapy atmosphere,
as, eyes tight shut, at midnight a Living She showers,
her blinds twitter with hand-shadows, she shampoos like she's at prayer,
turns round, is hidden in the dark, then the fridge blinks open;
forever like a wildcat, that hunk from the ads whirls away then
beyond the comets; the ice-cream sky, wisecracks everywhere...
...oh nightingale, right now you're in a different place,
                                        yes, sir, see,
the one who wasn't playing piano is also strumming,
a homeless wanderer, always going back, always returning:
neither much nor little, just happening to echo *Immemorial Tristesse* –
hey, Your Honour, tell me, how come cassia trees that are out of sight
are folded into our thoughts, stimulating the sequence of the night?

12

Can it really be a goodbye, September?
Your gaze, it decorates and furnishes some new interior:
a bronze figurine is this way, a swivel chair that way, leaves falling,
the girlfriend of this fresh, cool cosmos, fearless in all her doing:
right? Right? Eyelashes in chorus closely question
the instant's individual place, is it really right then?
The king, it falls beyond the chessboard; the west wind will blow
the financial arena of the clouds under the window:
noon, an individual person, arriving at the fast-food booth,
depicting the throughway for bread, fingers point to mouth;
Right? Poetry's this way, is the vagrant accordion
that way? Harvest's Katyushas lead me on
to the point I'm at right now: footsteps of the world, oh
halt! Right? How should we say 'No!'?

[BH]

XI CHUAN (*b.* 1963)

Exercises in Thought

Nietzsche said, 'Re-evaluate all values,' so in that case let's re-evaluate the value of this toothbrush. Perhaps the toothbrush isn't a toothbrush? Or perhaps the toothbrush isn't simply a toothbrush? If we refuse to re-evaluate the value of a toothbrush, we are re-evaluating the value of Nietzsche.

Nietzschean thought, when we are in thought, makes us brazen and shameless. But does that mean that we aren't brazenly and shamelessly mimicking the singing of the sparrow, brazenly and shamelessly mimicking the silence of white clouds? Does that mean that we aren't brazenly and shamelessly being brazen and shameless?

At times even if we can't figure out the whithers and wherefores, we still pretend to be in thought, like a fly crawling from one word to another, pretending to be able to understand a poem. Many people pretend to be in thought, which proves that thought is a beautiful thing.

But the bald man doesn't need a comb, the tiger doesn't need weapons, the fool doesn't need thought. The person with no needs is practically a sage, but the sage also needs to go and count great big rivets on an iron bridge as a diversion. This is the difference between the sage and the fool.

Nietzsche said that a person must discover twenty-four truths each day before he can have a good night's sleep. But first of all, a person shouldn't find that many truths, so as not to let the supply of truths in this world exceed demand; secondly, anyone who discovers that many truths would hardly be able to fall asleep at all.

So I guarantee you, Nietzsche never slept; or if he did fall asleep, he was a sleepwalker. A sleepwalker will never meet another sleepwalker. Nietzsche never met God, which is why he declaimed, 'God is dead.'

But did Nietzsche ever meet Wang Guowei? No. Did he meet Lu Xun? No. Did he ever meet brazen and shameless me? Still no. So perhaps this Nietzsche never existed after all, just as the word 'spirit' may mean nothing whatsoever.

Thought is like flying, though flying gives you vertigo, which is why I don't always want to be in thought. Thought is like a bad habit, though bad habits give you the full experience of life's flavour, which is the reason I sometimes want to be in thought.

I demand that turnips, *bok choy*, and I all be in thought together, I demand that chickens and ducks and cows and sheep and I all be in thought together. Thought is a kind of desire, and I demand that all ascetics admit it, and I demand all hedonists recognise it.

Those exercising athletes, they exercise and exercise till they collapse from so much exercise. Those people who see too much, they'd best go blind. To stop being in thought, you'd best think as much as you can. Think until you go stupid, so your incarnation as a person has not been in vain.

The depletion of a person, this was Nietzsche's work. To deplete a person, that is, to make him a superman, that is, to make him pull out all his lightning rods, and moreover to make him stick like a lightning rod out of the earth.

Regarding the principles of thought: 1. To be in thought in the hustle and bustle of the marketplace is one thing, to be in thought beside a stream is something else. 2. Thought isn't an exercise in filling in blanks, thought is making a fresh start. 3. Someone who has thought *ad infinitum*, even if he is a pessimistic cynic, will still clap his hands and laugh, and louder laugh all on his own.

[Lucas Klein]

from **A Sense of Reality**

My Grandma

My grandma coughed, and woke up one thousand roosters.
A thousand roosters crowed and woke up ten thousand people.
Ten thousand people walked out of the village, the roosters still
crowing.
Then the roosters' crowing stopped, but my grandma still coughed.
My grandma, still coughing, talked about her grandma, her voice
       growing dimmer and dimmer
as if my grandma's grandma's voice was growing dimmer and dimmer.
My grandma talked and talked and then stopped, and closed her eyes
as if my grandma's grandma actually died at that moment.

Grandma

Courtyard. A five-hundred-year history. She witnesses ninety-six of
these. She sits on a small bamboo chair in the west wing combing and
combing her hair.

The open door. Her profile. Around her, a brick stove, the pot on
the stove, a table, a bottle of soy sauce on the table, a plastic basket,
cabbage and carrot in the basket,

firewood in the corner. Above the roof of the west wing are white
clouds. Beneath the roof of the west wing are smoke-darkened walls

like a black cotton padded coat that hasn't been washed for ninety-six
years. Ninety-six years have turned her into a piece of land stricken
by a long drought,

only her eyes are wet, wet and opaque, like a well that isn't totally dry.
Ninety six years have made her sink into her body.

All her relatives have become ghosts. As if she was living in the west
wing as the ghosts' representative. Her husband, who was a Kuomintang
battalion commander,

was buried many years ago in the Communists' green mountains. She combs and combs her hair, meticulously, no longer afraid of repeating this simple gesture

over and over again. She has retreated to the bottom line of life, to even lower than this bottom line. Her dirty shoes have stamped the ground even lower than the ground.

She combs and combs, carefully so as to lack meaning, and the flowers are outside the door. She is the flower of those years...

Pei Ling

Later I got to know her name: Pei Ling.
Later she went back to her school to have a nap,
              and I kept on strolling down the street.
We had gone to the sugarcane stall as though by prior agreement.
The two of us, one big one small, together we chewed sugarcane,
together spat the husk of the sugarcane onto the ground
together saw the flies come –
              it turns out that flies are fond of sweet things too.
Then together we ate rice noodles, together ate rice balls,
then the most beautiful schoolgirl in this small town
         asked me where I came from.
I hope she grows up quickly so she can be my girlfriend
         in my old age.

[WNH & Xi Chuan]

4. EXPERIMENTAL POEMS

QIN XIAOYU

Word Square: On Experimental Poetry

The poet Suhui is popularly supposed to have constructed a famous word square in Pre-Qin dynasty times to send to her estranged husband. This square was made up of 29 horizontal lines and 29 vertical lines containing a total of 841 characters. Theoretically, this could be read in any direction and it would produce a text. In the Tang Dynasty, China's only female emperor, Wu Zetian (624-705 AD), tested the theory and discovered more than 200 poems. Then the Song dynasty emperor Gaozong (1107-87 AD, not to be confused with Wu Zetian's husband of the same name), a noted poet, separated it into 10 parts, and found 3,752 poems there. Kang Wanmin, a Ming dynasty scholar, studied it for his whole life, finally believing that he had uncovered 'a profound mystery' (this phrase in Chinese, '*xuan ji*', is a homophone of 'word square'). He put forward a complex theory which involved reading the grid in 12 different directions, adding another 4,206 poems, making a total of 7,958. This piece, created by Suhui to save her unhappy marriage, could be called the first masterpiece of experimental poetry in Chinese history.

The first line of 'X' by Barrett Watten, the US Language school poet, is 'Starting from anywhere...'. Watten is making both a joke and a paradox: you have to begin at his first line to understand that you can start his poem from anywhere. Here 'anywhere' is evidently an exaggeration: readers can start from any sentence of 'X', but can they start from any word or any letter? Suhui's word square, however, achieves this: within it, every character can be the beginning or end of a poem. Within the square are not only hidden about 8000 poems, but also the poet's name, and the title of the whole piece, which gives Suhui's own interpretation of her work: 'Poem without Beginning or End'. This was the ideal of Mallarmé's *Le Livre*, and of Joyce's *Finnegans Wake*, where the last word connects with the first word. This is also the spiritual goal of Yang Lian's *Concentric Circles*, which ends with an incomplete line – the book-length poem simultaneously stops here, and returns to the 'zero' at the beginning of its final section.

During the centuries since its publication there have been many imitations of Suhui's poem, of which the Rhombus Poem by the great Song dynasty poet Su Dongpo (1037-1101 AD), a relative of Suhui, is a very beautiful example. Inspired by this idea of circular poetry, Gu Cheng created a poem called 'Great Qing Dynasty' which, in his own words, has 'a thousand ways to be read'.

The experimental poetry selected for this anthology has some links with US Language Poetry in its foregrounding of language. Charles Bernstein, in his essay 'Artifice of Absorption', pointed out that language should be at the centre of poetry's concern but not as a proxy for things.[71] He developed the important idea of 'anti-absorption'. The artifice of absorption, he argued, is traditional, causing people to focus their attention, immerse and indulge themselves, to believe, be certain and be silent. But 'anti-absorption' disturbs the attention, its aim is to change the subject, break the rule, and counter the tradition, to break down and repel, thereby displaying the independent nature of language.

Language poets tried to break down the wall between poetry and other literary forms, even including non-literature. They intended this to bring a democratic spirit to the act of reading, with readers no longer passively accepting, but becoming interpreters and creative partners in their writing.

They also directed their attention to political usage of language. They saw their works as a direct challenge to existing power structures as these were reflected in language, believing that, under Capitalism, language has been gradually reduced to the level of exchange, sacrificed to a religion of commerce.

Among the experimental pieces gathered in this section of *Jade Ladder*, Yu Jian's 'Zero File' is a conceptual piece that brings together two distant modes of writing, the poem and the file, in just the manner expressed by Wang Pu, a poet born in the 1980s, in his poem, 'Non Poetry': 'Above is a new poem of mine, it's not a poem.'

Language poets intended to fight the monopolisation of poetry by an elite, thinking instead of writing as an invitation to the reader to create meaning. On the other hand, by setting out to disrupt the unity of the narrative voice and the rules of grammar, Language poets confused and alienated their readers.

Gu Cheng's 'Devices' (机关, '*jiguan*') also critiques the centralisation of power. '*Jiguan*' has several dictionary definitions: an intrigue; a mechanism, like a machine gun; the key part of a machine; an office

71. Charles Bernstein, 'Artifice of Absorption' in *A Poetics* (Harvard University Press, 1992).

or department. In autocratic China, these meanings are closely linked. Gu Cheng wrote:

These are your   troops
                    and small boxes
               that would sit, but cannot sit, on the concrete steps
snap!

'Troops' reminds us of Mao Zedong's, 'Power comes from the barrel of a gun'. 'Box' suggests dark rooms and plots. Then the poet refers to concrete steps to indicate an apparently peaceful office is in fact imperious ('steps' in Chinese can be related to class, and when linked to 'troops' carry a connotation of class struggle). 弶 ('*jiang*', trap) is a very strange character, meaning a machine for catching birds. Visually the character is made up of 惊 ('*jing*', scared) and 弓 ('*gong*', bow). Any Chinese person who had lived through the Cultural Revolution would understand the idea of a bird waiting to be picked off. The two final words *single pot* are made up of *single/alone* 只, and 盎 *pot with small mouth and big belly*. So to put them together creates an impression of centralised power. But 只盎 is a word invented by Gu Cheng, and it's impossible to know exactly what it means, rendering it as mysterious as a *Jiguan*.

From this poem, written at the end of 1980s, we can see the experimental aspect of Gu Cheng's writing. '*Jiguan*' is a part of the 'Liquid Mercury' series: he chose this title because one day he realised that: 'Chinese characters are just like plants that grow continually, they are alive, crawling very slowly, they have their own emotions, when you don't pay attention, they can combine themselves and become words, images and stories... Since then, I've given up control of the characters, and let them fall like liquid mercury onto a plate, so, when shaken a bit, they become thousands of little beads.'

Gu Cheng's later concept of Language could be explained by the Zen expression, 'abiding nowhere to give birth to Spirit'. 'Abiding nowhere' means not being attached to anything, therefore being totally free spiritually, able to travel without encountering any obstacles. But this doesn't imply an emptiness like a dead tree or cold ash. 'Abiding nowhere' must 'give birth to Spirit', that is it must let the heart and language, like still water, reflect and therefore include everything. Unlike the resistance of Language poets, Gu Cheng's writing stands apart from autocratic language, gaining its most extreme words and grammar from dreams: 'sometimes I wrote down the sounds I heard in dreams; sometimes the choice of characters didn't require thought;

307

sometimes it required clear thought, which I then translated into characters; sometimes it was, directly, poetry'.

In contrast to Gu Cheng's style, Yang Lian pushes towards the limits of language. He has written: 'I always think Poetry's only theme is language. What the poet is trying to do is settle every layer of thinking onto language, and therefore reach its limit with this energy.' His long poem *Concentric Circles* is built up in five parts, like five carefully constructed circles, developed layer by layer to establish the 'timeless situation of a human being'.

The most ancient picture of the cosmos was the Five Balances Diagram created by the Neolithic Hemudu culture of south-east China. This presented a universe made up of five 'concentric circles' centred on the North Pole. *Concentric Circles* could be seen as Yang Lian's own Five Balances Diagram, which has poetry at its centre. The fifth part is in three sections: 言 'Talking', 土 'Earth', and 寸 'Inch', derived from the three parts of the character 詩 ('*shi*', poetry). Each part then consists of seven poems, echoing the classical form of 7 characters per line, building up a world within each character. This is not simply a language-game, but an attempt to deepen the poem's meditation on this character layer by layer, until the concept of poetry stands out like a rock when the tide recedes.

言 ('*yan*', talk) was the unit of Classical poetry: forms were described according to the number of '*yan*' or characters per line. 'Talking' is engaged by the relationship between 言 ('*yan*', talk/speaking) and 文 ('*wen*', writing). Saussure thought words were the transparent medium of Language, existing only to express Language. But since Chinese characters are not only a symbolic medium, but also represent the inner form of Chinese civilisation, they don't just exist as an independent system, for they deeply influence or even control the language. This is perhaps why linguistics didn't exist in classical China, but the study of characters is found from antiquity.

The characters in the poem 'Sway' appear totally meaningless, but their tonal metrics precisely follow the pattern known as 浪淘沙 ('*langtaosha*', wave-beaten sand), according to the rules which govern the *ci* form. Actually, not all the meaning has been removed, for the flavour as it were of the characters continues to generate atmosphere, so that reading this poem is like watching an abstract painting being created while classical Chinese music is playing.

'Lies' would seem even more difficult to read, as not only are there characters which don't make words and words which don't make sentences, there's even a line made up of over twenty radicals, the constituent parts of characters, which have names, but neither meaning nor sound. 'Lies' doesn't just refer to the language of falsehood, but also to the language of dream. The earliest Chinese dictionary, *Shuowen Jiezi*, defined 'Lie' as 'dream speech'. A lie often follows normal speech but dream speech can throw out logic in favour of nonsense. The Diamond Sutra says 'All conditioned phenomena are like a dream, an illusion, a bubble, a shadow.'

It is significant that 詩 ('*shi*', poetry) is made up of 言 ('*yan*', talk), 土 ('*tu*', earth), and 寸 ('*cun*', inch). Could this ancient character for poetry perhaps suggest 'humans live poetically on the earth'? This has its origins in the Chinese creation story of Nüwa, who created man from the clay, which preserves old agricultural lore. Further, in Chinese, 'earth' originally had the meaning of 'root': in the poem 'Owl', from the *Book of Songs*, we find it used in this sense:

迨天之未阴雨
Before the evening rain began
彻彼桑土
I picked the mulberry leaf and root
绸缪牖户
to bind window and door

Here 桑土 ('*sangtu*') means the root of the mulberry tree.

In the 土 ('*tu*', earth) part of *Concentric Circles*, the section titles are visually linked: 土('*tu*', earth), 坛('*tan*', altar), 坤 ('*kun*', the feminine, the earth), 塚 ('*zhong*', tomb), 境 ('*jing*', place), 墟 ('*xu*', ruins), and 诗('*shi*', poetry), reflecting the depth of poetry deposited in the cultural history of these characters.

寸 ('*cun*', inch) becomes a unit of sensibility as well as a measure of length and, as in classical poetry, a unit of time

The sundial's inch is like three years
for the separated heart,
it's ten thousand miles.

    Qian Qi, 710-782 AD

This section rewrites the Tang dynasty poet Bai Juyi's 'Song of Unending Regret', which is the story of a love affair between an emperor and a dancer. In 'Inch' the opening sound '*wan*' from Bai Juyi's line. 宛转蛾眉马前死 ('*wanzhuan emei ma qian si*', beauty's grace-ful brow died in front of the cavalry), creates a chain of homophones which recur throughout the section: 挽歌 ('*wan'ge*', lamentation), 婉转 ('*wanzhuan*', grace), 宛如 ('*wan ru*', seem), 晚上 ('*wanshang*', evening).

Bai Juyi's line 夜雨闻铃肠断声 ('*ye yu wen ling, changduan sheng*', hearing bells in the night rain) has further connotations for 'Inch': 铃 ('*ling*', bell) is pronounced exactly the same as 零 ('*ling*', zero), so for Yang Lian, the sound of a bell is 'zero'. *Concentric Circles* could be described in one phrase as the poetics of zero.

YU JIAN   (*b.* 1954)

from Zero File

Volume 4 Daily Life

1 *Address*
the address he sleeps at is 6 Shangyi St.   public land
always used to build houses once with hoes carts saws nails roof
tiles
now with cement mixers   piledrivers   hammer drills   welding
torches   heavy lorries cement
marble steel bars casting punching stacking piling sealing
steel windows   steel doors   steel locks   against Richter 10 earthquakes
against fires against floods
ABCRm503   is the code in his residence permit   A for
the zone where he is   B for his building   C for his unit
5 refers to his floor   03, though, is his room

Sleep Situation
his bed is 1.3m above the floor positioned closest to the roof a
height for sleeping
not much noise dry and airy pretty good for storage keeping
putting aside stacking
10pm he draws the curtains locks the door switches off the light
this is formal sleeping
afternoons he sleeps on the couch in his shirt and pants only his
shoes off covers himself with a blanket
good days for sleeping are in spring sleep long sleep well sleep
not wanting to wake up
bad days for sleeping are from June to September hot stuffy one
sleep has to be divided
a number of naps could a sleep be completed sleep longest in
autumn not disturbed by mosquitoes and flies
no need to scratch carefree sleep deep and sound he goes to bed at
9 in winter with the electric blanket

Waking up

puts on shorts puts on t-shirt puts on pants puts on slippers goes
to the toilet squeezes toothpaste rinses
spits washes face looks into the mirror applies moisturiser combs
hair changes into leather shoes
has breakfast two deep-fried dough sticks a bowl of soya milk a
glass of milk a bun turn about
puts on a wool cardigan puts on a jacket takes his suitcase looks
into the mirror again locks the door
tests if the door is securely locked goes downstairs looks at the sky
looks at the watch pushes the bike leaves by the front gate

Work Situation

enters nods mouth open mouth shut face moves hands move
legs move
head moves eyeball and eyelids move stands sits face still walks 4
steps
walks 10 steps hands over takes over opens holds browses pats
pushes pulls receives
counts squats down comes out closes drinks chews spits
measures brushes copies bends
between longitude 35°E and latitude 20°N radius 200 meters
altitude 500 meters temperature
22° C force 3 SE wind time: eight to twelve two to six

Ideological Report

(according to comrades in control of secrets and their conjectures
suspicion exposure coordination)
he wants to shout counter-revolutionary slogans he wants to violate
public order he wants to be frenzied and go crazy he wants to be
degenerate
he wants to rape he wants to be naked he wants to kill a batch of
people he wants to rob a bank
he wants to be a billionaire a big landlord a big capitalist wants to
be king president
he wants wine, women and song to be dissipated and unashamed to
be a tyrant to abuse his power to ride roughshod over the people
he wants to surrender he wants to revolt he wants to confess he
wants to recant he wants to take revenge on his own people
he wants to riot take frequent actions agitate rise up overthrow
one class

A Set of Verbs Hidden in His Gloomy Mind
smash erect insert tidy up frame up falsely accuse add insult to
injury
fuck make fix shout till hoarse batter expose
bring down shoot stirrup in iron feet Up and at them! Advance!
instructions: this person should be for control and use by party
members only pay attention to and observe his movements send a
duplicate top-secret
internal circulation observe confidentiality transmission to non-party
members prohibited 'it's okay only you know don't tell him'

After-Hours Activities
worries about suburban scenery (far outside Xia Ma Village)
forges a good few fine verses wheat awns at 10k from the hometown
lucky to be mentioned by him
(see *In the Rain*) once in a while polishing up *Poems of Zhimo* (Xu
Zhimo contemporary poet
studied abroad in Britain graduated from Cambridge works include
Sayonara translated into Japanese
English French Italian Serbian and African 16 languages)
always strolls along a 19th century avenue (Shangyi Street is under
the Wu Hua Zone
with two public toilets 3 Szechwan flavour hotpot restaurants 12
electricity poles 1 post office
1 hairdresser 6 rubbish bins 3 back alleys 14 main doors 3 big
slogans
two billboards 10 posters about illnesses missing person notices
shop for rent)
every week washes the clothes once watches two movies buys
tabloids 7 times (evening papers weekly digest)
does 80 sit-ups shops for 6 hours (divided into three times two
hours each)
every day junk food 20g cake 20g sunflower seeds 3 sticks of
chewing gum 1 bag of peanuts
3g fruit candies looks at the calendar once looks at the watch 8
times sits down 9 times squats down for 20 minutes
lies down 11 times leans for 4 hours hands behind the back head
pillowed on the arms hands in
trouser-pockets hands on a cup hands hanging down hands relaxed
legs crossed on tip-toes on the floor
legs bent feet shod in slippers feet in a basin feet on a towel bare-
feet

every night   lifts the TV cover   presses ON   watches ads   watches
network news   watches weather forecast
watches *Animal Planet*   watches singing   watches dancing   watches 30
episodes of a soap
watches ads   watches foreigners   watches ads   watches *Our Lovely
Land*   watches ads   watches
balls   flowers   clothes   water   watches ads   watches tomorrow's
programmes   watches today's programmes come to an end
at this point   goodnight everybody   watches the snow on the screen
presses OFF

Diary
DD-MM-YYYY   sunny   bad mood   depressed   DD-MM-YYYY
sunny   good mood   sat a whole morning   DD-MM-YYYY   the sky
overcast again
lonely   raining   still sleeping in the afternoon   DD-MM-YYYY
slept the whole day
some year some month some day caught flu   some day the wind blew
some day hot   some day cold   some day waited for somebody
some year some month some day   new year   some day   birthday
some day   festival

[BH, LMK]

YANG LIAN   (*b.* 1955)

from Concentric Circles: Talking

Talking

a wrist watch dug up from the ground ticks away
wrist   vanishes
is timed

foreign trademarks on trainers
empty out toes

walk   into   a drop of blood

out   dripping   tick   tock

being killed exchanged decomposition

clay   smile
poppy   black red plump
bullet holes   oysterses

embrace Braille
raise   a touching spider

drip   tock

an even softer little brush can't wake
the sleeping sex sunk deep in each other

bring the time of us
time that the battery stammers
the other side   green radium light dazzles

arrive

unearthed
gliding black birds

archaeology of the now

Sway

yank so yeah you chin
fen sought bam show shin
choose ewe add fling sin
moat high ease door fin
eik wall gun gog

sigh you anti dan
squeak couching ban
doe hay bushy shan
coolie herring fan
fizz way chaw cog

Questioning

whether or not   death is deep as a chamber's shape

is the rainstorm of children driven again into the corner of flesh?

who rehearses cruelty on a piano?

revising   brutish ocean of tiny syllables

why do children conduct the brightly coloured age that is an avalanche?

whether   music turns humans into a foreign language

or not   window pauses   halting into sunlight's deathly pale frequency

where   which hand writes down the nursery on fire in the sky

page of sheet music   how does it demolish everything daily

five fingers   how do they lock composers in

what can a room hear   in children's pitch-dark centres

who   mad   ly   de   sires   to   ap   proach   ze   ro?

weakest   whether or not   deepest into a string's hidden pain

ink wash sky   dead children run   dis   tance

Lies

beauty sans home
beauty sans   home   sans its
colour   sans home may   Homeward Ho!   say
yellow red blue white black their rūpa vedanā samjña samskāra vijñāra
score pound foot shoal pint flock sheet leaf brace volume gaggle fathom
        dram
super al con ician mono ante ism per inity alysis cata intra ana ness pro
        ation ery
say hit drink play smile eat touch shoot fly co-in-cide pisc-itate hypno-tise
dying   attending to clarifying the foam on a glass of beer
stone borrows   masked experience
home   sans   its   beauty
is true

Obituary

this date is translated into our flesh and blood
chorusing fingertips
excavated music

concert   confirms ears
full moon   confirms
no performance not undressed   unroofed

cutting out the eyelids of stars

pink ribs
resonate   black

this date punishes the day that doesn't exist
a translation carefully listens
that vanished   that never pain-abandoning

that collective   left leg

317

throat
recollects

tenses of facial expressions
illuminate   our   flower   pond
the other side   green radium light dazzles

so many

deaths   powerless to overstep a number

syllables

both delving hands hold maggots
wriggling   synopsis of man

passing

confirming   there's no past
the same side   musical instruments clapping
a storm speeding up to pass through concrete

Knowing

Poetry

zero
>   date stops at a dangerous moment
translates as
>   art of losing blood from a tiny heart
boundaries between drop and drop of water
>   likened to history
the edge of bird call
>   Dante lies in Ravenna
the place where clouds originate
>   disinterred wristwatch worn on a Sarajevo street
plural darknesses
>   children compose music
gap between the winds
>   red marble sliced up
pain grasping the hands
>   dusk   withdraws from windows
leaves   nibbling their own green
>   shoot autumn's building in the back
linguistics
>   accommodates reality
tongues of fire
>   licking the vital part of love
one internal secretion   we're tottering
>   Dante   his back covered with the bullet holes of children's
voices
lying at the bottom of sea
>   be the reader of the orchestra of execution
by zero turned into
>   what looks like a zero   an obscure forefinger points to Chinese
>   *this second*   what isn't poetry

[BH & Agnes Hung-Chong Chan]

GU CHENG (1956-93)

Liquid Mercury

1 Names

Water poured from the stove
from the stove

looking at her face   looking at the sky
sawing the money in two   knocking twenty times
mist

Hauling West Gate with a cart, hauling it over to West Gate

Ya
Ya
Ya

14 Devices

This is the king you desired

Speaking to everyone
closing the window

This is the king you desired   a ladle lay in the snow

This is the former minister favoured by the king you desired
they say he   peeled   pushed along by water
sparkled slightly crossing the street

These are your   troops
and small boxes
that would sit, but cannot sit, on the concrete steps
snap!

A thousand troops for light

snapping shut!

15 *Willow Jar*

With a small bumping sound
two people stand

> There is a city wall in the mountains
> there are trees near the wall
> there are women under those trees

Oh how their flowers   fade and fade some more
> eyebrows so delicate
> knives and clubs in hand

[Joseph R. Allen]

YANG XIAOBIN (*b.* 1963)

Super-Cutie Language
A Tongue-Twister to Try

say there's a bird called a bride bird
and there's a board called a breadboard
and, maybe, there's a face called a bored lid

suppose, you put all the bared faces together
would they join up to make a blinded blackbird?

say I'm blacking my face – that's also
blocking my face. but if the black leaves the board
can the bread-head, eyes barred, draw a bead on the bride?

is it only a bird face painted with panting pigment?

the things they also call blackheads, compared to bods
and spods and bards who hoard more boards than beards,
basically don't hold with folding breeds and barring holds.

say there's not a single broad that can be called
'the bored bird brooding in your burred beard.'

[BH, LMK, WNH]

YA SHI (*b.* 1966)

Wa Hoo

WA HOO...WA WA HOO WA HOO...HOO
THOU HIPBONE WIDE RIVER DENSELY COVERED AND WIDE, WIDE
WA HOO WA WA HOO...ROSY & CHUBBY
QUEEN WIDE ROSY & CHUBBY BIG-FOOT QUEEN FRESH AND WIDE
WA HOO WA HOO WA HOO HOO...
FLOCK OF SHEEP ON GRASSY SLOPES...WA HOO WA...ON GRASSY SLOPES
FLOCK OF SHEEP LICKING YOUR FINGERS YEA...WA HOO...HOO
HOW ABOUT A SHEPHERD 'IRON EGG' THE SHEPHERD FOOLING
CRAZY OFF TO WHERE?
WA HOO...WA HOO HOO WA HOO HOO...
INSIDE THE DRIPPING WET FLORAL GOWN WA...HOO WRAPPING UP
AN ARMY THOUSANDS STRONG YEA...
WRAP OH...WRAP...WRAPPING UP A WHOLE SLOPE OF HOARSE-HOO
FLYING STONES YEA
WA HOO WA HOO WA   HOO...WA HOO HOO
WRAP WRAP OH WRAPPING UP THE VIOLENCE OF THE TANGERINE MOON
WA HOO WA HOO WA WA...WA HOO HOO...

[BH, LMK, WNH]

5. LONG POEMS

QIN XIAOYU

Approaching the Origin: On Long Poems

The first poet in the history of Chinese poetry whose name we know is Qu Yuan (*c.* 340-278 BC). His given name Yuan (原) sounds the same as another character, 元 '*yuan*', which means primary, or original. This might be coincidence, but it also points to a truth about Chinese poetry. For over two millennia, Qu Yuan has inspired Chinese poets and artists.[72]

As discussed elsewhere, Qu Yuan is best known for his long poems, including '*Tian Wen*' (Heavenly Questions), a poem which established the image of the poet as questioner, and, arguably, suggested that the true poetical motive must be the questioning of oneself.

Qu Yuan's other long poems also provided important elements on which later poetry could build. In '*Li Sao*' (Song of Leaving), a poem which recounts his exile and the reasons for his eventual suicide, we discover a hidden structure made up by the different levels of his spiritual pilgrimage.[73] It begins with autobiographical details of the poet's painful experiences, then his continuing search through mythological and historical realms in a vivid, even surrealist manner; then, as neither heaven nor hell provide a satisfactory answer, the poet must return to this world, and finally resolves to live in solitude amongst nature.

Qu Yuan selected a unique language and rhythm for each long poem: '*Tian Wen*' is written in the four-syllable line characteristic of ancient folk songs, while '*Li Sao*' is written in couplets, usually of two seven-syllable lines, inspired by the rituals of the Chu Kingdom's shamanistic tradition. The '*Jiu Ge*' (Nine Songs) each have a voiced caesura in the middle of each short five- to seven-syllable line of mainly five to seven characters.[74] More than two thousand years later, when Yang Lian suggests that there should be a sense of necessity linking concept and form in poetry, this principle is derived from the work of Qu Yuan.

---

72. Qu Yuan, et al, tr. David Hawkes, *Songs of the South* (Penguin, 1985).
73. Translated by Hawkes as 'On Encountering Trouble'.
74. Brian Holton (Scots translation): 'The Nine Sangs' in *Lallans* 67. Blackford, Perthshire, Hairst 2005.

How long does a poem have to be to be called a Long Poem? Many ancient epics such as the Iliad or the Ramayana are more than ten or twenty thousand lines long, but in the Chinese tradition, such poems are generally much shorter. Qu Yuan's poems were mainly 300-400 lines, and he was the only poet to write to that length for the next 300 years. Modern poetry also offers widely-differing examples, Pound's *Cantos* runs to thousands of lines while Eliot's *Waste Land* is only a few hundred lines.

In his introduction to *Narrative Poem*, Yang Lian said, 'I want to see three elements in a long poem: psychological maturity; mature philosophical and poetic understanding; and a high degree of conceptual finish to the writing.' Within a long poem, we need to see that its poetical and philosophical depth of thought is directly linked to the concept of the poem – this demands the development of a unique structure; in its details and its whole the poem must operate as a single completed system, a symphony, the greater creative energy of which demands greater control. A long poem cannot just be a number of short poems placed together. It is an independent world created through language, one which sums up or rewrites our memories, so becoming the origin of our subsequent journeys.

The root of the long poem in contemporary Chinese writing is found in the extremely painful experience of the Cultural Revolution. This man-made nightmare woke up the Chinese people's most traumatic memories of the 20th century, and linked these back to the main cultural impulse of the period: how could we rethink the classical Chinese cultural tradition in a modern context? Over and over again, instead of dreaming of the future, we found ourselves waking up in the darkness of the past.

When we think of the Chinese language as the basis of a unique mode of thought, when we learn about classical philosophy as a complete system of thought, when we read thousands of literary masterpieces as proof of the achievements of our tradition, then we must ask: is this a living tradition, or just a very long but nonetheless dead past?

The crisis made not only poetry, but life itself seem epic. Perhaps as a result, during the 1980s and 1990s a group of long poems suddenly appeared, as if from an erupting volcano. Among the Misty poets, Jiang He was writing socially-powerful pieces under the title of 'The Monument'. Mang Ke transformed himself from a lyric to a philosophic poet and published 'Timeless Time'. Yang Lian produced a series of long poems: *Yi* in China, then *Concentric Circles* and *Narrative Poem* during his exile. Bei Dao wrote his one venture into the long poem 'Day Dreams'.

More long poems were written by Post-Misty poets: Ouyang Jianghe's 'Hanging Coffin'; Xi Chuan's 'Salute' and 'Eagle's Speech'; Meng Lang's 'The Edge of Dreadful Times'; Liao Yiwu's 'Death City'; Chen Dongdong's 'Total Lunar Eclipse'; Lü De'an's 'A Suitable Place' and, among many more, Xiao Kaiyu's 'Salute to Du Fu'.

Xiao Kaiyu's model is the Tang dynasty poet Du Fu (712-770), because of his Confucian attitude toward social responsibility and his command of form. In this long poem, arranged in ten chapters, Xiao Kaiyu paid tribute to Du Fu in several ways: the notion of a poetry that could convey painful experiences; the use of narrative; and a rich, linguistically-complex style. The Confucian understanding that 'the nation and the person are one' provides the soul of 'Salute to Du Fu', becoming a basic element in its structure. The beginning of the first chapter is already a judgement upon the nation:

This is another China.
What is it living on for?
No one answers, nor is there
an echo to answer either.
This is another China.

Then from the second to the ninth chapters Xiao Kaiyu paints different sides of this other China: family, language, city life, culture and arts, politics. The poem portrays the desires of a modern Chinese city: a boy escapes from school; a patient plays chess with pain; a prostitute flies in an aircraft. All these figures – and their betrayals, their fears, their hopelessness – point to a deep crisis in modern society. Every chapter is focused on a little narrative, and together they create the larger narrative of another China. In the final chapter he writes:

I am a young lady, mouth open to the section chief.
I am the driver, given my destination by all of you.
I am the cleaner and the broom. I am the nauseating smell of sweat
dispersed by a hairdryer, I am the man and woman
grappling in ecstasy. but I am not the po-faced
hypocrites of the world of letters

When the 'I' is everyone, then everyone's crisis becomes 'my' spiritual crisis. Xiao Kaiyu wanted to follow Du Fu closely, to maintain sincerity when engaging with normal life without being 'normal', thus preserving a Confucian concern for the world he lives in. He said in his essay 'Personal Passion and Reflections on Society', 'Contemporary Chinese poetry seems more and more to have become separate, it needs to be pulled to the land by a strong political force to be linked with life again…' Here, Du Fu became the means of re-establishing that link. However, if Xiao Kaiyu stopped here, he could only become a modern mandarin, trying to judge others from above, but the fifth chapter ends with the 'I' making love to a country girl, a woman as passionately described as Dante's Beatrice, although she is actually a prostitute:

> I pay tribute to this girl in her fake couture!
> this temp, this country girl, this whore
> presents the other side of the New Year,
> I worship her tears, her thick waist, her lies.

We don't know what system of values lie behind these actions: is this a poet's cynicism or a symbol of the rebuilding of some link with the lost countryside? A complete break from Du Fu is made here: morally, the 'I' makes himself lower than a prostitute. This other China is at once introspective, and at the same time, a piercing critique of all our lives.

'A Suitable Place' is a 2000-line poem composed over nearly ten years. It is divided into a 'Prelude', and four main parts – 'Tao Di's Land', 'One Midsummer Day', 'Postscript for the Rocks', and 'It's Not Eden, But It Is Paradise' – with 'Dream Song' for a coda. Each of the main parts is composed of 20-30 smaller sections written in couplets.

When Lü De'an came back from the US in 1992, he built a new home in the mountains of Fujian Province, in south-east China. He said of the form of 'A Suitable Place', 'the couplet has always been used in folk song, and it can be richly expressive.' Not only the language but the structure of 'A Suitable Place' is inspired by folk song. It follows the practice in performing Chinese folk songs of starting with an overture, followed by two main songs and a refrain, then finishing with another song.

This gives 'A Suitable Place' stability of mood. The poet watches life and the world from a settled point. The poem attempts, amid contemporary uncertainty, to engage anew with the themes of love and home, ultimately looking for a return to self-identification that will allow the poet to resolve his life.

Lü De'an acknowledged the decisive influence of Robert Frost, who 'rediscovered and confirmed my own nature and taste… sometimes I gained the opportunity to see my own truths from his viewpoint'. Echoing Frost's line 'I chose to be a farmer in New Hampshire,' he said, 'I wished myself to have been born a peasant.' As in Frost's poems, Lü De'an's poems appear simple and natural, initially very easy to understand, but the more you read the more their mystery deepens.

The first five chapters of 'A Suitable Place' consist over seventy sub-sections, often beginning with 'It is a new day', 'That night', 'At the end of the day...' This makes the poem feel like the diary of a couple's working life. They move into the mountains, work the land, build their house, seek out a spring, cut grass, burn back the hillside, observe animals, and make love. This diaristic structure is different from a linear narrative. It focuses on every fragment, opening it up as a dramatic yet lyric space, meaning the poem moves lightly, with its own distinct rhythm.

From his earliest work, Lü De'an was already a poet of locality. His poems are deeply rooted in Fujian, his home province, and he renders the image of rock as both concrete and metaphysical. He first confronts the object, then digs deep into it, making it in the end a symbol, even a faith:

> I serve again as foil to a loneliness
> And again the humble stonemason's image
>
> He is the highest fabrication.
> ...
> Surrounding these stones
> We will be utterly free of doubt.

The deepest theme of 'A Suitable Place' is home. We as readers have seen its construction as a physical place, and how much pleasure the 'we' of the poem take in it. But 'home' is also the destination of a spiritual journey, and to find it is a close equivalent to finding oneself.

Each of Yang Lian's three book-length poems is an independent project with its own theme, structure, and different layers of form and language. Beyond that, all three books constitute a further larger project which could be seen as a spiritual journey. Yang Lian separates his writing into 'Chinese Manuscripts', 'South Pacific Manuscripts' and 'European Manuscripts', with his long poems occupying the central role in each group. *Yi* was written between 1984 and 1989, *Concentric Circles* between 1994 and 1998, and *Narrative Poem* between 2005 and 2009. They show the poet's spiritual journey from deep within China, to his being a world traveller in exile, and finally to his crossing all borders in search of a synchronic text.

Yi was the last work he wrote in China: with the political and cultural consequences of the Cultural Revolution on his mind, Yang Lian tried to sum up his understanding of China – its language and tradition – and the possible role of poetry in reaching the root of Chinese culture and opening up its future. In and of itself the title was surprising, as it is an invented character combining the archaic script forms for person and sun from the earliest unified Chinese writing system. Yang Lian said it was pronounced 'yi', the same as the Chinese for the number one, to imply and echo the classical idea that the heavenly and the human are one, while further suggesting that the intrinsic nature of humanity is one with the external world. He said he invented the character in order to represent humanity's first encounter with language.

The structure of *Yi* is rooted in the symbolic system of the 64 hexagrams in *Yi Jing* (Book of Change). Its 64 parts consist of seven different forms of poetry and three different styles of prose. By the end of the poem, Time is cancelled, and a synchronic space is established within the poem.

Yang Lian has said about *Concentric Circles*, 'there could be no book without two conditions: my experience of exile, and the nature of the Chinese language'. 'Exile' has no meaning for him if it cannot become a creative force both poetically and politically. The title establishes this point: 'concentric' indicates the synchronous nature of the human situation, while circles brings our experiences together across any and all cultural borders.

The five parts of the whole have no verbal titles as such, being marked only by the geometrical progression of ever-increasing circles. In each circle, there are always three designed sections, each organised in a radically different way, but echoing each other structurally. Like ripples in water and annual rings in a tree, they increase in circumference, while at the same time, always emanating from the centre.

Narrative Poem completes the cycle. This book goes back to personal experience, and sets up the theme of how deeply history is involved in individual destinies, and how individual minds construct a deep understanding of history. The whole is in three parts beginning with 'Photo Album: A Dream with Time (Allegro ma non troppo)', which is based on a series of photographs covering the period from Yang's birth up to the completion of the book, the day before his mother died. The second is 'Elegies of Water-Mint: Reality without Time (Lento)', five long poems focussed on five big themes: reality, love, history, home, and poetry. The third is 'Philosopher's Side: Synchronicity. No Dreams (Allegretto)'. Here the poems are formed into three groups travelling into the depth of the heart, from which all thoughts set out and return.

Narrative Poem is itself a return to the art of writing classical Chinese Poetry. Each poem is given a unique form with its rhyme, rhythm and visual appearance, all musically arranged in relation to the other parts. It is an attempt to resolve the long-held dream that has troubled Chinese poetry for a century: how do we make poems which are the equal of those from our ancient tradition? And how do we make this living tradition an inspiration to world literature?

JIANG HE (*b.* 1949)

from The Sun and His Reflections

Heliotropy

The day he took to the road, he was already getting on
or else he never would have gone chasing the sun
the sun is green youth itself
the day he took to the road he made offerings
saw glory in his blood again, heard
drumming in earth in blood in sky
he stood and swayed in silent recollection, a man apart
he ranged a long way back   to the left   to the right
found besides ritual nothing but years of empty show
he coiled snakes hung them on his ears
pulled the snakes straight took them in his hands
dementedly tormenting them
The sun doesn't like tranquillity

Like sharp flames the snakes' forked tongues recalled his boyhood
flickering back and forth all through his heart

Legend has it he was so thirsty he drank both Wei Water and Yellow
          River dry
in fact he poured himself out and offered himself to the sun
in fact he and the sun were soon drunk on each other
he washed and dried himself in the sun
he laid himself down creakily-crackly on the ground
there was the road there were the wrinkles there was the dried-up lake

When it settled down in his heart
he found the sun was soft, so soft it hurt
it could be touched – he was old
his fingers trembled like sunlight
he could just leave, throw his walking stick toward the horizon
people could gather wood from the spring grass
lifting their heads   as peaches fell down every hill and dale

[BH, WNH]

MANG KE (*b.* 1950)

from Timeless Time

16

in this place where the numberless dead are buried
now fresh green days are sprouting again
plaster has peeled off the walls of an old house
and I will never again be the me I once was
in the eyes of people today
I am old and useless, like a fossil
in my time it seems there is no blood flowing
now I have been abandoned by the now
and my past has been forgotten by the now
each day there is only me keeping watch on myself
myself dragging my own shadow
dirt fallen all over me
and my life seems a life no longer
no one browses or reads my history
I too will no longer browse or read myself
I don't want myself to look at myself again
so this is how I'm waiting for myself to rot
I am slowly rotting
I don't die, but it's not like I'm alive
and I will never again be the me I once was
I have no smiling face any more
and I will never smile again
I by chance I bare my teeth
and look so ugly
now I can't be like before
drawing people in
drawing people in to pick my smile
I have no smiling face any more
my face is cold and cheerless
my lifeless eyes are like two dry leaves
drifting down from on high
drifting to the ground
slowly getting filthy dirty
there's still one small place in this human world

displaying this useless head of mine
my carcass, like a broken boat
that hasn't sunk yet
daily I steep as always in
the current of human life's immensity
it's only that my life isn't a life
my brain has been utterly emptied
no past, and no present
and even less way to imagine the future
in my heart is an uninhabited desolation
more and more gruesomely dark
my heart is lonelier than me
now I am like a tomb
myself burying myself
but I still fear death
and I also fear life
in this place where the numberless dead are buried
now fresh green days are sprouting again
plaster has peeled off the walls of an old house
and I will never again be the me I once was
there is no memory in my memory
my memory is quite deserted
if there are still things left
they're blurry and indistinct
I feel no more pain, and no more happiness
I will feel no more pain because of my unhappiness
I will soon finish
throw everything away
I have squandered all of it by myself now
the great door of my dreams will never open again
the grave of my thought has begun to seal itself up
I am saying goodbye to me
I'm happy to go
after I part from me I won't own a thing
I am finishing
what finishes is me
death will get nothing from my life

[BH]

332

YANG LIAN (*b.* 1955)

from **Yi**

Earth 1   *(King Zhou of Shang)*

Dusk   Stillness

An altar is born

Words   One by one flee
Yellow earth surges in a mass
Stars perish in the distance
Tranquil at the core
Sitting in the tyrant's court   Rocks radiate like circles of light

This day has chosen him, fire has chosen him
Rebellion's wilderness howls ferociously, wolf smoke draws near
High platform solitarily abandoned like a huge tripod
Flaccid muscles, precious bow falcon dogs disperse into evening colours
The jade suit
He says, is death: Heaven commands the Vermilion Bird
                              Descend and give birth to Shang

Mountains prostrate before the plough
The seed after four seasons
Swells up into a cicada about to burst from the soil
Night strikes   A white poplar is born
Like a rotting corpse hanging in mid-air
The sun basks in its offerings, blood of abortions a pool of potent wine
Splashing the earth the swirling dance of rebellious women
Too late, already not a wine cup can be raised
Night-wandering fires heaven-beseeching fires, music of skeletons
          hissing revenge

In the clouds wanton grandeur   This unprecedented hour
Slaughtering the sense of smell in every bird
Omens are burnt into glazed tiles
Die in fragments everywhere

Unmoving veins like water carry fuses: lust branded on huge
        bronze pillars
Tired of playing, the sky shakes forth a blinding flurry of bats
As the spirit at dusk gives the final command
It transparently infuses the jade heaven
He says, Enough: Indomitable is heaven
                                        Omniscient its command

   Carried up stairs
   Thrown by the legs into a marble dish utterly mute
   Trampled earth   Earth ultimate and supreme
   Yellow   Red   Blue   White   Black
   Deaf at the core
   Pushing open a door   Moonlight's crimes in deep layers
   On mountains pure smoke curling
   Is piled-up snow

[Mabel Lee]

from **Narrative Poem**

Ballad of Water Mint
An Elegy for Love, for Yo Yo

                V *Ocean, requiem, the first time and once more*

      sluggishly the boat's prow presses into blue   in these seconds
         something is broken forever   the look in the seagulls' eyes
   is beautiful and violent   bends toward the gunwale's horizons
   the leisurely dolphins that lead the way, swimming under our keel
   have penetrated something   sharper than sunlight-painted skins
                    deep as their little shiny black blowholes
      looking down over them our arms wave in imitation of fins
      and   our hearts have just smoothed out the breaking waves

            the thoroughest smash can't be seen   drops of water
                  gently break two hands   blue metaphor
   is for the soul and for the sea   dip in and crack like stained turtle-shell

pull out   shadow too late to retreat learns to be a composer
            our two notes are linked by a water-line
        twice performed   making every distance stealthily double
    the splinter that peels the sea   the meat of cactus-fruit red as
        blood ties   has spattered our gums with one another

    oh, we have sailed across so many oceans   so much lustre
        keeping its young   whetted penknives like wings
            a bed dragging the boat's trace   sailing into our
    maturity   home   looking out from this word the sea is vaster
        doubts spread over the tabletop of tides   once again defer
            a line of verse and then it's a pumice stone   farther
        oh, very near   we can feel it hatch in our inner being
    love   from this word we conjure up the image pounded out by the
        waves' roar

        only two people   plus a starry sky   seeking no less
    only one day   a rhythm squeezed bright then quenched
        scours away the gunwales' world of painted waterlines
    our lips, yours and mine, fix a structure where nothing is passed over
    a perfect vortex   only awaiting a swordfish's long and deep kiss
        dawn like the last left-over   most blinding reason worth
            swapping for the shallow hollows on my cheeks
                as you awake   there is your forehead's berth

        as time   this music's grammar   doesn't discuss endings
            but illuminates that ending with every life of madness
                going to die stuck in a cave where warmth lingers
    is not infinity   on a commonplace afternoon a surprise attack of loneliness
        pretends infinity   the room where we quietly sit facing each other
        drips with a fine drizzle farther away than infinity   listen closely to
            the telegram the waves decode   two hearts surprised still
            by how colourful we are   even though the days are speechless

        so they seem identically beautiful, the ocean and the requiem
        a love poem waits for the first time   trembling blue recurs
            times without number   each time an unendurable world
                holds a carefully-carved phoenix-tail fern toward you
        beach roads without number run to seek refuge in the spume
            use the one we have   to conduct a dazzling orchestra
                giving you the tonality of a sun-trimmed waistline
                you're wringing seawater from your dripping hair

                            335

restore my vision   oh   having lived
is to spread out the score of one's own flesh and blood
write down the ancient undulations   fondle
the immensity of blue waves from where one pair of eyes falls into another
snow-bright   equal to the dark night below the skin
the huge whale's bones like wan lamps faintly tumble
our beauty is like our brokenness   held in whose hand
come the clouds   the masterpiece of the storm in pen point scribble

put your hand in mine   an itinerary
memorised once then experienced once more   so a poem is born
in a million years water mint's fibres have only once woven
so green you and so green me   appointing a bitter poetic
learning to love is learning how to stand on the street's deck steady
learning to die   nothingness how deep gentleness how deep   so delight
is born   the heat in your palm has seeped into my marrow
once two water birds' wingtips collide   it brings our created images to a hal

[BH]

LÜ DE'AN (*b.* 1960)

from A Suitable Place

III *Postscript for the Rocks*

1

Ah, a whole day hiding from the blazing heat
until nightfall, when thunder was heard,

and then came rising wind and falling rain, until the rain
actually fell into the valley

filling the nearly dried-up stream
forming what's called a spate, only then understood as

the slightest bit real. Until someone
shouted on some winding path, faint

and fainter, and displaced, sunburned for three days
while using a broom of bulrushes,

calling for someone else to take all this away –
it was already too late.

– This was a real mess, we thought at first that it wouldn't rain,
that nothing unexpected could happen in this world;

until those white rocks
stuck out, only then did we

finally discover ourselves
to be a crowd of objects, near or far away –

primitive, and so easily frightened!

2

Under a gallows-like winch,
a rock slowly rising up –

the one time a rock will rise like the sun.
I saw the whole process with my own eyes.

As it rose mournfully up, chain pulled tight
to halt any sudden downward slide,

this seemed a kind of premonition,
it too was far from its native soil, a sigh

escaped from this skull as it left its body.
Faint and fainter, in my heart,

there was another rock bound like that,
dangling in mid-air, framed by a cloud whitened by memory

like a promise, or like a daily prayer,
or, even more, like a luminous cave,

only that surrounding cave
was Michelangelo's brain,

and the silence of slaves down the ages.

3

Honeybees in threes and fours, rising up from deep in the rock,
does this make a difference to the surface of the ordinary?

That mysterious drill-hole,
storing water, is it like God's dwelling-place?

And yet right there, the honeybees'
screw-propellers are blowing up a little tornado,

invisible to the naked eye.
And, higher still, one bee suddenly ascends,

its shadow almost vanished;
we know this is their existence:

one bee steadies another there
using the power of a buzzing snore,

wings like eyes interlock,
bodies face different directions:

we know this is summer's zenith,
as they split up, the air

is heavy with a post-coital emptiness,
the sky cleaner still.

There's also a slender replenishment
as they fall back down like rain; the rock floats,

objects emerge into light:
this is an inexhaustible form.

4

Oh, make these masons shout and roar, and find someone
to help truss up a rock, hoist it,

and poise it exactly on the tractor, then jolt it around the whole way,
or push it into the stream, or pack it on a lorry and ship it off.

Now I can say, if I could wake up my dozy cleaver,
I would, with appropriate prayers, evade the locusts

otherwise, not giving a damn, I'll mumble away
as I go back to the night, bury myself in my writing, repeat

all night what they said all day, inside and
outside their heads – tell me what else can I do?

They tried to talk me out of it, but my writing
has already recorded what they said:

every single word hits the spot,
and is as proper and humble as a day-trip to the country.

[BH, WNH]

339

XIAO KAIYU (*b*. 1960)

from Salute to Du Fu

10

why them, why not me,
    why them, why not a person emitting light?
        a secretary standing on the roof of a high building;
why a prostitute in flight,
    why is there no thinking, only recall and misconception,
        no successful dialogue, only guesswork?

(sometimes hidden, sometimes manifest, as if someone is there...)

the business people I've known well or just bumped into
    cheerful but dying in their deceitful business,
        would they give the time it takes to drink a Coke
to contemplate their unconsidered *spirit-flying-device*?
    so I follow the trail of their corporeal selves,
        extinguished like electricity beneath the tank tracks of dawn.
the doctors I understand and loathe
    covet and take possession of other people's pain,
        their superiority derives from donating the Demerol.
they just love ECGs, they push air into
    the embryo's heart, bung a necrotic liver into
        a black plastic bag, and, as I thread through streets and lanes
toward some family home, I am the doctor.
    I am the slightly feverish relations who, spellbound by medication,
        wait for their doctor. I am the one who signs a contract with you,
white-coated youth flashing by.
    I am a young lady, mouth open to the section chief.
    I am the driver, given my destination by all of you.
I am the cleaner and the broom. I am the nauseating smell of sweat
    dispersed by a hairdryer, I am the man and woman
        grappling in ecstasy. but I am not the po-faced
hypocrites of the world of letters
    I am elsewhere, I am downtown, I am a sleepwalker
        – I have no self the future might seize.

I open the cardboard box,
  I open the photo album and the diary,
    I see a child quickly winning prizes from the enemy.

so my sense of respect comes from my balls, from my unease.
  (might I, in a five square metre room,
    receive the sincere admonishment of artists?
as they leave, raincoats folded on the carriers of their bikes,
  they think the days have been ravaged
    layer by layer with *Peony* cigarettes.)
in the letters from these damp, ordinary afternoons
  I haven't found the part about the poets' heaven, about suddenly
          flying toward
    that free province, ringed by savage peaks, that Li Bai reached
      through drink,[75]
or the rhymes that Du Mu discovered for Cao Cao's empire,[76]
  their uncontrolled flow handling its endless factions,
    or the *schadenfreude* that Dante felt, guided by the girl next door,
      who had died so young, until, finally,
he entered that same lofty realm of light, for which Pound consulted
  so many unread books, or Ulysses in the city, riding the commuter bus
    back to his New Ithaka of the suburbs, when what he really wants is
      to go back to Bloom & Bud Mountain of the Waterfall...[77]

but I'm a student of Confucius, dense fog strands me
  at the ferry port, I see I have turned into
    a leopard invading government offices,
their panicking circus troupe urgently
  advertise for an animal trainer and a clown, the Pig Year accountants
    hand a happy new balance sheet to the Rat Year.
the past is a Chicken, numbers are Dogs, and afterwards is a Tiger.
  but I see tanks coming right at me
    gun barrels not camouflaged in green nylon.

75. Li Bai (701-762 AD) the other great Tang poet, often paired with Du
Fu. Also known in the west as Li Po, and to the Japanese (and Ezra Pound)
as Rihaku.
  76. Cao Cao (155-220 AD), famous warlord, King of the state of Wei, central
figure in the Three Kingdoms period, and an accomplished poet. Du Mu
(803-52 AD), accomplished poet and essayist of the late Tang period. Both he
and Cao Cao commented on Sunzi's *The Art of War* and both wrote poems
on the Battle of Red Cliff.
  77. Hua Guo Shan, where Monkey, the divine hero of *Xi You Ji* (Journey
to the West) grew up.

I beg Lao-tzu to take me on the escape route
    from his obscure verses
        to Nowheresville and vanish, vanish,
but I am a disloyal reader of *Reference News*,[78]
    so I believe that Mars and the Moon
        will soon be setting up colonies.
alone and arrogant, I perch on red ore,
    I open my wallet to the universe,
        and watch helplessly as the sand rivers flow.
soot, discarded silicon chips, mutant white mice escaped from labs,
    and, just as weird, gigantic or cold-blooded: dubious philosophical dinosaurs
        the poor old moon consuming its own pure light.

the flat-pack kitchen which two skint artists helped me assemble
        in the corridor is the only album of realist painting I can open,
            the artworks inside are all surrealist.
tantalising, useful, sometimes wonderful, but without style.
    I shuffle sideways, a half-starved, half-stuffed chef,
        it belongs to me alone, illegally.
what am I doing, borrowing the stained glass of a western kitchen –
    its greasy braggadocio has long since turned into shit:
        the stained glass and pews of churches – and the stale clichés of elders
and my belly, breast and brain – and my desire,
    and my actually-illegal good works – are totally unconnected,
        so I renounce their images and their names.
my computer is like my kitchen,
    like my raindrops, my sudden thunderclap, my insecticide –
        they are all compatible, non-programmatically
constituting another cosmos: if at beef and potatoes time[79]
    the addition of poppy heads is not ungenerous, its print-out
        will bring hallucinations.

in the revolving space of nothingness,
    I met a teacher, baseball cap on his bald head,
        he no longer works, his short-arsed son has married,

78. Nowheresville refers to the Chinese title of William Morris's *News from Nowhere*; *Reference News* is the limited-circulation CCP newspaper.

79. A Khrushchev quotation: communism equals 'beef & potatoes'.

80. (*See opposite page.*) Pigsy is Zhu Ba Jie from *Xi You Ji* (Journey to the West); the Monkey King is Sun Wukong from the same novel.

he is amazed I'm still besotted with Pigsy,[80]
    when he has cast away the Monkey King and the secrets of outer space,
        'you're hung up on such bloated interests, you and the country'.
my radiator replies for me: when the cold draught causes me
    to hunch over my knees, a flying saucer
        takes me to a place of brilliant light,
maybe a room in the machine, a feeling close to the truth
    muddles my shaken confidence,
        haloes and bright spots, clouds of butterflies,
soon convince me of the aliens' evil intent,
    from far away I see their star on the keyboard.
        and our souls' heaven.
I take my interstellar journeys inside my room.
    in our hell, our bank,
        it's possible to hold God's hand.
yet in the night club, in an absent-minded moment,
    an immortal girl appears before me,
        and takes me back to my room.

I pay tribute to this girl in her fake couture!
    this temp, this country girl, this whore
        presents the other side of the New Year,
I worship her tears, her thick waist, her lies.
    her undersea paradise cannot be contained by death
        all along she's been leaping, leaping and striking her shuttlecock.
oh, I worship the blue of the sea, its turbulence.
    it makes me like a fish, like an amnesiac,
        like summer evenings competing with each other.
the clothes I stripped off then are exactly like dark waves,
    my putrescent flesh is really not the door-handle to the study –
        and to say it again, neither is this self-incineration the end.

20 December 1996, Shanghai
[BH, WNH]

MENG LANG (*b.* 1961)

from The Edge of Dreadful Times

Freshly-ploughed earth steals up to my pillow
Then waves and a sunken boat, a boat of loosened frame
Intact and unperturbed
With all the dead belonging to it still aboard
Rises from the ocean's surface
To touch the heel of my foot.

Men who travel on foot
Who are late for their execution, with hurried steps
Converge at my side
The blot of sun in the sky, concealing its role
Forces my eyes to open
On the final terrible scene
As the sea sinks into its own depths

Those self-engulfing possibilities
Utterly destroy themselves into reality
The sunken boat, on its return voyage
Endures trials much told about in history
I stand erect before the dialogue concludes
With water freely draining off my body
Then I said: my hands are a pair of anchors
I will cast them into the depths of the sky

Mouth full of other people's bashed-out teeth
Wishing I could spit them out
Cries of disaster victims
Blameless hostages take a position in a room
On the right side of food from an uninspected factory
The meaning of all of these
Connects with the blood coursing in my veins

Pondering on the banks, sitting immobile
I eclipse the broad desk before my chest
Here behind a flammable wooden wall

In this room, I cannot let myself be
A hostage in a cold-storage locker

They might walk into this room
At a pivotal juncture of history
While some are just getting to their feet
And wiping their faces clean
Of other people's teeth or blue teeth-marks.
A well-meant saying, a curlicue of shavings
Wilfulness is holding a drawn-out conversation
With a champion sprinter and a shaven-headed killer
No one is about to surrender to the clock.

On the boat a clock that dares not show its face
Is coming into the home stretch
I observe the part that is incomplete
Is the part suffused with living blood
Blueness of veins, blueness of ocean
Our no-longer resisting hands
Now move behind razor-like peaks
So very ancient – this minute's setting sun

Leaving someone's finger traces, the powerful ocean surface
A convoy that pain prevents our bodies from reaching
Lost voyage past a twisted coastline, white book paper on the shore
People with places to go are walking
Not sensing the danger and passion of chaos encroaching

Fragments of memory are just fragments of flesh
Each drop of blood is coming awake
Even the blood spattered on the wall
Pure whiteness makes us silent
A school of fish that will never rise, under the water in darkness
Is able to see my lips, the salt of mankind.

[Dennis C. Mair]

BRIAN HOLTON

Phrases That Shall Be Musical in the Mouth

Outsiders usually imagine the translator working alone with the text in a solitary and unfrequented corner of the library, but, since relatively few translators are bilingual, literary translation could be much more of a collaborative process than it is at present. We could, and perhaps should, use native-speaker informants or special subject informants more, talk to our authors more (or to specialists and scholars, if our author is dead), and to each other. In my own practice, I have been working more and more with other translators, and I would recommend collaboration to literary translators: this is in fact how we have proceeded in the preparation of this book.

Jade Ladder began with Bill Herbert's first idea and Yang Lian's enthusiastic acceptance of it. Yang then collaborated with Qin Xiaoyu on the first selection of the poems. Next, I had the pleasure of collaborating with the talented young translator Kay Lee (Lee Man-Kay), who produced first drafts which she and I polished together, then sent to Yang to check, not just for howlers (of which there were enough – good collaborative translation involves a lot of laughter), but also for subdued and not-so-subdued allusions, idioms, puns, jokes, and hidden meanings – the sort of things which a fifty-something Beijing native would see, but which could – and did – escape the scrutiny of a middle-aged Scotsman and a Cantonese-speaking Hong Konger in her 20s. Yang and Qin also proposed a list of poems which they thought were likely to have been translated by others. Finally, I sat down with Bill Herbert to read through the drafts Kay and I had made, to see what was and wasn't working as poetry.

And that was a fascinating experience. To work closely with a target-language poet who doesn't speak the source language is to enter a different world, and to see your carefully-polished drafts from a completely different angle. Many of the dangers which Robert Louis Stevenson pointed out long ago, in an elegant essay that should be on the curriculum of every translation department, apply as much to translators as they do to writers in general: we all suffer from a tendency not to notice intrusive or clumsy rhythms, unplanned runs of consonant or vowel sounds, mismatches between style and sense, and so on. This is his conclusion, and it merits close consideration:

We have, peculiar to the prose writer, the task of keeping his phrases large, rhythmical, and pleasing to the ear, without ever allowing them to fall into the strictly metrical: peculiar to the versifier, the task of combining and contrasting his double, treble, and quadruple pattern, feet and groups, logic and metre – harmonious in diversity: common to both, the task of artfully combining the prime elements of language into phrases that shall be musical in the mouth; the task of weaving their argument into a texture of committed phrases and of rounded periods – but this particularly binding in the case of prose: and, again common to both, the task of choosing apt, explicit, and communicative words. We begin to see now what an intricate affair is any perfect passage; how many faculties, whether of taste or pure reason, must be held upon the stretch to make it; and why, when it is made, it should afford us so complete a pleasure. From the arrangement of according letters, which is altogether arabesque and sensual, up to the architecture of the elegant and pregnant sentence, which is a vigorous act of the pure intellect, there is scarce a faculty in man but has been exercised. We need not wonder, then, if perfect sentences are rare, and perfect pages rarer.[81]

To our tale, though – the Herbertian inquisition to which each poem was subjected was a close one, and since Chinese routinely omits pronoun subjects and objects, it is often a real puzzle to work out who is doing what to whom. Chinese verbs are not marked for tense (tense is shown, if at all, by adverbs – I yesterday go, I tomorrow go); nouns are not marked as singular or plural, and Chinese has no articles, so when it comes to decisions on tense, number, definiteness or indefiniteness, and the supply of pronouns, all of which English demands, these decisions are almost entirely up to the translator alone, and since the translator can only rely on his or her own judgement in the reading of the text, all of these decisions had to be put to the question as Bill and I worked our long and often painful way through each poem. Close reading, in its highest form, is one of the greatest and most transformative tools of our trade, for no one reads as closely as a translator – unless it be a poet reading someone else's work. I watched, fascinated, as the draft poems on which Kay and I had laboured so long the year before revolved, in the light of Bill's interrogation, to present whole new facets of meaning.

As a versifier, Bill Herbert is a *non pareil*, and that introduces another element of our work together. Not only syntactical and logical muddles had to be sorted out: incompletely realised sound structures had to

81. 'On Some Technical Elements of Style in Literature', *Contemporary Review* 47 (April 1885).

be dealt with too. You can now be confident, reader, when you see rhymes in this book, that rhymes exist in the Chinese: we were not always able to rhyme in exactly the same places – like Italian, Chinese rhymes with much greater ease and felicity than English does – but we aimed to have the same *density* of rhyme. Kay Lee and I managed fairly well, but many of the rhymed poems were transformed by Bill's touch.

The majority of Chinese poetry in our period has used *vers libre*, though in recent years poets have been returning to stricter forms. It is relatively easy to render unrhymed free verse into English, though to my ear, few American translators seem able to create a rhythmic pulse on the page, and that tends to make their poems into rather unpoetic collages of cut-up prose. We were all more interested in the structured musicality of each poem – each example of Auden's 'contraption of words' – and we have gone to great lengths to re-create or construct a convincing sound structure in our English poems that mirrors or echoes the structure of the Chinese text. Hugh MacDiarmid said it in the 1920s: *It's soon', no' sense that faddoms the herts o' men*,[82] and I believe that this emphasis on making Chinese poems into working, musical English poems is what distinguishes this book from other collections of modern verse from China.

Not all poems in Yang and Qin's original selection survived the transition into English.[83] Some were discarded because the joke just wasn't funny in English. Others went because we felt they were speaking only to Chinese readers whose experience did not carry over into another language, and some because, no matter how we tried, they fell flat in translation.[84] We had decided to keep our texts as free from footnotes as possible, unless there were footnotes in the original poem, or unless we felt that a small explanatory whisper of an intervention from the editors would transform a poem that otherwise would be closed to the reader into something more accessible and enjoyable. What we did not do was omit poems because of their difficulty. This was a matter of professional ethics: the student or the beginner complains, 'It's too difficult' – but the professional is more likely to complain

82. *Gairmscoile* in *Complete Poems*, ed. M. Grieve & W.R. Aitken (London: Martin Brian & O'Keefe, 1978), vol 1, p. 74.

83. Some would have required either an intimate knowledge of party slogans on the part of the reader; others would have needed pages of footnotes explaining the puns (had we succeeded in translating the puns, of course).

84. While I take issue with the idea that all poetry is untranslatable, some individual poems just fail to thrive away from their original cultural and linguistic home. Do they die of homesickness, I wonder...?

that a task is too easy, because, where no challenge exists, there is no chance to extend your craft skills, or to become a better practitioner.

A translator who dodges difficulties is a liar: our job in this book is to show the English reader contemporary Chinese poetry, and to use every means at our disposal to show as much of it as possible, warts and all, complexity and all, glory and all. If the Chinese poets are worth reading, then it's worth making more of an effort so that their poems read better in translation.

A first draft is a question – it says 'Is this what the text means?' To talk of mistakes is not helpful at this point, because we can only learn by making mistakes. The author of the original text may have known exactly what he or she wanted to say and succeeded magnificently in saying it with power, precision and elegance, but it's often not immediately obvious to the translator what the essential sense of that text might be, since being a translator is not at all the same thing as being a mind-reader. The second or third draft is more or less the point at which native-language input becomes less useful to the translator, since at this stage, many of the translator's word choices must inevitably be operating on a level below what is obvious to the non-native speaker. I know that when I try to translate from Chinese, there are depths and subtleties that I don't see at first, and I'm sure there must be some I never see, because all good writing relies on these below-the-surface connections such as rhythm, rhyme, running metaphors, slant-rhyme, half-rhyme and other echoic devices.

There is an important mirror-image of this myopia of mine, in that once the translator has embarked on the stage of slowly polishing sound and sense into the singular and one-pointed contraption of a new poem in the target language, then he or she has left the source language behind. The late great translator David Hawkes wrote to me once, '...as a translator, all my failures have been failures of rhythm'. And it is the often unnoticed sound structure underlying a poem that makes that collection of words and phrases into a functioning poem. Sound, and the structures of sounds that shape and give life to a sentence or a line of poetry – that's the most difficult thing to get right, and that's what a translator will be working on after the initial, sense-fixated drafts. Neither of us in this transaction is master of the other's craft. I'm not a poet and the poet is not a translator, and that is why we can work so well together, our voices raised in happy unison, because each complements the other, each filling as best he or she can the lacunae in the other's knowledge and practice.

Why doesn't China win more Nobel Prizes in literature? Well, of course, the government's habit of jailing, exiling, or otherwise silencing the brightest and the best has something to do with it, but, I would contend, an equally important reason is the poor quality of much literary translation from Chinese. As translators, we have failed to give enough attention to literary quality, to the music of the language, to the sophisticated balancing act that is good writing, to those essential nuances of sound and sense which turn a collection of words into a poem that soars and sings and changes readers' lives. Go back and read that Stevenson paragraph again, and ask yourself how often you have read a translation from the Chinese which is 'musical in the mouth', or which is 'perfect' in his sense.[85]

We, the readers, don't want to be told what information the poem contains, nor do we want to be presented with a text that only makes sense if you can read the original. Translators must work solely for those who cannot read the original texts, and not for those who can read Chinese (they don't need us). And here I must address native Chinese translators: substituting English dictionary definitions for Chinese words does not make a poem, nor can you translate allusions to stories that Chinese people all know, because your readers won't know the stories that you do. Chinese names, too, whether of people or of places, however resonant they are in Chinese, have no connotation in English, and do not evoke anything at all: you must summon up a great deal more cleverness, dear translator, to make names cross the cultural and linguistic divide with which we are confronted.

The idea is still current in China that, since non-native speakers cannot read Chinese with the necessary sensitivity to nuance, then all translation of China's astonishingly diverse and accomplished literature should be done by Chinese people only. The first part of that statement is perfectly true: I will never see all the subtleties, I will never be alive enough to all the nuances, I will continually fail to get the joke, because my command of the language is not as good as a native speaker's. That is why we collaborate: a native speaker of Chinese to read the source text better than a non-native can, and a native speaker of English (in our case) to re-state the poem in the target language, better than a non-native can.

To state, however, that only Chinese people should translate out of their mother tongue – in the context of literary translation, which is to say, the attempt to take a poem from one tongue and make from it a poem in another tongue – this is, quite simply, nonsense. Of all

85. I exempt the work of the late David Hawkes, of John Minford, and of Burton Watson, to name a few only: my principal target is the academy, far too many of whose members appear to be afflicted by a deafness to rhythm, and a numbness to style.

the millions of Chinese speakers of English, only a vanishingly small proportion have mastered the language to the point where they can produce literary texts of any quality. The vast majority of Chinese-English literary translation done by Chinese speakers simply does not work, because *fluency* is not at all the same thing as *mastery*. And what is worse, young practitioners and students in China are taught to revere the work of people like the self-proclaimed 'greatest living Chinese-English translator', Xu Yuanchong. I can't help quoting myself:

> ...[Xu Yuanchong] is the worst possible role model, and a pernicious influence on younger scholars and students in China, who are not aware that seniority and self-advertisement alone do not confer literary merit in English...his repertoire includes the stanza
>
> > *While young, I knew no grief I could bear*
> > *I'd like to go upstair* [sic]
> > *I'd like to go upstair* [sic]
> > *To write new verses, with a false despair.*

These lines are ridiculous, firstly in that the first line...says almost the exact opposite of what the Chinese text means (its sense is more like *in my youth I didn't know the taste of sorrow*); secondly, in that *I'd like to go* is the wrong verb form, because it does not mean *I used to like going*, which is what the source text is expressing; thirdly, *upstair* is plain wrong, both because it is inadmissible as an adverb and also because it is an unbreakable rule that the writer should never break the rules of grammar in order to find a rhyme... At his best, Xu Yuanchong rises no higher than the level of the truly dreadful English poetaster, and thus he travesties the authors he attempts to translate, by making them appear to be as clumsily inept as he is – and that is his sin: one old gent making a fool of himself may be forgivable, but making imbeciles out of great poets is altogether beyond pardon.[86]

If you're Chinese and want to translate Chinese poetry into English, or any other language, for that matter, then you only need one thing, and that is a collaborator with a high level of competence as a writer who is a native speaker of your target language. And please, don't think that you can edit, revise or rewrite a native speaker's work, because essentially you can't do it without breaking the poem.

Poems change, mutate and evolve into different creatures through the process of restatement in another language, and what works in one language doesn't always work well in another, which is another

86. 'When the Blind lead the Blind: A Response to Jiang Xiaohua' in *Target* 22, December 2010, pp. 348-49.

reason why non-native versions rarely work as poetry: the non-native can never see the text in the same way as the native speaker – in effect, they are reading different poems, as each brings a different set of values and expectations to the text, and the text can't not be read through the lens of these values and expectations. This, in our case, is an unavoidable result of the gap between the cultures of China and the cultures of the English-speaking world.

In this project, cultural gaps were everywhere: between Chinese culture and western culture, between the English language and the Chinese language, between Mainland China and Hong Kong (which is also to say between Mandarin and Cantonese), and between generations too. To take an example from our team, the historical experience of someone like Yang Lian, who spent his early life under the rule of the Chinese Communist Party and was a teenager during the ten years of terror known as the 'Cultural Revolution', was very different from that of Kay Lee, who was educated in 21st-century Hong Kong at an English-speaking high school and an English-speaking university: they not only speak different languages – Mandarin and Cantonese are about as close as French and Portuguese – but they are from very different societal backgrounds – Yang is descended from Manchu and Mongol aristocracy, and grew up among the Communist Party's intellectual elite, while Kay is from a middle-class Cantonese family who work in banking and the stock market. Add into this mix a working-class Scottish baby-boomer and ex-hippy of half-Irish descent, who grew up partly in Nigeria, and who is Chinese by marriage, and you will see that the possibilities for misreading are nearly infinite.

But then, in the richness of this mix, the possibilities for creative reading are nearly infinite, too. Proust once remarked that all great literature is founded on misreading, for few readers can divine the mind of the author, and as they read (that first and most basic act of translation, from page into thought) all readers misread, re-make, and rewrite the text in their own way. The greatest literature is that which survives this process of being endlessly re-read and re-cast. Yang Lian talks of Ezra Pound's 'magnificent mistakes', too, those beautiful poems of his which are founded on misreadings of the Chinese text. Pound's howlers are much the same as undergraduate howlers, but from them he made great poetry.

The question then arises: who owns this poetry in translation? Who has the right to edit or alter it? I would say, only the translator and his or her collaborators. If the original Chinese poet could write that specific poem in English, then he or she would not need a translator. If a Chinese editor thinks it is permissible to make changes to the work of a native English speaker, then I would say that he or she is wrong, and actually has no right to do so, for the Chinese ownership of a poem ends once that poem is remade in another language, because, from that point on, its audience is no longer a Chinese one. This is the grand and fundamental paradox of our trade: the translated poem, like a Beethoven quartet arranged for the piano, is still the same poem in terms of its logic, its narrative, its programmatic and imagistic thrust, but there comes a point when it must be handed on by its mother-tongue curators, when it must become a new poem, no longer the same in terms of its sonorities, its tone colours and its textures, or its sense of being 'musical in the mouth'.

Our job as translators of poetry is to aspire to that perfection of musicality, to make and re-make our poems in search of the rhythmic and syntactical structures that permit a text to sing, and to engage in that life-or-death struggle with the text which is the daily bread of poets – in other words, if we translators do not treat our texts with the high seriousness, the craftsman's precision, and the titanic struggle for meaning that poets bring to bear, then we are not doing our job as well as we should. Samuel Becket famously laid it out for us: 'Try again. Fail again. Fail better.' [87]

As Chinese-English translators, we have too often failed our readers and traduced or even parodied our poets, by failing to try harder. This anthology represents our own attempt at a better failure.

---

87. *Worstward Ho* (1983) available in *Nohow on* (New York: Grove Press, 1989).

ACKNOWLEDGEMENTS

Special thanks are due to the Department of Chinese & Bilingual Studies, The Hong Kong Polytechnic University, and to the Faculty of Arts & Humanities, Newcastle University for their funding, and to Arts Council of England for two grants made under the Grants for the arts scheme, one for editorial and translation commissioning costs and the other to cover copyright fees for previously published translations. This funding made it possible for new translations to be commissioned from Brian Holton along with other translators, all of which are first published in *Jade Ladder*, except for Brian Holton's translation of Jiang Tao's 'Tribe of Palaeopithecus', a runner-up in the first *MPT* Poetry Translation Competition, which was published on *MPT*'s website.

The rest of the poems in this anthology are reprinted from the following books, all by permission of the publishers listed unless stated otherwise. Thanks are due to all the copyright holders cited below for their kind permission:

Bai Hua: 'Things Past', Under-Sky, *Underground: Chinese Writing Today, 1*, ed. John Cayley, Jonathan D. Spence & Zhao Yiheng (Well-sweep Press, 1994) by permission of John Cayley; all other poems taken from *Anthology of Chinese Poetry* (Yale University Press, 1992) by permission of the publisher.

Bei Dao: 'Accomplices', 'Window on the Cliff', 'On Tradition', 'It Has Always Been So', 'The Art of Poetry', 'Starting from Yesterday', 'SOS' from Bei Dao: *The August Sleepwalker*, tr. Bonnie S. McDougall (Anvil Press Poetry, 1988); 'To Tomas Tranströmer', 'A Guide to Summer' from Bei Dao: *Forms of Distance*, tr. David Hinton & Yambing Chen (Anvil Press Poetry, 1988); 'Landscape Over Zero' from Bei Dao: *Landscape Over Zero*, tr. David Hinton and Yanbing Chen (Anvil Press Poetry, 1998); 'Moon Festival' from Bei Dao: Unlock, tr. Eliot Weinberger & Iona Man-Cheong (Anvil Press Poetry, 2006); 'Picture (for Tiantian's 5th Birthday)' from Bei Dao: *Old Snow*, tr. Bonnie S. McDougall & Chen Maiping (Anvil Press Poetry, 1992); all by permission of Anvil Press Poetry. 'Black Map' and 'To My Father' from *The Rose of Time: New & Selected Poems*, ed. Zhao Zhenkai, tr. Eliot Weinberger (New Directions, 2010), by permission of New Directions Publishing Corporation.

Duo Duo: *The Boy Who Catches Wasps: Selected Poems* (Zephyr Press, 2002) by permission of the publisher.

Gu Cheng: 'Nature', 'Butterflies', 'Blood Relatives' and 'Wolf Pack' from *Sea of Dreams*, tr. Joseph R. Allen (New Directions, 2005) by permission of New Directions Publishing Corporation. 'Truly, This Is The World', 'Distribution', 'Source' from *Selected Poems*, ed. Sean Golden & Chu Chiyu (Renditions, 1990, reprinted by Research Centre for Translation, 1996), permission granted by The RCT at The Chinese University of Hong Kong. 'We Write Things' from *Under-Sky, Underground: Chinese Writing Today, 1*, ed. John Cayley, Jonathan D. Spence & Zhao Yiheng (Wellsweep Press, 1994) by permission of John Cayley; 'The End' from *Anthology of Chinese Poetry* (Yale University Press, 1992) by permission of the publisher.

Mang Ke: *Anthology of Chinese Poetry* (Yale University Press, 1992) by permission of the publisher.

Meng Lang: *An Even Prouder Heart* (Chapbook, 1994) by permission of the translator Dennis C. Mair.

Wang Xiaoni: 'White Moon' originally published in *The Guardian Online* (22 August 2008), and 'Four Typhoon Poems' originally published in *Brand* (2008), both reprinted by permission of the translator Pascale Petit.

Xi Chuan: 'Exercises in Thought' from *Notes on the Mosquito: Selected Poems*, tr. Lucas Klein (New Directions, 2011), reprinted by permission of New Directions Publishing Corp.

Yang Lian: 'Talking' from *Concentric Circles*, tr. Brian Holton & Agnes Hung-Chong Chan et al (Bloodaxe Books, 2005); 'Where the Sea Stands Still' and 'Darknesses' from *Where the Sea Stands Still: New Poems*, tr. Brian Holton (Bloodaxe Books, 1999); all others from *Riding Pisces* (Shearsman Books, 2008) by kind permission of the publisher.

Yi Sha: *Starve the Poets! Selected Poems*, tr. Simon Patton & Tao Naikan (Bloodaxe Books, 2008).

Zhai Yongming: *The Treekeeper's Tale* (Seren, 2008), by permission of the translator Pascale Petit.

Zhang Di: *Chinese Writers on Writing*, ed. Arthur Sze (San Antonio, Texas: Trinity University Press, 2010) by permission of the translator Murray Edmond.

Every effort has been made to trace copyright holders of the poems published in this book. The editors and publisher apologise if any material has been included without permission or without the appropriate acknowledgement, and would be glad to be told of anyone who has not been consulted. All poems included in this anthology are copyright © the poets and translators.

Finally, many thanks are also due to Lee Man-Kay, Daniel Hardisty, Stevie Ronnie and Susannah Pickering for research assistance.

BIOGRAPHICAL NOTES

W.N. Herbert is Professor of Creative Writing at Newcastle University and has co-translated poems from a diverse range of languages. Born in Dundee, he established his reputation with two English/Scots collections from Bloodaxe, *Forked Tongue* (1994) and *Cabaret McGonagall* (1996), followed by *The Laurelude* (1998), *The Big Bumper Book of Troy* (2002), *Bad Shaman Blues* (2006) and *Omnesia* (2013). He has also published a critical study, *To Circumjack MacDiarmid* (OUP, 1992), and co-edited *Strong Words: modern poets on modern poetry* (Bloodaxe Books, 2000) with Matthew Hollis. Twice shortlisted for the T.S. Eliot Prize, his books have also been shortlisted for the Forward Prize, McVities Prize, Saltire Awards and Saltire Society Scottish Book of the Year Award. Three are Poetry Book Society Recommendations. He lives in a lighthouse overlooking the River Tyne at North Shields.

Yang Lian was one of the original Misty Poets who reacted against the strictures of the Cultural Revolution. Born in Switzerland, the son of a diplomat, he grew up in Beijing and began writing when he was sent to the countryside in the 1970s. On his return he joined the influential literary magazine *Jintian* (Today). His work was criticised in China in 1983 and formally banned in 1989 when he organised memorial services for the dead of Tiananmen while in New Zealand. He was a Chinese poet in exile from 1989 to 1995, finally settling in London in 1997. Translations of his poetry include three collections with Bloodaxe, *Where the Sea Stands Still* (1999), a Poetry Book Society Recommended Translation, *Concentric Circles* (2005), and *Lee Valley Poems* (2009), as well as his long poem *Yi* (Green Integer, USA, 2002) and *Riding Pisces: Poems from Five Collections* (Shearsman, 2008), a compilation of earlier work. He was awarded the International Nonino Prize in 2012.

Brian Holton was born in Galashiels in the Scottish Border country but grew up partly in Nigeria. He was the son of an Irish father who was bilingual in English and French, fluent in Hausa and West African Pidgin and competent in Yoruba. After being educated in Greek, French and Latin, he studied Chinese at the universities of Edinburgh and Durham and was the first Programme Director of the Chinese-English/ English-Chinese translation programme at Newcastle University. He taught translation for ten years at the Hong Kong Polytechnic University and in 1992 he began a continuing working relationship with the poet Yang Lian, which has so far resulted in a dozen books of translated poetry, including *Where the Sea Stands Still* (Bloodaxe Books, 1999), a Poetry Book Society Recommended Translation, *Concentric Circles* (with Agnes Hung-Chong Chan) (Bloodaxe Books, 2005) and *Lee Valley Poems* (with Agnes Hung-Chong Chan and seven poets) (Bloodaxe Books, 2009). He also translates into Scots and is the only currently-publishing Chinese-Scots translator in the world.

Qin Xiaoyu was born in 1974 in Hohhot, Inner Mongolia. A writer and critic, he is a graduate of Tianjin University, Editor-in-Chief of *Northerner* magazine, and author of *Random Notes on Poetry*, which has been praised as 'the finest critical work on the history of the new Chinese poetry'. He is recognised as having 'created a new genre of modern poetry criticism', and is one of the most original and influential of the younger critics now writing in China.

INDEX OF POETS

(Italicised numerals are references to the poets in the essays.)